Bruno Latour

French sociologist and philosopher, Bruno Latour, is one of the most significant and creative thinkers of the last decades. *Bruno Latour: Hybrid thoughts in a hybrid world* is the first comprehensive and accessible English-language introduction to this multi-faceted work. The book focuses on core Latourian themes:

- contribution to science studies (STS – Science, Technology & Society)
- philosophical approach to the rise and fall of modernity
- innovative thoughts on politics, nature, and ecology
- contribution to the branch of sociology known as ANT – actor-network theory.

With ANT, Latour has pioneered an approach to socio-cultural analysis built on the notion that social life arise in complex networks of actants – people, things, ideas, norms, technologies, and so on – influencing each other in dynamic ways. This book explores how Latour helps us make sense of the changing interrelations of science, technology, society, nature, and politics beyond modernity.

Anders Blok is a Lecturer in the Department of Sociology, Copenhagen University. Combining an interest in STS with a background in socio-political theory and environmental sociology, his research focuses on the knowledge politics of science in global processes of environmental governance.

Torben Elgaard Jensen is a Senior Lecturer at the Department of Management Engineering, Technical University of Denmark. His current research focuses on the practical ways in which companies construct knowledge about their users, and the current Danish efforts to develop a national innovation policy with an emphasis on so-called user-driven innovation.

Bruno Latour
Hybrid thoughts in a hybrid world

Anders Blok and Torben Elgaard Jensen

Routledge
Taylor & Francis Group
LONDON AND NEW YORK

First published 2011
by Routledge
2 Park Square, Milton Park, Abingdon, Oxon OX14 4RN

Simultaneously published in the USA and Canada
by Routledge
711 Third Avenue, New York, NY 10017

Routledge is an imprint of the Taylor & Francis Group, an informa business

First issued in paperback 2012

© 2011 Anders Blok and Torben Elgaard Jensen

The right of Anders Blok and Torben Elgaard Jensen to be identified as authors of this work has been asserted by them in accordance with the Copyright, Designs and Patent Act 1988.

All rights reserved. No part of this book may be reprinted or reproduced or utilised in any form or by any electronic, mechanical, or other means, now known or hereafter invented, including photocopying and recording, or in any information storage or retrieval system, without permission in writing from the publishers.

Trademark notice: Product of corporate names may be trademarks or registered trademarks, and are used only for identification and explanation without intent to infringe.

British Library Cataloguing in Publication Data
A catalogue record for this book is available from the British Library

Library of Congress Cataloging in Publication Data
Blok, Anders.
  Bruno Latour : hybrid thoughts in a hybrid world / by Anders Blok and Torben Elgaard Jensen.
    p. cm.
  Includes bibliographical references.
  1. Sociology–Philosophy. 2. Technology–Social aspects. 3. Social networks. 4. Actor-network theory. 5. Latour, Bruno–Political and social views. I. Jensen, Torben Elgaard, 1967- II. Title.
  HM585.B56 2011
  301–dc22

2010048556

ISBN: 978-0-415-60278-5 (hbk)
ISBN: 978-0-415-64298-9 (pbk)
ISBN: 978-0-203-83527-2 (ebk)

Typeset in Times
by RefineCatch Limited, Bungay, Suffolk

Contents

Preface   vi

1 On the trails of Bruno Latour's hybrid world   1

2 Anthropology of science   26

3 Philosophy of modernity   52

4 Political ecology   75

5 Sociology of associations   102

6 Conclusion: The enlightenment project of Bruno Latour   130

7 "We would like to do a bit of science studies on you . . . ": An interview with Bruno Latour   151

Glossary of key terms   167
Notes   175
Bibliography   184
Index   194

Preface

The works of Bruno Latour have emerged as some of the most original, wide-ranging and provocative calls for a radical re-examination of the key issues of our times. Difficult questions about the internal workings of science and technology, the history of modernity, the political challenges of globalization and the moral significance of the ecological crisis are all scrutinized in his far-reaching thinking – and surprising results always follow. Latour is one of the most astute interpreters of our hybrid, chaotic and ever-changing world, and it is our conviction that his thinking deserves a wider audience. That, at least, is our rationale for writing this book, which is set to be the first introduction to the (so far) complete authorship of Latour.

Latour's approach is notoriously difficult to capture in a few simple characteristics. He was educated in theology, philosophy and anthropology, but spent many years working as a sociologist at *École des Mines*, an elite school for engineering students, before moving to his current position as dean of research at *Sciences Po*, a Parisian center of political science. His name is often associated with actor-network theory (ANT), which he developed with colleagues Michel Callon and John Law during the 1980s. But even a cursory look at his formal career and publications indicates a considerably broader field of intellectual engagement. Similarly, Latour is often identified with the interdisciplinary field of science studies known as STS (Science, Technology, Society; or Science and Technology Studies), which also emerged during the 1980s, primarily in British and American settings. However, while Latour is certainly recognized as a pivotal figure in this field, his theoretical position remains distinct, in part because it reaches well beyond the thematic boundaries of science and technology.

In short, it is quite difficult to simply categorize Latour in terms of academic disciplines, thematic interests or theoretical currents. And it would be just as problematic to try to pinpoint his theoretical position by using a few philosophically charged concepts. Despite persistent rumors to the contrary, Latour is neither a social constructivist, a postmodernist nor a relativist. He *could*, however, be reasonably linked with a number of subtly different labels, such as constructivism, non-modernism and relationalism. But unlike their more well-known counterparts, the theoretical significance of these labels is not immediately apparent. Latour develops his position in ongoing dialogue with a number of intellectual figures from the sidelines, ranging from theologian Bultmann to sociologist Tarde and philosopher Whitehead. This quick glance at Latour's sources of inspiration is enough to suggest that we are dealing with a highly original and vigorous intellectual project. Overall, an adequate picture of Latour needs to embrace the *intrinsically* interdisciplinary nature of his thinking, together with the sheer diversity of his philosophical, empirical and public engagements. As authors of this book, it is our (admittedly ambitious) goal to create an account that retains the complexity of Latour's intellectual pluralism, while highlighting those common threads that will help readers navigate his hybrid universe.

One of the central points of this book is that there *are* indeed common threads running throughout the better part of Latour's 35 years of work as an intellectual – and as a prolific writer of a dozen books and a wealth of scientific articles. These threads are merely difficult to find, and it requires a bit of perseverance to discover and describe them. Put briefly, however, Latour is arguably *the* contemporary intellectual who has most radically investigated, deconstructed and carefully re-described the divide between *nature* and *culture*, which he (and others) believes to be constitutive of modernity itself. In Latour's case, this investigation takes the shape of a sustained attempt to better understand the practice through which our modern society recognizes nature: the practice of natural science.

Since his first anthropological studies of science, which took place in a Californian laboratory in the 1970s, Latour has pursued the fundamental point that "nature" must be viewed not as the *cause*, but as the *product* of scientific practice. Scientific facts are constructed in a process where human interests and non-human technologies are both negotiated and brought together to work as one. In this way, the very existence of an ontological gap in the given order of things between nature and culture – and between science and politics, technology and society – is called into question. Latour's exquisitely detailed studies of the close interconnections of science and society show that, in practice, we have *never* been modern (to paraphrase the theoretical slogan for which he is best known). "Nature" and "society" have never been separate domains; they have always been interwoven in hybrid networks of human and non-human elements; therefore, these terms require a new set of definitions. Since the end of the 1990s, Latour has written books and articles that re-describe these two domains as part of a single, ecological and negotiating assembly. The central question now is, how can we live together peacefully in a world that exists beyond the unshakable truths created by science? If we Westerners have never been modern – then what have we been, and what should we strive to become?

What we just said might be read as an ultra-short outline of how the argument of this book is structured; a structure based on a thematic and a philosophical thread running through Latour's writings, as we elaborate in the introductory chapter. It is worth noting that, as readers and writers, we have had to undergo a significant learning process to reach the point where these connections seem evident to us. There are many possible routes into Latour's multifaceted universe, and together we represent merely two of these possibilities. One of us, Torben Elgaard Jensen, was educated as a psychologist but re-trained in the interdisciplinary field of science studies (STS). Working at *Danmarks Tekniske Universitet* (DTU),[1] Torben (like Latour!) teaches technology—society relations to engineering students.

Anders Blok trained as a sociologist, focusing on environmental sociology, and had no real connection to science studies – only discovering Latour's work through research in social theory and political philosophy. By now, we obviously share a professional interest in and enthusiasm for Latour's thinking, but as our respective biographies indicate, we have reached this conclusion from quite separate starting points. Torben first encountered Latour through the latter's early work in the anthropology of science (and ANT), and the construction of techno-scientific networks has remained central to Torben's own research. Anders started out reading Latour's much later texts in political ecology and the sociology of associations, and then gradually worked his way backward through the authorship. Writing this book has been a mutual discovery process where we, as writers, have come to meet in the middle, so to speak – and quite appropriately, given that the subject of this book is a thinker for whom "The Middle Kingdom" (of nature—culture hybrids) always takes center stage.

We hope that, through our different yet converging approaches, we have managed to create a richly textured portrait of Latour, while also opening a broad range of theoretical, philosophical and thematic interests for the reader. This book is written with higher-education students in mind (although, others are obviously very welcome to read it). However, it is *not* directed at audiences within any particular academic field. Such an approach would, in our view, deviate too far from Latour's intrinsic interdisciplinarity. In this context, it is worth emphasizing that we are also deliberately avoiding a particular tendency in much of the previous reception of Latour: namely, the tendency to read his works as *primarily* philosophical in nature, whether that refers to philosophy of science, philosophy of modernity or to metaphysics.[2] As interesting as such philosophical explorations are, we want to maintain throughout this book the (only slightly) polemic argument that Latour's intellectual universe is exciting and original mainly because it *breaks away* from the dominance traditionally held by philosophy over key questions of knowledge, facts and modernity.

Despite our taste for interdisciplinarity, we must admit that our own approach leans rather systematically toward the sociological and the anthropological. By flagging this inclination, we wish to stress that, above all, Latour outlines an *empirical* program for alternative explorations in a hybrid world of constant dynamism and change. We thus hope to inspire our readers – across academic segments – to experiment with the analytical tools made available by Latour. Our ultimate aim with this book, then, is to provide readers with the means and the inclination to navigate *themselves* through Latour's *own* texts and intellectual universe. In that sense, this book is a bridge, not a destination in itself. While Latour's thinking is challenging and at times difficult to access, we hope to communicate the subject matter in ways that engage the reader and provide a glimpse of the inspiring and entertaining experience that may *also* be found by moving around in Latour's hybrid world.

It remains only to thank the many students, colleagues, advisers and friends whose constructive criticisms have been an invaluable support in our work with Latour and in the making of this book. In particular, we wish to thank the following people, who either made valuable comments on one or several earlier chapter drafts, or who otherwise provided tangible assistance to the work: Niels Albertsen, Heine Andersen, Christoffer Andersson, Margareta Bertilsson, Christian Borch, Christian Clausen, Paul du Gay, Casper Bruun Jensen, Mette Jensen, Lars Bo Kaspersen, Liv Nyland Krause, Martin Letell and Estrid Sørensen. A warm "thank you" to Astrid Jespersen, who has supplied *both* valuable comments and practical support on the home front to one writer.

The rapidly growing Danish STS environment – including many who, like us, are affiliated with the Danish Association for Science and Technology Studies (DASTS) – has played a vital role in nurturing our Latourian interests. This energetic network of mostly young researchers has given us the belief that the majority of effects, applications and discussions of Latour's work lies in the future, not the past. At the same time, this STS community – together with its international counterparts – forms an important part of our imagined audience for this book.

In the course of writing the original Danish version of this book (published by Hans Reitzel; Copenhagen, 2009), we had the pleasure of collaborating with Social Science Editor Martin Laurberg. We are grateful to Martin for his encouraging, extraordinarily precise and always well-directed commentary, which helped us improve the manuscript substantially. We would also like to thank the editors and staff at Routledge for their unwavering support, experience and professionalism.

Since this book started out its life in the Danish language and has since been translated and modified, we wish to gratefully acknowledge the invaluable translation work and language assistance provided by Amy Clotworthy and Luci Ellis. As anyone familiar with the work of Bruno Latour is likely to acknowledge, translation is neither easy nor innocent. Working with native English speakers who are simultaneously competent in the obscurities of the Danish language has provided us, as authors, with much-needed guidance on how to balance linguistic curiosity against the strains of working in our second language. Needless to say, we remain solely responsible for whatever shortcomings can be detected in this collective endeavor.

Finally, we owe special thanks, of course, to the main character himself: Bruno Latour. Not just for the inspiration his writings have provided us, but also, and more specifically, for his generous involvement in the interview printed toward the end of this book. Having first endured the fate of seeing his voice translated into Danish, at least we are now back to a language he understands! The irony, of course, is that this book as a whole translates the writings of an author renowned for his own well-articulated translations, not least across the Atlantic of French– American relations. Not that this seems to bother a man for whom *translation* as *transformation* represents a general truth about the world, inside and outside social science. Nevertheless, we conclude by emphasizing that any deficiencies in this book should of course be blamed on us, the interpreters, rather than on Latour, the interpreted.

1 On the trails of Bruno Latour's hybrid world

> I would define myself as an "empirical philosopher," not as an empiricist philosopher, but as someone who tries to get at classical philosophical questions through the methods of fieldwork and case studies. [. . .] It is just that sometimes I identify myself more with philosophy and sometimes more with anthropology. In fact, deep down, my real interest is in metaphysics.
>
> (Latour, in Crease *et al.* 2003: 15f)

Prologue: "Do You Believe In Reality?"

On a hot afternoon in June 1996, two researchers – from two different scientific disciplines and two different parts of the world – meet for an informal conversation by a lake in the tropical mountain region of Teresopolis, near Rio de Janiero, Brazil. They are both middle-aged, Western men, participating in the same scientific conference; both are highly respected for their research efforts, although in entirely different fields. One is an American psychologist, and as such, a recognized member of the natural-science establishment. His counterpart belongs to another domain of scientific culture: He is a French philosopher and anthropologist of science, known for his work within the growing interdisciplinary field of Science and Technology Studies (STS). The psychologist is anonymous. The anthropologist is Bruno Latour, and he is the focus of our attention here, based on his own re-telling of this meeting (Latour 1999b: chapter 1).

The conversation itself is amicable, but the context is dramatic: At this time in the United States, the psychologist's homeland, an intense discussion is raging about the relationship between the "hard" and "soft" sciences – that is, between the natural sciences and the humanities. In fact, conflicts between the disciplines are so intense that they are later dubbed "the science wars." At stake in these verbal wars are the relations between science, politics and society – relationships that are undergoing dramatic transformation in the so-called "knowledge society." As an anthropologist of science, Latour analyzes – but is also deeply implicated in – these extensive changes. In his view, science is essentially a social matter. But this approach makes him the object of suspicion in certain academic circles: Mainstream philosophers of science, and some quite vocal natural scientists, view such "social constructivist" and "post-modern" standpoints with skepticism and concern.[1] This sentiment of concern is shared by the American psychologist by the lake at Teresopolis.

Only in this context are we able to understand the bizarre exchange that takes place during this meeting – an exchange of words that, deep down, touches upon the status of scientific knowledge, and thus one of the foundations of our modern world. Is scientific knowledge really as compelling, objective and universal as it is usually presumed to be in our high-tech society, influenced by the ideals of the Enlightenment? If not, then what are the implications for our world-view, our self-perception and our very relationship with the world around us? These are the kinds of thoughts that prompt the American psychologist to seek out Bruno Latour, and then to ask, with a slight quiver in his voice, the following cryptic question: "Do you believe in reality?" Latour is completely taken aback by the naiveté of the question. "Why, of course!" he replies. "What a question! Is reality something one needs to believe in?"

Encouraged by this response, the American psychologist asks two further questions: First, whether we now have greater knowledge than before, to which Latour answers, "Of course. A thousand times more!" And second, one of the classic questions of the philosophy of science: whether science generates cumulative knowledge. Once again, Latour responds in the affirmative – although this time, he adds that scientific disciplines also have an unfortunate tendency to forget their own past. The psychologist is clearly pleased and relieved by these answers. Latour, on the other hand, is shocked: How has he managed to put himself in a position where others feel the need to pose such questions, so obviously misguided and bizarre? How could his, and his colleagues', efforts to create a more *realistic* image of science, by studying the sciences as dynamic social activities, have been so fundamentally misunderstood? How could his profound respect for the diversity and intricacies of the scientific world be so casually confused with cheap anti-science?

Even a cursory understanding of the theoretical landscapes of the social sciences and humanities since the early 1980s leaves no doubt that this exchange is a caricature: a caricature of debates between "realists" and "social constructivists," between "modernists" and "post-modernists," and between stereotypes of the natural and social sciences. In his book *Pandora's Hope* (1999b), Latour uses this anecdote as the basis for clarifying his theoretical position – and he comments on the ongoing scientific controversies using the motto: "We are not at war!"

In order to clarify his approach, Latour must propose a position that fundamentally diverges from modernist ways of thinking – by at once relating epistemology, ontology, politics, psychology and theology, and by encompassing all of nature, society and God. In Latour's view, such a position is considerably more realistic than the so-called "realism" produced by modern philosophy of science. As such, he uses the anecdote to pointedly highlight the absurdity of a range of those categorizations that we all, as modernist Westerners, use in our everyday interpretation of the world. To understand how the question "Do you believe in reality?" can become meaningful – indeed, how it can be articulated at all – we must first, according to Latour, understand the deeply entrenched categories of the modern world. Next, we need to transgress these categories by realizing that, in fact, we have never really been modern in the first place (Latour 1993).

Our book, which deals with Bruno Latour's far-reaching intellectual project, examines all of these issues (and much more). For the moment, we simply employ the anecdote as a sign of warning against the error of wanting to understand Latour's ideas via a few compact, (over)simplified interpretive categories – categories such as "social constructivism," "post-modernism" or, indeed, "philosophy of science." We claim that understanding Latour's thinking requires a fundamental willingness to rethink categories and intellectual habits. With this introductory book, our aim is to assist readers in such a process of reconstruction.

Bruno Latour, the actor-network

To start this book with a categorical definition of who Bruno Latour *is* – using biographical data, theoretical traditions, philosophical positions and the like – would be tantamount to being out of step with his own way of thinking from the start. Indeed, one of the principal ideas expressed in every aspect of Latour's wide-reaching authorship is that no one entity is significant in isolation, but instead attains meaning through its numerous – and changeable – relations to other entities. Often, these multitudes of relations are called actor-networks, and this constitutes the foundation of the theoretical tradition known as *actor-network theory* (ANT), with which Latour's name is intimately associated. Such actor-networks are hybrid, which means that they consist of both humans and material objects; and everything exists within actor-networks – including, of course, Bruno Latour himself. This relational and hybrid approach to the world has broad implications, and this book aims to capture a number of the essential implications for the theory of science, methodology and politics.

However, the point relating to Bruno Latour is self-evident: It makes little sense to attempt to separate the person from his many books, his academic career, his colleagues, discussion partners and sources of inspiration, or his academic disciplines. Neither would it make sense to separate Latour's works from their numerous enthusiastic, indifferent or indignant readers: Without them, there would be no "famous and increasingly influential French anthropologist of science and philosopher of modernity" to write about. The authors of this book are some of his more ardent readers, and as such, we are small nodes in the "Bruno Latour" actor-network. Our book is an attempt to expand this network by presenting Latour's thoughts in a compressed form to an interested readership. With Bruno Latour, the world is always full of new connections.

With this in mind, it may no longer be all that obvious what we actually mean when we refer to "Bruno Latour" – let alone whether we mean to refer to one single entity or to a plurality of relations. Are we talking about the man born in the year 1947 in the village of Beaune in the Bourgogne district of France, son of a vineyard owner? The man who studied theology, philosophy and anthropology in Dijon and Tours? The man who later became a professor at the elite engineering institution *L'École des Mines* in Paris? The man who developed a particular version of a "sociology of innovation," and who has been teaching this version of sociology to engineering students for most of his academic career? Or are we perhaps referring to the numerous books (those low-tech devices from the 1400s) through which the author and label "Bruno Latour" has by now spread to many different countries? The books that have been translated into several languages, and which have achieved recognition while also awakening intellectual resistance? If that is the case, then are we talking about one, some or all of these books? And does it make any difference that Latour refers to himself as an "anthropologist of science" in certain places, a "metaphysicist" in others and a "sociologist" in others still?

Alternatively, are we perhaps referring to the various theoretical positions associated with the labels "Bruno Latour," "ANT" or "(social) constructivism" in a growing number of articles, textbooks and reference works – although Bruno Latour can hardly be considered a philosopher of science in the classical philosophical sense of the term? Of course, the name Bruno Latour covers all of these facets. For the time being, we are referring to all of them at once. Only gradually do we insert a number of demarcations into this chaotic jumble, and thereby create an ordered image of a complex whole. Bruno Latour, then, is neither a singular entity nor a plurality, but rather an extensive and partially connected network.

This book introduces Bruno Latour's texts and thoughts, as he has presented them in around a dozen books and numerous scientific articles, commentaries, interviews and art-exhibition catalogs. Our ambition is to encompass most of the essential aspects of this vast universe – well aware that such an enterprise requires a considered approach, involves a number of difficult omissions and creates its own risks. With regard to the omissions: Apart from a short overview of Latour's academic career, there are only a few details about the man himself in this book. This is not a biography, and certainly not an intellectual biography, but rather a catalog of one of the most far-reaching, inventive and provocative intellectual projects of our times. In addition, we do not feel that the most interesting aspect of Bruno Latour's intellectual universe is his (more or less explicit) philosophical position in relation to classical epistemological, ontological and metaphysical questions. Although we are aware that he is often read this way, we do not think that Latour is *primarily* interesting as a philosopher of science. Of course, he is interesting in this respect, but he is also a significant contemporary thinker precisely because he *removes* philosophical epistemology from its dominant intellectual position – replacing it with something we might call "empirical philosophy." Another word for this is anthropology, or as Latour would say, "symmetrical anthropology"; other terms would be "sociology of associations" or "political ecology." The most important goal of this book is to clarify and expand upon the meanings Latour gives to these complex designations. We aim to show how, despite internal differences, they form elements in *one* undertaking, *one* intellectual project.

What, then, does this project consist of? Strictly speaking, readers should go through the entire book before they can expect a clear answer to that question – but we give an initial response in this introductory chapter, which also serves as a reading guide for the subsequent chapters. We begin with a short overview of Latour's academic biography, calling attention to the many threads that run from his early authorship through to the later. Next, we attempt to pinpoint Latour's combined intellectual endeavor, which, in essence, concerns the relationship between science and politics over the last 300 to 400 years of (so-called) modern Western society. In short, if "facts are fabricated",[2] where does this place our understanding of science, politics, society, technology, nature, modernity, God – and the other essential ingredients in our collective life? This also involves a discussion of the principal philosophical currents to which Latour's thinking is related, especially in a French (and thus Continental) philosophical context. Following this tentative overview, we go straight to a different kind of dissection: We then explain our rationale for dividing Latour's authorship into four "phases" or, more precisely, four "professional identities." We also define the contours of two of Latour's largest collective projects – ANT and STS – that still play a constitutive role in his own intellectual project.

This review of "phases" and projects in Latour's thinking – a preview of the chapters in this book – leads us to a discussion of the fluid transitions and definite shifts that have occurred during the course of his authorship. This is a complicated discussion, and we save the details for the concluding chapter. Likewise, most of our evaluation and criticism of Latour's contribution to science studies (and a variety of other disciplines) is to be found in this concluding chapter. We round off this introductory chapter with a series of practical and stylistic guidelines for the reader, including a few remarks on the choices and omissions manifested in this book, its strengths and limitations, and our aspirations on behalf of the reader. There is no reason to deny it: Bruno Latour can be a complicated acquaintance to make. This book attempts to facilitate the introduction to his work, but nothing is gained without effort, and everything comes at a price when one attempts to take shortcuts.

Fragments of Bruno Latour's academic biography[3]

Let us begin by eliminating one potential misunderstanding: Although Bruno Latour is indeed the son of a French vineyard owner, his family is in no way linked to the famous vineyard *Château Latour* in the Médoc region in northwest Bordeaux! His family owns the lesser known, but still quite impressive, *Maison Louis Latour*, a family business of wine growers and merchants in the Bourgogne district.[4] This information is taken from Bruno Latour's personal web site – a web site recommended to readers looking for a quick overview of his intellectual universe.[5] The fact that this information appears on the web site of a French elite university professor is a telling indication of the colorful, and at times playful, temperament that characterizes Latour's work. In addition to standard lists of academic and popular publications, the web site contains a virtual, illustrated and hyperlink-based book (*Paris: Ville Invisible*; see Chapter 5). It also displays photographs from two techno-art exhibitions – "Iconoclash" (2002) and "Making Things Public" (2005) – mounted at the *Zentrum für Kunst und Medientechnologie* (ZKM)[6] in Karlsruhe, Germany; Latour co-curated both exhibits.

Even this short overview indicates a far-reaching intellectual engagement that is rooted in a creative approach to contemporary challenges, particularly those of a technological bend. Leafing through Latour's academic works, it becomes clear that this creativity is also reflected in his prose. Latour writes energetically, with humor and in a polemic tone. He often experiments with different genres and narrative structures. His stylistic experiments include texts that read like an anthropological travelogue (*Laboratory Life*; see Chapter 2), a courtroom drama (*Science in Action*; Chapter 2), a detective novel (*Aramis*; Chapter 5) and a classical philosophical tract (*Irreductions*; Chapter 3). Indeed, Latour approaches the craft of writing with passion and a sense of pride. His declared ambition is that his readers take as much pleasure from reading a Latour book as from drinking a Latour wine.[7]

Latour describes the environment in which he was raised as being a "typical provincial bourgeoisie" (interview, Crawford 1993). This provincialism may explain why (in spite of everything) he broke with his family's winemaking tradition and embarked on an academic career. Latour studied philosophy and Biblical exegesis at the *Université de Bourgogne* in Dijon in the late 1960s. Later, he studied theology at *Université de Tours*, and in 1975 he received his Ph.D. in philosophy, for a thesis titled "Exégèse et ontologie: une analyse des textes de resurrection."[8] In retrospective interviews, Latour strongly emphasizes that – in contrast to a number of his well-known French academic colleagues – he was not educated at the *École normale supérieure*, an incubator of France's bureaucratic elite. In fact, the combination of ontology and theology is far removed from the dominant theoretical currents of his student time, notably Marxism and structuralism. This may explain why Latour – unlike his slightly older but almost contemporary fellow countrymen, Michel Foucault and Pierre Bourdieu – has never undertaken any detailed critique of either Marxism or structuralism. Latour was simply trained in quite different philosophical and theological traditions, and his subsequent work is much closer to, for instance, the Christian metaphysics of Alfred N. Whitehead than it is to the social theory of Karl Marx or the structuralism of Ferdinand Saussure. We return to Latour's philosophical sources of inspiration later.

As we mentioned earlier, Latour also studied anthropology. These studies, however, did not take place in a traditional university environment. He encountered anthropology during his military service in the early 1970s, when he was stationed in the Ivory Coast, West Africa, and affiliated with an organization called ORSTROM (*Institut Français de recherche scientifique pour le développement en cooperation*).[9] This organization works to improve economic conditions in developing countries through education in, and transfer of, science and technology. At that time, the Ivory Coast office was under the leadership of anthropologist Marc Augé, who later became a well-known figure within his academic field. Latour received inspiration from Augé and learned the fundamental principles of anthropology, especially long-term fieldwork as a scientific method. As early as 1974, the year before receiving his Ph.D. in philosophy, Latour had already published an anthropological and ethnographic report on the French tradition of technical education and training, which he compiled while staying in the Ivory Coast.

This simultaneous encounter with anthropology, the non-Western world (in the form of West Africa) and the complex histories of science and technology was arguably to become more significant to Latour's career than his theological and philosophical studies in France. A direct line extends from here to the anthropology of science and technology that Latour begins in earnest in the mid-1970s. This new work likewise consists of close-up, ethnographic studies of everyday activities. The subjects, however, were to be changed from poor African peasants to highly esteemed Euro—American scientists.

Consequently, Latour's first comprehensive and influential study, published in 1979 and co-authored by sociologist Steve Woolgar, is called *Laboratory Life: The Social Construction of Scientific Facts*. To make this happen, however, yet another historical coincidence was required: Roger Guillemin, whom Latour knew from his time in Dijon, had since become an internationally acclaimed researcher in the field of neuroendocrinology. Guillemin invited Latour into his laboratory in La Jolla, California, and Latour stayed there for two years (1975–76), financed by a Fulbright scholarship. Latour enjoyed full access to every nook and cranny of the laboratory, and this unique opportunity allowed him to make one of the first and most significant contributions to the emerging field of interdisciplinary science studies. To Latour, this also laid the foundation for his theoretical thinking about science and anthropology, which developed into ANT in the early 1980s. (We elaborate on the history of both ANT and science studies later in this chapter; Latour's anthropology of science and technology is the topic of Chapter 2.)

Upon his return from the U.S., Latour was employed by the *Centre de Sociologie de l'Innovation* (CSI),[10] where he achieved the status of professor in 1982; he remained there until 2006. CSI is a center for sociological research and education at *L'École Nationale Superieure des Mines* in Paris, an elite institution focused on the education of engineers – traditionally, a rather powerful profession in France. The center was founded in 1967 as part of a restructuring of the engineering education. Later on, CSI found itself in the middle of a maelstrom of political changes in France, characterized by an increasing focus on applied research in science, technology and innovation throughout the 1970s and 1980s (see Fuller 2000). In this context, Latour had ample opportunities to pursue his broad, cross-disciplinary research interests, in line with ongoing developments in science and technology.

Around 1980, Latour began closely collaborating at CSI with Michel Callon, a sociological researcher educated in physics and economics. This collaboration laid the foundation for the initial formulations of ANT, originally conceived of as a "sociology of translation." The term "translation" became the fundamental concept used to describe technological innovation as a process of translating (forcing, bending, seducing, organizing) a multitude of heterogeneous elements into the hands of a few powerful representatives. Such translation processes occur within specific relations or networks of actors – hence, the name of the theory (see Chapter 2). Latour and Callon developed these basic theoretical principles using a number of case studies of important, but ultimately unsuccessful, techno-innovation projects. These projects, set in the contemporary French research – political context, included: the electric car (Callon & Latour 1981); a global communication system called Minitel; and a computer-driven public transportation system in Paris (Latour 1996a).

Based on these cases – as well as close collaborations with British sociologist John Law (e.g., Callon, Law & Rip, eds. 1986) – ANT gradually developed into a recognized, and increasingly dominant, research program within the interdisciplinary field of STS. Given that STS is mostly practiced in the English-speaking world, one consequence of the development of ANT was that Latour's work became read and referenced more widely in England and the U.S. than in his native France. Almost all of Latour's books and articles have been translated into English, if they were not originally written in English.

During the developing phases of ANT, Latour became increasingly interested in the history of science. This interest led to a (by now well-known) book about French scientific icon Louis Pasteur and his work with microbes in the 1860s (Latour 1988b). Compared to existing historical accounts, Latour assigns a prominent role to the microbes themselves, thus illustrating the central position envisaged by ANT to technology, machines, animals and organisms – all designated by the common term "non-human actors." This interest in the non-human actor is similarly apparent in his lengthy collaboration with primatologist Shirley Strum, whose work he uses extensively (and provocatively!) in his own sociology from the late 1980s onward (Strum & Latour 1987; see Chapter 5).

In the 1990s, Latour continued to work on the distinctly philosophical and metaphysical aspects of ANT, notably in the book most people consider to be his major philosophical work: *Nous n'avons jamais été modernes* (1991) or *We Have Never Been Modern* (1993). In this book, Latour presents, with visionary clarity, the intellectual program for an exploration of the "modernist" history of ideas in the Western world, a project he dubs "symmetrical anthropology." At least two of his later books continue, or elaborate on, the threads started in this principal work: the aforementioned *Pandora's Hope* (1999b), which sums up Latour's philosophy of science; and *Politics of Nature* (2004d), which focuses more on political philosophy. In this latter book, Latour expands on his notion of political ecology in the context of contemporary environmental threats, a central theme of his research during the 1990s.

All of these themes are discussed later in this book: the philosophy of modernity of *We Have Never Been Modern* in Chapter 3; the political ecology of *Politics of Nature* in Chapter 4; while Chapter 5 introduces the successor of the sociology of translation, now dubbed the "sociology of associations." This latter chapter is based primarily on Latour's book *Reassembling the Social* (2005), which reads as an expanded introduction to ANT, in which the theory emerges as a fully fledged sociological research program.

In 2006, after 25 years at CSI, Latour was appointed professor at *Sciences Po*, a Parisian university of political science. Here, he is affiliated with The Center for the Sociology of Organizations, while also currently (2011) serving as vice president of research. Latour's chair at *Sciences Po* is named after sociologist (and psychologist) Gabriel Tarde, who was until recently little known outside of France. Tarde's work originates in the end of the 1800s, a period when the social sciences were being institutionalized in France. Latour has increasingly heralded Tarde as his intellectual role model and as an unaccredited forefather of ANT (Latour 2002a).

In these ways, Latour contributes significantly to a rising interest in Tarde's work outside of France; for instance, Latour wrote the foreword to a republication of Tarde's major work on the "psychological economy" (Latour & Lépinay 2009). Similarly, Latour entered into a famous dispute from the earliest days of sociology: Tarde versus Émile Durkheim, his younger, victorious and better-known counterpart (see Candea 2010). Latour's interest in this dispute concerns nothing less than the future of the sociological (and anthropological) sciences. While sociology in the 20th century was "Durkheim-ified," Latour now pushes for a "Tardification" of the 21st century (see Chapter 5). Toward such an end, Latour was one of the driving forces in reviving this classic social-science dispute when he personally played the role of Tarde in a verbal duel with modern-day Durkheimians at Corpus Christi College, Cambridge, UK in March of 2008.[11]

This endeavor is typical of Latour: he seems to like nothing better than a good intellectual controversy, particularly when the stakes are high – for the future of both the sciences and politics. So although Latour is not at war with the natural sciences as such, he *does* admit that he "won't mind firing a few shots" (1999b: 23) in the direction of his intellectual opponents and toward the central debates of contemporary philosophy, social science and politics.

Latour's thematic axis: "Facts are fabricated"

From this brief overview of Bruno Latour's intellectual project, it should be clear that any attempt to sum it up in a few words is likely to be incomplete and unsatisfactory – if not downright misleading. He simply moves around too much: both in historical time (Pasteur) and geographical space (Africa and the U.S.), as well as in the zones between established scientific disciplines, philosophical questions and thematic points of reference. But behind all of this mobility, there are nevertheless strong patterns to be found.

In our view, Latour's multifaceted engagements converge into one relatively coherent intellectual project, which can be traced along two axes: one thematic, and one ontological–metaphysical. The thematic axis centers around Latour's lifelong fascination with the worlds of science and technology – especially science's innermost, highly esteemed and quasi-holy core: the scientific fact and its place of production, the laboratory. The ontological–metaphysical axis is harder to capture. Its roots and connections in the history of ideas are somewhat fleeting, and these relations are often only minimally mentioned in Latour's own writings. Latour is not a philosophical "system builder" in any strict sense – as he himself declares: "I produce books, not a philosophy" (interview, Crease *et al.* 2003: 19). For this reason, there is always a risk of presenting his thinking in *overly* coherent philosophical and theoretical terms. Nevertheless, we find it meaningful to single out three of his significant sources of inspiration in the history of ideas: Whitehead's process philosophy; Gilles Deleuze's conception of immanence; and Michel Serres' ontology of mediation (see the following section). With this narrowed-down selection, we merely intend to sketch the conceptual landscape and history in which Latour's thinking emerges. It goes without saying that Latour engages with a considerably larger number of significant authors than just the three philosophers on our list; at the same time, Latour does explicitly acknowledge Whitehead, Deleuze and Serres as deep sources of inspiration.

But let us begin with the thematic axis: the complex, often inaccessible and esoteric worlds of science and technology. As others have also noted (Fraser 2006: 59), Latour's lifelong project may be described as a multifaceted, interdisciplinary investigation into the intricate ways in which scientific facts are produced (constructed, fabricated) and then distributed far beyond their original site of production. His project may be considered a practical, as well as philosophical, attempt to "de-naturalize" the scientific fact as a social category: A fact is *not* a given, inevitable nor universal entity. On the contrary, it has a very specific history of production, which may be analyzed by means of thorough empirical and historical studies.

Looking at Latour's academic biography reveals some of this project: His entry into an American laboratory and his attempt to document the practical work of scientists using anthropological methods form the crucial vehicles for his de-naturalization of scientific action. As Latour later recounts: Prior to the ethnographic studies of laboratories, we had only the scientists' own accounts of their work to rely on (Crease *et al.* 2003: 20). Such autodescriptions, it should be noted, often combine with highly normative philosophical ideas as to the proper conduct of science, such as the principle of "falsification" developed by philosopher of science Karl Popper. By contrast, Latour's interest in science is anthropological before it is philosophical: The aim is to describe, in as much detail as possible, how scientific facts emerge from the practical tasks, negotiations and literary inscriptions of laboratories. Early on, Latour and other pioneers of science studies formulate a radical motto, which has significant bearing on his later work: "Nothing extraordinary and nothing 'scientific' [is] happening inside the sacred walls of these temples" (Latour 1983).[12] In laboratories, facts are fabricated – nothing more, nothing less.

Such a motto is clearly set forth in full confrontation with age-old epistemological traditions, as well as the attempts of the normative philosophy of science to distinguish true scientific knowledge from all sorts of pseudoscience, superstition and "common sense." This is indeed the fundamental point of Latour's anthropology of science and technology: Scientists and engineers are historical, social and political "world builders" like everyone else – although the laboratory provides them with a unique set of material tools (see Chapter 2). In this sense, Latour's "anti-epistemological" approach is a thread that runs through his entire authorship (see Bowker & Latour 1987), and it raises a host of issues that all seem to challenge prevalent Western ways of thinking. Because if "facts are fabricated" – rather than elevated above the rest of social reality in any absolute sense – then we need, first of all, to re-evaluate the entire relationship between science, epistemology and society. Furthermore, such a claim also necessitates a re-examination of some fundamental problems of social science: the question of modernity and relations to the non-Western world (Chapter 3); the relationship between scientific and political forms of representation (Chapter 4); and the relationship between scientific activity and other types of social practice, such as religion, law and art (Chapter 5).

Latour's intellectual project may be considered a sustained investigation of how to re-describe the "modern" world *beyond* the dominance of science and epistemology. For this reason, his thematic interests have also increasingly moved outside of the boundaries of the scientific domain. In his own words: "My longer-term project has always been to visit successively and to document the different truth-production sites that make up our civilization: science, of course, but also techniques, religion, law, etc." (interview, Crease *et al.* 2003: 16). Thus, the constitution of valid knowledge is always at stake in Latour's work: How can we learn to recognize, appreciate and transform our world – including its most basic elements, such as time, space and agency? It is in this sense that Latour considers himself an "empirical philosopher" or a kind of "experimental metaphysicist": Once we move beyond the idea of given and universal facts, reality may always surprise us in its diversity and unpredictability.

Latour's ontological–metaphysical axis: Process, immanence, mediation

The second axis that characterizes Latour's intellectual project is the ontological–metaphysical. As mentioned earlier, we are on much shakier ground here, and we can only hope to make a few principal observations on the theoretical landscape in which Latour's ideas emerge. As a starting point, it could be noted that Latour's anti-epistemological approach to scientific facts is merely one element in a much broader endeavor to break with the idea that the world should consist of two fundamentally distinct types of elements: spirit and matter, for example, or culture and nature. This so-called anti-dualist venture (see Newton 2007: 28ff) is expressed in various ways and on many levels of Latour's thinking. Throughout this book, we encounter Latour's continual attempts to develop analytical repertoires that reformulate or transgress dualisms – between scientific and non-scientific knowledge, modernity and non-modernity, reason and power, and between nature and society. Indeed, the four dualisms just mentioned form important subjects of the four main chapters in this book, respectively.

However, Latour's anti-dualism is not confined to particular thematic or analytical projects; it also reaches an ontological, and even a metaphysical, substratum. From an ontological standpoint, it is expressed as an attempt to transgress fundamental modernistic and philosophical dichotomies: between subject and object, facts and values, and between the primary and secondary qualities of natural objects.

In this ontological sense, Latour should be categorized as a highly unconventional and uncompromising revisionist, for whom the majority of the history of philosophy – from Descartes and Kant to Hegel, Heidegger, Habermas and Derrida – amounts to nothing more than a worsening of the dualistic fallacy! These philosophers base their thinking on firmly held beliefs about a radical division between the subjective and the objective, or between language and the world. This forces them to develop ever more speculative (and ever less successful) theories on how these elements can ever be brought together (see Latour 1993: 55ff).

In more positive terms, Latour's thinking inscribes itself mainly in the complex chain of metaphysical traditions known as *monism*. One common point of reference here is Gottfried Leibniz's theory of monads, and many of Latour's intellectual role models indeed relate themselves (directly or indirectly) to Leibniz: philosopher Alfred N. Whitehead (1861–1947); sociologist Gabriel Tarde (1843–1904); and the more contemporary, French-speaking philosophers Gilles Deleuze (1925–95), Michel Serres (b. 1930) and

Isabelle Stengers (b. 1949). Among these intellectual heroes, Serres is worthy of particular emphasis, since he is the closest we get to a Latourian mentor – as demonstrated by the fact that Latour conducted a lengthy interview with Serres on the latter's philosophical oeuvre (Serres & Latour 1995).

Even a brief summary of this Leibniz-inspired monism would be too exhaustive for our purposes; not to mention the futility of any attempt to situate Latour's thinking in the only partially cohesive networks of ontological and metaphysical hypotheses represented by the aforementioned philosophers (but see Harman 2009). Listing these sources of inspiration is therefore only meant as a reminder that Latour's intellectual project involves itself in some quite fundamental controversies in the history of ideas – conflicts between dualism and monism, or between "cartesianism" (after Descartes) and "vitalism."[13] Nevertheless, to illustrate how such sources of inspiration have profoundly influenced Latour's thinking, we briefly highlight three select philosophies, each of which we believe represents particularly paradigmatic examples.

Alfred N. Whitehead

The first point of reference here is Whitehead and his cosmological-cum-Christian "process philosophy," which implies and develops a metaphysical concept of nature that reaches well beyond the traditional materialism of the natural sciences (see Van Der Veken 2000). In his later writings, Latour often refers to Whitehead when attempting to transgress the deeply rooted ontological–metaphysical dichotomies between subject and object, society and nature, language and the world (e.g., Latour 1997; 2004a). This inspiration is also evident on the conceptual plane, where Latour borrows a number of basic categories from Whitehead – such as, for instance, the notions of "event," "proposition" and "prehension."

These categories are all embedded in the basic idea that the fundamental phenomenon in nature is *process*. According to Whitehead, nature does not consist of discrete entities of matter distributed in time and space – as (certain) natural sciences claim. Instead, nature consists of *events*; events through which time, space and experience become dynamically related to each other. For Whitehead, reality (that is, nature) is fundamentally processual and relational: Reality comes to us in experiences that take the shape of "propositions"; as actual events laden with sensations, values and causal relationships (see Schinkel 2007: 713f). Whitehead's concept of nature, in short, deals with a notion of dynamic becoming.

A number of threads run from Whitehead's process–philosophical approach to nature and into Latour's work in science studies and political ecology; we highlight two of the most notable. First, Whitehead seems to provide a metaphysical language that transgresses a number of the modernist dichotomies that – according to Latour as well – obstruct our understanding of the dynamic relations between culture and nature, humans and non-humans, society and science. Such dynamic relations form the central points of reference in ANT. As we discuss throughout this book, Latour consistently articulates his actor-networks in terms of processes and relations. For him, dynamic relations – known as "translations," "mediations," "circulations" and the like – are ontologically primary, whereas static entities such as "society" and "nature" are seen as secondary effects of such relations.

Second, and more specifically, Latour's affirmative political philosophy is strongly inspired by Whitehead's polemic against the so-called "bifurcation of nature." According to the theory of bifurcation, nature consists of primary and secondary qualities. For example, John Locke (the father of empiricism) believed that an apple consists of a series of *primary* qualities, independent of an observer – shape, size, weight, etc. But the apple also consists of subjective or *secondary* qualities that are observer-dependant – color, odor, flavor, etc. In a famous passage from his book *The Concept of Nature* (to which Latour refers several times; e.g., 2005c), Whitehead criticizes this concept of bifurcation, because *everything* available to the senses is equally part of nature: "For us the red glow of the sunset should be as much part of nature as are the molecules and electric waves by which men of science would explain the phenomenon" (Whitehead [1920] 2007: 37).

It is quite evident why such an anti-dualist concept of nature should appeal to Latour, especially when he attempts to rethink the relationship between scientific and political forms of representation (see Chapter 4). To Latour, Whitehead's non-bifurcated concept of nature is helpful in making the sciences more compatible with democracy, because it is no longer assumed that natural science enjoys any monopoly on knowing *true* nature.

Gilles Deleuze

The next case of significant inspiration that we wish to highlight is Gilles Deleuze's conception of immanence. Certain core Deleuzian concepts – such as "plane of immanence" and "rhizomes" – form configurations of ideas that seem to have had a significant theoretical effect on Latour's most consistent figure, the (actor-)network.[14]

Generally speaking, philosophies of immanence represent an attack on widespread notions of transcendence, in the shape of something absolute, fundamental and "other" (such as God, History, the Subject or Nature). Transcendence is often expressed in distinctions between "inside" and "outside," "body" and "mind," "nature" and "culture" and so on. Contrary to such dualisms, philosophies of immanence take their metaphysical starting point in the assertion that there is only *one* substance, *one* level of existence – or, to use the Deleuzian term, *one* plane of immanence. All experience, action and change unfold on this single plane. Conceptions of immanence thus relate to monism, and Latour's experimental metaphysics may be understood as enacting a sustained revolt against a whole range of (quasi-)transcendent substances: Science (with a capital S), Nature, Society, the Subject and the

Cause. This does not imply that Latour *denies* the existence of science, nature, society, subjects and causes – instead, he depicts these phenomena as being produced (and temporarily stabilized) through dynamic relations that play themselves out together on the same plane of immanence.

Once again, dynamic relations (translations, circulations) are of primary importance, since these give rise to various displacements and mixtures – or, to use a concept central in Latour's work, *hybridizations*. If hybridization is the ontological point of departure for Latour, then his argumentative strategy is often to show that things that may *appear* to be ontologically separate phenomena (as in the formula "*either* nature *or* society") are in fact ontological displacements (hybridizations) of each other's heterogeneous elements (see Holbraad 2004). Such elements and processes are related on a pluralistic, multidimensional plane of relative and dynamic differences. In Latour's work, this plane of immanence is simply known as a *network*. This Latourian use of the term "network" thus has very little to do with any notion of stabilized infrastructural networks like sewage systems or Internet hubs. Latour's network consists of erratic hybridization processes that resemble the so-called *rhizomes* of Deleuze and Félix Guattari (1988) – named after the horizontal, branch-like network of roots found in certain plants, such as ginger. Latour himself recognizes that his notion of "network" is greatly inspired by Deleuze and Guattari's immanentist theory of rhizomes – to the extent of once remarking that he would have no objections to renaming ANT "actant-rhizome ontology" (see Latour 1999a).[15]

Michel Serres

The third – and arguably, most important – point of interest in this short review of key Latourian sources of inspiration is Michel Serres, the thinker who comes closest to being Latour's true philosophical mentor. Serres embodies a highly idiosyncratic approach, and his almost-encyclopedic writings span – and investigate the relationships between – a number of significant knowledge regimes of the Western world since antiquity: philosophy, science, literature and mythology. Serres' work may be metaphorically characterized as an extended journey: He guides his readers through unexpected sequences of ideas, logics and phenomena that would commonly be viewed as incompatible fragments belonging to entirely different times and spaces. In this constant search for surprising similarities and continuities, Serres navigates the "Northwest Passage" of the history of ideas – and connects seemingly disparate phenomena, epochs and forms of knowledge. In *Atlas* (1994), for instance, Serres maps an alternative topology in which disparate fields – including chaos theory, political publics, the cartoon character *Tintin*, history of religion, classical mechanics, interactive computer systems and astronomy – all come to be related on partially overlapping plateaus of ideas (see Boisvert 1996: 63f).

In this alternative topology – or relational metaphysics – the movements, the connections and the mediations *themselves* are of primary importance, whereas the often rigid intellectual, discipline-based and genre-specific boundaries of modernity are thoroughly sacrificed. Serres never focuses on the elements that stand in explicit relation to one another (ego/alter, nature/culture), but instead always on "the excluded third." His intellectual universe is populated by go-betweens, messengers, angels, parasites – and especially by Hermes, the ancient Greek god of travelers and those who cross borders.

To say that, broadly speaking, Latour seems to inherit Serres' intellectual style and to carry it forward, points exactly to their shared focus on mediation, on movement and on the excluded third. In Latour's work, mediation is often known as *translation, circulation* or *association*; in *We Have Never Been Modern* (1993), the excluded third is simply dubbed "The Middle Kingdom" (see Bingham & Thrift 2000; also see Chapter 3). Another term for the excluded third is *hybrid*: In Serres' ontology of mediation, Latour finds an extensive analytical focus on the movements that break down established lines of demarcation – the boundaries separating temporal epochs, spatial territories and analytical categories. It is no coincidence, then, that Latour adopts the concept of "quasi-object" (the hybrid that ties social relations together) straight from Serres (1982; see Chapter 2). According to Latour himself (Bowker & Latour 1987: 731), Serres' most significant contribution is precisely his consistent mixture of discursive genres. Via his method, Serres succeeds in eliminating the "meta-languages": Science, religion, literature and mythology come to be placed on the same plane (of immanence). Latour's lifelong endeavor to de-naturalize scientific forms of knowledge should also be viewed in this light.

Other sources of inspiration

We wish to end this selective review of Latour's sources of inspiration by emphasizing once again its main purpose: Our goal is simply to indicate how Latour's thinking inscribes itself in a number of extensive ontological–metaphysical traditions that all converge on what might be called a monistic theory of immanence (see also Harman 2009). Much more could (and should) be said about the exact conceptual relationship between Latour and the thinkers highlighted here: Whitehead, Deleuze and – above all – Serres. Further, we should note that Latour has many other significant philosophical and intellectual role models. In addition to Gabriel Tarde and Isabelle Stengers, thinkers more associated with political philosophy, such as Niccolò Machiavelli, Thomas Hobbes, Friedrich Nietzsche, Carl Schmitt and John Dewey, all play vital roles in Latour's writings. Latour's analyses of conflicts and strategic alliances in the worlds of science and technology are explicitly inspired by Machiavelli's classic theory of power, developed in response to political conflicts in Italy during the early 16th century. With respect to Nietzsche, Latour himself states that Nietzsche's "will to power" inspired his own consistent focus on struggle as a focal point for social and technological change (Crease *et al.* 2003). However, as we point out (particularly in Chapter 4), such sources of inspiration in political philosophy have gradually shifted throughout Latour's authorship, giving way to more significant dialogues with both Whitehead and the American pragmatist John Dewey.

In addition to the inspirational figures mentioned here so far, we also want to stress the crucial roles played by a number of authors not usually considered to belong in the realm of "high" philosophy. These authors may roughly be categorized in terms of their disciplinary affiliations: Marc Augé and Phillipe Descola in anthropology; Harold Garfinkel in sociology; and Algirdas J. Greimas in semiotics (a branch of linguistics). From this list, Greimas, a Lithuanian (but francophone) semiotician, needs to be highlighted. In a very concrete way, he inspired Latour to analyze how scientific statements are built up, or undermined, by adding and removing linguistic "modalities" (see Chapter 2). Greimas also coined the term *actant*, which plays a crucial role in Latour's social analyses, and which allows him to juxtapose human and non-human actors on the conceptual plane. In this respect, the role of Garfinkel, an American sociologist and founder of ethnomethodology, should also be singled out. Garfinkel authored several exemplary accounts of how meaning and order are produced through practical and local methods, and how these methods are employed by all social participants whenever they cooperate, disagree and attempt to make themselves understood, either by themselves or others. Latour's account of how scientists, engineers and other "world builders" mobilize specific resources, in their attempts to persuade others and create orderings, shares substantive traits with Garfinkel's sociology (see Chapter 5).[16]

Throughout the four main chapters of this book, we continue to revisit such connections to these (and other) significant thinkers, as and when they are activated in Latour's respective inquiries and domains of argumentation. It should become clear that, while Latour is certainly inspired by a wide range of thinkers, his originality is to be found exactly in his ability to juxtapose and reinterpret their work, thus breaking new ground. However, before we delve deeper into that discussion, we need first to clarify the principles that serve to justify our claim that – despite the continuities of the two axes (the thematic, and the ontological–metaphysical) running through his intellectual project – Latour's authorship may nonetheless reasonably be divided into four "phases" or professional identities.

Four tracks in Latour's authorship

When dealing with great intellectual figures, commentators often divide their respective works into "phases" that can then be characterized by concise narratives about significant "developments" within these authorships. One example here would be the fairly well-entrenched distinction between an early ("political") and a late ("scientific") Marx. But the reception of Latour's work is still in its infancy, and clear categorizations – both of phases and emphases – are conspicuously absent. Some commentators have suggested that we may observe a drift from primarily descriptive to primarily normative research interests in Latour's authorship during the 1990s (see Crease *et al.* 2003). Others point to the significance of changes in the global political situation – in particular, the end of the Cold War – to the way Latour positions his arguments in *We Have Never Been Modern* (Elam 1999).

Indeed, over the years, Latour's basic analytical approach and vocabulary seems to have shifted somewhat, from metaphors of war to metaphors of negotiation and diplomacy (see Chapters 2 and 4). In other contexts, there is now talk of ANT and "post-ANT," whereby authors recognize that this theoretical school of thought, to which Latour's name is intrinsically linked, has seen significant developments since its earliest formulations in the 1980s (see Gad & Bruun Jensen 2010). However, it remains unclear as to what extent Latour's own thinking since the 1990s can reasonably be dubbed "post-ANT" – a confusion, we should note, to which Latour himself has substantially contributed. Hence, in the context of a collective self-reflection on this very theme, published as *ANT and After* (1999), Latour (1999a) writes that only four things are wrong with *actor-network theory*: the term "actor," the term "network," the term "theory" – and the hyphen! Six years later, in *Reassembling the Social: An Introduction to Actor-Network-Theory* (2005b), Latour explicitly (and apologetically) adopts the exact opposite position: Instead of critically rejecting these concepts, he is now prepared once again to defend and clarify each and every one of them.

This anecdote may also lead us to the general impression that Latour's style of writing is characterized by a somewhat slippery and metaphorical use of terminology – in fact, a number of concepts developed in quite different settings seem to be used more or less as synonyms (see Lewowicz 2003). The most obvious example here is the concept of *translation*, which Latour also dubs – depending on the context – *hybridization, mediation, circulation* or (more recently) *association*. All of these terms share the same basic meaning, but with slightly different connotations. Such shifting terminology – both within individual books and over time – only makes it more complicated to divide Latour's authorship into distinct phases.

We believe that all of the interpretations listed here have some validity: the shift from the descriptive to the normative; the significance of the international political context; and the transition from ANT to post-ANT. However, for the purposes and the genre of an introductory book – a text that must attempt to "cut" the entire authorship into a somewhat logical sequence of clearly demarcated chapters – none of these interpretative schemes seems precise enough to serve as our stabilizing foundation.

For this reason, we have chosen a different strategy: Rather than dividing Latour's work into "phases" defined in purely temporal terms, our focus is on his multiple and shifting identities – his many intellectual "faces," as it were. For the most part, these identities (or versions) are closely linked to changing settings and domains of discussion – contexts in which Latour both actively positions his thinking and becomes placed via the reception of his works.

In an intellectual landscape that, by the early 21st century, is still predominantly characterized by disciplinary specialization, it should come as no surprise that many of the nuances of Latour's thinking emerge through his movements across the boundaries of several disciplines. In different contexts, as noted, Latour calls himself an anthropologist, a metaphysicist or a sociologist – and his primary intellectual affiliation is to the field of STS. In line with such self-designations, we dedicate each of the following four chapters to a particular professional-identity label, by which Latour has come to "filter" (so to speak) his engagement in shifting academic debates.

By way of interpreting and reconstructing these four significant professional identities, we speak about Latour as the "anthropologist of science," the "philosopher of modernity," the "political ecologist" and the "sociologist of associations." Each of these identities – which, to reiterate, is our own (re-)construction of Latour's work – represents a deliberate blend; part academic discipline, and part thematic marker. On one side, we put the academic traditions of anthropology, philosophy, political theory and sociology; on the other, the themes of science, modernity, ecology and associations (in the broadest sense).[17]

What we said in the earlier section on Latour's academic biography already suggests important reasons as to why these exact four academic disciplines should take center stage, and also how Latour's respective works may be grouped within such a grid of disciplines and themes. The term "anthropology of science" then refers to some of Latour's earliest books (including *Laboratory Life* [1979] and *Science in Action* [1987]); "philosophy of modernity" refers to his magnum opus *We Have Never Been Modern* (1993); "political ecology" refers mainly to *Politics of Nature* (2004d); and "sociology of associations" primarily to *Reassembling the Social* (2005). As such, there is a certain element of temporal "phases" in our system of divisions: Anthropology of science comes to be associated with the "early" Latour; philosophy of modernity marks a "middle point"; and the two remaining identities may be said to belong to the "later" part of his authorship (since the mid-1990s). Given the fact that Latour is still a prolific writer at the time of this introductory book's release, the provisional nature of such designations, however, should be obvious. Moreover, we consider the different professional identities as partially concurrent and overlapping, rather than as clearly distinct from each other in time or substance. The identities highlight different tones, thematic points of reference and central domains of discussion – they are fluid transitions rather than definitive shifts.

While it is the role of each consecutive chapter to unfold and expand the precise meaning of our professional-identity designations, at this point we find it fruitful to briefly describe Latour's various domains of discussion and the links that exist between them. As an anthropologist of science (Chapter 2), Latour uses fieldwork methodology to compile a detailed account of how facts are constructed in the scientific laboratory. In the process of doing so, he mounts a comprehensive attack on traditional epistemological explanations as to what scientific facts are. This anthropology of science comes to serve as a foundation for the rest of Latour's authorship, in the sense that he repeatedly draws upon and refers back to it. This applies in particular to his work in the philosophy of modernity (Chapter 3), where Latour analyzes the so-called "modern Constitution"; that is, the official scientific, political and theological organizing principles of modernity. Among other things, this Constitution creates and upholds clear distinctions between politics and science, between society and nature, and between modern and pre-modern cultures. Latour's main argument is that this official Constitution has never been valid – "we have never been modern." Moreover, he argues that the Constitution is becoming increasingly problematic, as the number of unruly entanglements (or hybrids) of nature and culture increases – as evidenced, for instance, by the alarming signs of present-day ecological crises. As an alternative to the modern Constitution, Latour outlines a cultural self-understanding and practice that he dubs "non-modern" – set up in explicit opposition to widely held notions that our contemporary world should be either "late-" or "post-modern."

Through his political ecology (Chapter 4), Latour now attempts to draw those implications for political theory that stem from his science studies and his theory of modernity. He strives to rethink the problematic relationship of human beings to their non-human surroundings in terms of new "parliaments of nature," designated as hybrid collectives of humans and non-humans. Latour's consistent focus on hybridity affects both sides of this equation, so to speak. On one hand, he argues that, correctly understood, political ecology has nothing to do with any transcendental Nature. On the other hand, the notion of a transcendental Society (with a capital S) – as it is traditionally studied by sociologists – will likewise have to be abandoned. This line of argument is continued in the sociology of associations (Chapter 5), where Latour suggests a complete revision of the social sciences, still using the umbrella term of ANT. Whereas traditional sociology studies a society that consists merely of human beings, Latour argues that in a non-modern world sociology needs to trace heterogeneous connections (or associations) among human and non-human "actants" – hence, the sociology of *associations*. This completes the analytical circle: Starting with an anthropological re-description of scientific knowledge, Latour has now conjured up a vision of a non-modern collective of humans and non-humans – beyond dichotomies of subject and object, society and nature. As authors, we hope that our partition of Latour's thinking into four professional identities serves not to cloud, but rather to clarify, this kind of evident continuity running through Latour's intellectual project.

One significant side effect of partitioning Latour's work into four partially overlapping disciplinary identities is that this principle of organization does not allow for any free-standing introduction to the background, main characteristics or dynamic developments of ANT itself. However, what we discuss (in Chapter 2) in terms of Latour's anthropology of science is, in many respects, identical to the "core" of the original formulations of this theory. Except, of course, that ANT was and is a collaborative project, which means that our rather one-sided focus on Latour's contribution may come across as an underestimation of the constitutive efforts of Michael Callon, John Law and others (although this is certainly not our intention). In more positive terms, however, we might also argue that there are good reasons for omitting a full review of ANT in this introductory book: By focusing explicitly on *Latour's* anthropology of science, we avoid creating the misleading suggestion that his version of ANT should be the only version, or indeed the only valid version, that exists.

The same point applies, with even greater force, to the wider field of science studies, a primary audience for Latour's work. In this context, Latour should most emphatically *not* be seen to represent every position in this diverse field – although basic tenets of his views on science have undeniably gained a stronghold here. We turn next to some more in-depth remarks on the issue of how Latour's thinking is received in various important contexts of discussion.

Positioning this book in the reception of Latour's work

It is certainly not easy to summarize in a few short sentences the numerous ways in which Latour's work is read, discussed and used across diverse contexts. One appropriate place to start, however, is to follow the American philosopher of technology Don Ihde in suggesting that, above all, Latour has emerged as an "often controversial pre-eminence" in the interdisciplinary field of science studies (2003: 2). Indeed, Latour's work is widely read, quoted and discussed in STS, a field of research that has by now become widely and internationally institutionalized, possessing its own theoretical paradigms, journals, training programs, textbooks and conferences. The field remains strongest in the English-speaking world – and, as Latour points out, this occasionally leads to translation issues, given that he himself traces his intellectual roots to the French academic scene (Bowker & Latour 1987). Translation problems aside, Latourian ANT has clearly become one of the most compelling theoretical paradigms of the field; and one that unites philosophers, historians, sociologists, geographers and engineers (among others) in exploring how scientific knowledge gets applied in complex, (non)-modern knowledge societies (see Guggenheim & Nowotny 2003). International research statistics simultaneously indicate that Latour is quoted extensively by academics from a variety of disciplines: Besides science studies, Latour's work is used in such diverse subject areas as research policy, sociology, management, social medicine, geography and psychology. In short, Latour enjoys a wide and heterogeneous audience.

Based on our experiences as authors, and in order to clarify how we read and interpret Latour's work throughout this book, it may be useful to provisionally divide the Latourian readership into two ideal–typical groups.[18] The first group consists of researchers and practitioners with a stated interest in STS. This group generates an ever-expanding amount of STS-inspired research; an increase, we might note, that in many ways runs parallel to a heightened political interest in interdisciplinary research and issues of the "knowledge economy." From diverse regions of the world, there are multiple indications of such growing institutional and individual interest in STS.[19] These research environments mostly work within qualitative and interpretive social science, with a strong empirical focus. Thematically, they focus on things like technology, culture, organization, policy, markets, and health and education practices. In such contexts, Latour is one of several significant STS thinkers whose works are read, discussed and eagerly applied to new empirical topics. Whenever Latour's work is evaluated in these circles, criticisms tend to be formulated from within broadly "compatible" theoretical positions, such as symbolic interactionism or feminist critique of technology.

The second ideal–typical group of ardent Latour readers is typically found outside of STS circles, in contexts dominated by philosophers and historians of ideas. This group tends to read Latour as a philosopher of science in the epistemological sense; a reading that often bases itself primarily (or exclusively) on *We Have Never Been Modern* (1993). We may point to several sources manifesting such tendencies in the international reception literature – and where Latour is sympathetically criticized by authors who employ philosophically more "realist" or (in Latour's terms) "modernist" standpoints.[20] Interestingly, among sociologists as well, there has been a similar tendency to read Latour primarily as a philosopher of science, who is then dismissed for not being sufficiently "sociological" in his theorizing. This reading is most paradigmatically exemplified by the acclaimed French sociologist Pierre Bourdieu (2004), who directs a very aggressive criticism toward Latour's entire sociology of science (we return to Bourdieu in the concluding chapter of this book).

As authors of this book, we share a professional background in (or closely around) the disciplines of sociology and anthropology. We work with qualitative empirical studies in our everyday research practices. In these and other ways, we are clearly positioned much closer to the first group of ideal–typical Latour readers (empirical STS) than to the second (philosophy of science) – and this position lays much of the foundation for the interpretations we express. However, we want to emphasize that we obviously do not consider philosophical readings of Latour's work to be inherently misguided, misleading or uninteresting. Rather, our point is that such readings, interesting as they may be, easily risk painting a somewhat one-sided picture of Latourian "empirical philosophy" – and at worst, risk reducing the empirical aspect of his work to mere "illustrations" of some predetermined and stable philosophical "position."

This brings us back, then, to the serious point of our satirical prologue: In the case of Latour, philosophically laden categories like "social constructivism," "postmodernism" and "philosophy of science" should be used with the utmost care. Indeed, we believe that Latour's thinking stands out exactly because of the dense and seamless ways in which he weaves together abstract theoretical (even metaphysical) investigations with concrete empirical case studies coming from different social domains, and particularly from the world of techno-science. We hope that our sociological and anthropological approach in this book helps to bring about a more versatile, multifaceted and (dare we say?) loyal depiction of Latour's hybrid universe. We aim to avoid the use of philosophy as a "meta-language" through which to understand and filter the intellectual practices of Latour (and others). On the other hand, we make no pretension of encapsulating Latour as representative of a clearly defined epistemological "position." On this point, we instead want to insist that Latour remains first and foremost an "anti-epistemologist"!

Guidelines for readers

In his recent introduction to ANT (Latour 2005b), Latour retells an amusing (and probably fictional) story of a young Ph.D. student at the London School of Economics, whose encounter with ANT turns out to be a disappointing and frustrating experience. The student has conducted extensive empirical inquiries into the management structures and communication channels of a major British company. Now, all he needs is a theoretical framework capable of explaining his empirical observations. He seeks out Latour and ANT because the buzz around the university says that this theory is "hot stuff." The company he is studying is absolutely full of networks – money, computer chips, standards, corporate boardrooms... It would seem that our student is well on his way to an ANT analysis, right?

But the response from Latour is disheartening: ANT, Latour patiently explains, does not work like other social theories that can be "applied" to an endless variety of domains. ANT is first of all a *negative* argument: a method to study how elements relate to each other, *not* a substantial theory of the character of these relationships – whether they be capitalistic, power-based, functional or otherwise. This theory is a tool that allows the researcher to trace associations, translations and negotiations. ANT prohibits only one thing: the idea that we already *know* the nature of such hybrid associations – including any belief we might have that they should resemble a classic network. The student leaves Latour's office slightly agitated, convinced that he would rather use Niklas Luhmann's systems theory as his underlying theoretical framework!

By now, readers of our book should have a fairly accurate impression of the contours of the terrain to be covered – and this ought to preclude the kind of vain expectations embodied by the student in Latour's anecdote. As emphasized several times, any journey into Bruno Latour's hybrid universe will lead one in many directions, and into the nooks and crannies of space and time, thematic issues, analytical categories and metaphysical abstractions. Latour's universe is original, idiosyncratic and, at first glance, perhaps somewhat strange. It exists in dialogue with a wide range of significant intellectual traditions and domains. In many ways, Latour's universe also mirrors – and is a sophisticated reflection upon – some of the most pressing analytical and practical issues of our times, as summed up in fashionable concepts like *knowledge society*, *networks*, *modernity*, *ecology* and *technological innovation*. In short, many elements come together in Latour's pervasive analytical network, and patience is a necessary virtue for readers looking to navigate these unique theoretical landscapes.

In this introductory chapter, we have indicated a number of themes and connections that we hope will guide readers safely through this book – and beyond, into the Latourian universe. We have identified Latour's sustained thematic focus on the construction of scientific knowledge, as well as his ontological–metaphysical substrate of processes, monistic immanence, relations and mediations. Further, we have sketched the contours of a complex analytical narrative as one way of ordering Latour's writings, which is also reflected in the structuring of our book. This narrative leads us first into the innermost core of science: the laboratory and its facts (Chapter 2). In turn, this takes us to a reworking of the fundamental coordinates of modernity (Chapter 3), including Nature (Chapter 4) and Society (Chapter 5) – the elements of which end up forming a single, heterogeneous, non-modern collective. In light of this principle of ordering, one piece of practical advice to readers is that this book ought to be read progressively, from beginning to end, just like any other narrative. Readers with specific thematic or professional interests may, of course, prefer to read only the relevant chapters, but in this case, they should be aware that some conceptual and analytical details might have been addressed in other chapters.

Latour has spent more than 35 years in his social-science laboratory. Throughout this period, he has made forays into the knowledge practices of natural sciences, engineering, art, law, religion and politics. To Latour, whether or not "reality" exists has never been the issue – indeed, can we even think of people who do not "believe in reality"? (Latour 1999b). On the contrary: He seeks to *expand* our sense of reality, to increase our respect for the diversity of realities, while refusing to acknowledge that "Reality" (with a capital R) should count as a final, definitive statement. Here, reality is indeed political, since realities are constantly being created and re-created, and may thus potentially be practiced in novel ways. Latour prefers to live in a non-modern world – and his anthropology of science, philosophy of modernity, political ecology and sociology of associations, as we present them in the following chapters, all represent essential tools in this endeavor. As readers, we do not necessarily have to accompany Latour on his entire journey. We may choose to focus on select points, concepts and analyses, and we should certainly scrutinize Latour's arguments as critically as we would any other knowledge claim. For these reasons, we hope that our book may inspire readers to experiment in their own ways with Latour's dynamic and wide-ranging ideas.

Latour's general statement about texts also applies to this book: Its destiny lies in the hands of future users (see Chapter 2). One possible fate is that readers will want to jump-start their acquaintance with Latour by reading the interview in Chapter 7. Another possibility is that this book will be put aside in favor of one of Latour's own texts – a destiny which we would certainly welcome. Overall, we gladly entrust such decisions, and other unpredictable uses, to our readers. After all, a guidebook does nothing more than guide.

2 Anthropology of science

This chapter introduces the first part of Latour's authorship, which we have chosen to call his "anthropology of science." This phase, or professional identity, refers primarily to a 10-year period in which he produced three books: *Laboratory Life* (Latour & Woolgar 1986 [1979]), an anthropological examination of the scientific work in a Californian laboratory; *The Pasteurization of France* (1988b [1984]), a historical analysis of the work of the famous French microbiologist Louis Pasteur; and *Science in Action* (1987), a summary of his own earlier work and a systematic theoretical account of science, technology and facts. If we want to maintain the term "anthropology" for this phase, then we need to clarify that Latour practices anthropology in two senses of the word: He produces thick descriptions based on field studies, and he develops general reflections on the overall nature and logic of the field. And both of these endeavors are pushed to the extreme: Reviewers have described *Laboratory Life* as one of the most thorough and detailed studies of scientific practice ever produced (Tilley 1981; Haraway 1980; Knorr Cetina 1995). *Science in Action*, in turn, has been described as a comprehensive and integrated research program for the social study of science (Shapin 1988), and as an independent and original theory of knowledge in line with – or rather, in opposition to – other more mainstream traditions, such as realism, social constructivism and deconstruction (Ward 1996).

The focal point for Latour's work during this period is the question of what a scientific fact *is*. The usual answer provided by *epistemologists* – that is, philosophers specializing in theories of knowledge (epistemology) – is that a scientific fact is a description or an idea that corresponds to the objective world. For example, epistemologists would say that it is a fact that "water consists of two hydrogen and one oxygen atom" *because* this linguistic statement accurately reflects the nature of the objective, material world out there. Such an epistemological definition of scientific facts – often referred to as the *correspondence theory* of knowledge – is so integral to Western culture that it is hard to imagine a fundamentally different understanding or definition of facts. But Latour does just that. He claims that a thorough anthropological investigation of the work carried out by researchers in scientific laboratories reveals that the epistemological definition of a scientific fact is based on unrealistic assumptions. First of all, it is a gross oversimplification to imagine that science operates with, on one side, a universe of pure ideas and, on the other side, a universe of objective, material realities. And if this dual-universe imagery is wrong, then it follows that the epistemologists' key notion of correspondence is also seriously misleading. But if facts are not ideas, then what are they? What do they consist of? Latour's response is quite surprising. First, imagine a state of disorder. Then imagine that certain actors – let us call them scientists – mobilize a variety of resources and materials that gradually allow them to establish, register and repeat a number of orderly patterns. Finally, imagine that such locally constructed orders are distributed and stabilized in other contexts, through the active participation of numerous actors and tools. Each step along the way requires work, resources and participants, who must all be enrolled one way or another. Facts are orders that are forced onto a world that is not always receptive. Facts exist only in and through networks of actors and material objects; just as electricity, gas, mail services and parking regulations in a big city only exist in and through complex and well-ordered networks.

In a nutshell, Latour's anti-epistemological understanding of facts is more about *logistics* than logic. The secret of science and technology is not some higher form of rationality, or a peculiar form of conceptual leap that in a magic split-second will allow scientific geniuses to discover the existence of a universal fact. Instead, the secret lies in the painstaking and creative efforts that go into scientists' work of constantly relating countless different kinds of materials: machines, texts, people, animals, linguistic statements and so on. According to Latour, any serious attempt to understand the nature of science and technology, including their enormous effects on the world, must involve an anthropological approach. We need to follow laboratory scientists and engineers into their workplaces to see how they construct and distribute particular types of orderings, or networks, in actual practice.

This chapter focuses on Latour's anthropological studies of scientists and engineers, starting with his analysis of how facts are created in a laboratory, based primarily on his (co-authored) *Laboratory Life* (Latour & Woolgar 1986). We include a fairly detailed account of this work, because Latour's study of laboratory practices remains a key point of reference for all of his later work. This is the case, for instance, when Latour presents his philosophy of modernity as an attempt to extract the philosophical implications of science studies (see Chapter 3). Similarly, in his more recent work on so-called "regimes of existence and enunciation," he uses his laboratory studies as a basis for comparison between different regimes (see Chapter 5).

The latter part of this chapter contains three examples of how facts and orderings are stabilized and distributed *beyond* the laboratory. The first example is Latour's analysis of technology and *machines*; the second concerns *rationality*, considered a form of constructed order; and the third deals with the establishment of so-called *centers of calculation*, a key point in

28 Anthropology of science

Latour's analysis of how science and technology become worldwide phenomena.

Finally, this chapter summarizes the theory of facts, knowledge and power that Latour develops through his work on the anthropology of science. This theory is developed in close collaboration with Michel Callon and John Law, and has since become known as *actor-network theory* (ANT).

The background for the laboratory studies

As noted in Chapter 1, Latour formulates a question during his stay in West Africa; a question that may appear rather innocent, but which is actually a direct attack on one of the fundamental principles of epistemology: "What would happen to the Great Divide between scientific and pre-scientific thinking if the same field methods used to study Ivory Coast farmers were applied to first-rate scientists?" (Latour & Woolgar 1986: 274) Behind this question lies a strong skepticism – developed through dialogues with the anthropologist Marc Augé, and through Latour's own studies of African leaders – with regard to the tendency of anthropology at that time to explain phenomena through the idea of an "African mentality." If French teachers complain that their African students "cannot think in three dimensions," then this is probably due to the students' lack of experience with motors and engineering diagrams, rather than some "mental deficiency." The question is now whether an equivalent focus on the practical circumstances, instead of epistemological (cognitive, mental) factors, can also be applied in the study of Western science. Two years later, Latour is given a unique opportunity to investigate this question. He meets Roger Guillemin, head of the neuroendocrinology laboratory at the Salk Institute for Biological Studies in California. Guillemin praises the openness of the Salk Institute, and in this spirit he invites Latour to conduct a two-year "epistemological study" of his laboratory – provided that Latour can obtain his own funding. Latour takes him up on the offer and starts his inquiries in the autumn of 1975. Latour thus arrives in California as a foreigner with relatively poor English skills, with a strong anthropological curiosity and a special interest in the practical circumstances under which scientific knowledge is established.

In California, Latour meets a small group of younger researchers who are involved in anthropological field studies of scientific laboratories. Among them are Steve Woolgar, Mike Lynch, Karin Knorr Cetina and Sharon Traweek, who later become significant parts of Latour's academic circles. In a retrospective article on the resultant laboratory studies (1995), Knorr Cetina observes that this was the first time social scientists took an explicit interest in the very *core* of scientific work. Previously, sociologists had examined external circumstances, such as funding and recruitment patterns, but they had never conducted in-depth studies of the actual work processes of natural-science laboratories. The earlier avoidance of the core of scientific work was probably due to a certain feeling of awe toward the natural sciences, which were considered an entirely objective, logical and rational endeavor. In other words, the epistemological view of science as a distinct form of thought was widely accepted. As a consequence, the common view of science would leave little room for anthropological or sociological explanation – except perhaps in cases where the knowledge of specific scientists was later shown to be incorrect.

However, in the 1970s, this reverential attitude toward the rationality of the natural sciences was somewhat lessened, in part due to the groundbreaking book on *The Structure of Scientific Revolutions* (1962) by historian of science Thomas S. Kuhn. Kuhn argues that the scientific view of nature is determined by particular social and cognitive frames called *paradigms*, acting as pre-set boundaries on what can be seen, and on which questions can even be raised. Kuhn's description of science is mainly epistemological, since its focus is on cognitive frames, but at the same time, he raises serious doubts about the notion of correspondence. After Kuhn, it is difficult to maintain the idea that science simply reflects or discovers a pre-existing and pre-given Nature. By implication, there is every reason to investigate the internal work processes of science, in order to understand the results that are produced; there *is*, after all, something for anthropologists and sociologists to explain. The laboratory studies of Lynch, Knorr Cetina, Traweek, Woolgar and Latour can be seen as a continuation of Kuhn's interest in the internal workings of science, but by different means. Rather than a historical approach, the new wave of laboratory studies deploys methods from anthropology and discourse analysis to analyze scientific debates and knowledge in the making, in order to provide an in-depth picture of the technical, material and linguistic processes of laboratory work.

The laboratory as a fact-producing factory

A good place to begin our journey through scientific work processes is with Latour's own description of the numerous impressions that greet an anthropological observer who visits a laboratory for the first time:

> Every morning, workers walk into the laboratory carrying their lunches in brown paper bags. Technicians immediately begin preparing assays, setting up surgical tables and weighing chemicals. They harvest data from counters which have been working overnight. Secretaries sit at typewriters and begin re-correcting manuscripts which are inevitably late for their publication deadlines. The staff, some of whom have arrived earlier, enter the office area one by one and briefly exchange information on what is to be done during the day. After a while they leave for their benches. Caretakers and other workers deliver shipments of animals, fresh chemicals and piles of mail. (...) Every ten minutes or so, there is a phone call for one of the staff from a colleague, an editor, or some official. There are conversations, discussions, and arguments at the benches:

'Why don't you try that?' Diagrams are scribbled on blackboards. Large numbers of computers spill out masses of print-outs. Lengthy data sheets accumulate on desks next to copies of articles scribbled on by colleagues.

By the end of the day, mail has been dispatched together with manuscripts, pre-prints, and samples of rare and expensive substances packed in dry ice. (. . .) Minute hints have dawned. One or two statements have seen their credibility increase (or decrease) a few points, rather like the daily Dow Jones Industrial Average. (. . .) Now the place is empty, except for the lone figure of an observer. He silently ponders what he has seen with a mild sense of bewilderment.

(Observer's story; Latour & Woolgar 1986: 16–17)

This description provides a kaleidoscopic introduction to the field, the actors and the materials that Latour sets out to examine in more detail. The challenge will be to reshape this disorganized pile of observations into one coherent account. But where should one begin? What is the first step? If one believed that laboratory work could be explained by epistemological processes, then one would probably focus on the researchers' intelligence, their scientific methods, rationality, their logic, and perhaps their ability to "see in three dimensions." But skepticism toward this kind of explanation is precisely what brought Latour to California. Instead, Latour chooses to focus on the practical sequence of events in the laboratory. He aims to describe the entire production process, which in the end leads to the publication of a scientific article.

This process starts in the area of the laboratory where technicians are preparing animals for experimentation. Various fluids are injected into small rodents, which are then hooked up to specific apparatuses. Later, these apparatuses will produce print-outs that are to be processed by the technicians. For example, the print-outs will be cleaned up and compared. The resulting pile of papers is brought into the offices of the scientists. Here, the newly arrived and internally produced papers are placed onto a desk that already contains a number of externally produced papers, that is, scientific articles. The scientists start relating the two piles of papers to each other and create rough drafts for new articles. These drafts will be discussed in depth and revised several times. Finally, they will be proofread and sent out of the laboratory.

This description of the scientific production process gives an initial insight into the functioning of the laboratory. Latour has taken the first step toward his goal of describing science as a practical endeavor, rather than as a logical or cognitive achievement. However, it remains something of a mystery as to exactly how researchers are able to "conjure up" a scientific fact from using rats and chemicals. To get closer to an explanation, Latour shifts his attention to the wide range of instruments in the laboratory.

Inscription devices

Following the sequential chain of work processes in the laboratory, Latour discovers that certain types of material get transformed into other materials, and that the interest and attention of participants closely follows this flow of transformations. For example, once technicians have printed a graph from some machine, this print-out is made the object of their collective interest, while the laboratory animals and chemicals that served as input to the machine are now simply disposed of as waste. Latour considers such situations – where material substances serve as input, and some mark or graph on a piece of paper becomes the output – to be particularly significant links in the chain of scientific production. With these transformations, a kind of bridge is formed between the practical and material processes of the laboratory on one side, and the phenomena and objects that scientists talk about on the other. Latour calls this process *literary inscription*. In the laboratory, literary inscription is achieved by way of particular instruments, or "inscription devices."[1]

Latour defines an inscription device as a combination of technicians, machines and apparatuses, which together are capable of transforming a substance into a kind of visual display that can become part of a scientific article (Latour 1987: 67). Some inscription devices assume the form of a small machine; others fill an entire room – such as, for instance, the *bioassay* of the neuroendocrinology laboratory. Here, a cell, a muscle or a laboratory animal is connected to a registration mechanism, such as a gamma-counter or a myograph, a device used to record muscle contractions. First, the organism is injected with a substance of known effect, in order to establish a frame of reference. In the next step, a substance of unknown effect is injected, and the response of the organism is once again measured. The *difference* that emerges between the two response registrations is now the result of the bioanalysis. Technicians may note that "It is the same" or "There is a peak." If there is indeed a difference, this is an indication of "activity" in the as-yet unidentified substance (Latour & Woolgar 1986: 58–59).

As will be clear by now, Latour and Woolgar's account of inscription processes and devices is quite meticulous and "slow." There is an important point to this. If one were to quickly sum up the previous description by saying that "Scientists investigate substances by means of instruments," then one would indirectly assume (as in epistemological explanations) that substances are pre-given in the order of things, as if they were merely waiting to be discovered by the scientists. However, this depiction is not consistent with the actual sequence of events in the laboratory. *First*, scientists work on and with materials and inscription devices; *next*, they obtain increasingly stable inscriptions; and *finally*, they determine the existence of a new substance. The anthropological observer, attuned to details and not inclined to simply accept the scientists' own accounts, must conclude that substances are a kind of ordering, painstakingly constructed with the help of inscription devices. Latour and Woolgar articulate this core point as follows:

> The central importance of this material arrangement is that none of the phenomena 'about which' participants talk could exist without it. Without a bioassay, for example, a substance could not be said to exist. The bioassay is not merely a means to obtaining some independently given entity: the bioassay constitutes the construction of the substance. (...) It is not simply that phenomena *depend* on certain material instrumentation; rather, the phenomena *are thoroughly constituted by* the material setting of the laboratory. The artificial reality, which participants describe in terms of an objective entity, has in fact been constructed by the use of inscription devices. (...) It follows that if [we] were to imagine the removal of certain items of equipment from the laboratory, this would entail the removal of at least one object of reality from discussion.
>
> (Latour & Woolgar 1986: 64).

This statement demonstrates a position within the philosophy of science that has since come to be called *constructivism*.[2]

Constructivism has been (and still is) the subject of much debate. In reaction to the Latour and Woolgar citation, for instance, many commentators would raise the objection that atoms, social classes and biochemical connections are all objective phenomena, and therefore, cannot simply be constructions. Latour would respond that this objection creates a false contradiction. The constructed objects of the laboratory are indeed objective in that they constitute real, material arrangements of machines, laboratory animals, inscriptions and so on. Constructed entities are real, whether they are biochemical substances, buildings or traffic regulations. It is thus misleading to say (as critics of constructivism often do in caricatures) that science is "simply" a matter of constructed objects, as though these would be random mirages or fleeting ideas. Objects constructed in the laboratory are hard-won – and hard-hitting – achievements.

However, skeptics may continue by asking whether Latour and Woolgar really believe, in all honesty, that there are no real "pre-determined" objects "out there"? After all, that would seem to be a prerequisite for the laboratory to be able to discover anything at all. Is it not, then, a given fact that water consists of one oxygen and two hydrogen atoms? Latour and Woolgar have answers to these questions as well. But in order to understand their arguments, we must follow the anthropologists a little further into the laboratory, by once again turning our attention to the work processes of the neuroendocrinologists.

Articles, types of statements and the struggle between laboratories

In his investigation of laboratory logistics, Latour has reached the point of the further processing of literary inscriptions. At this juncture, he observes yet another interesting aspect of the scientific work process that he calls the *juxtapositioning of documents*. At their desks, researchers compare two types of writings to each other: on one hand, literature that comes from external sources, usually scientific articles; and on the other, the new texts produced within the laboratory itself. It is immediately apparent to the outside observer that articles are of the utmost importance to laboratory participants: They work incessantly on comparing texts, which leads to the writing of new draft articles, which are then discussed, adjusted and transcribed before being shipped away by mail. Latour is thus faced with another fundamental aspect of scientific work that he must attempt to explain, even though the articles themselves make very little sense to him. Fortunately, he finds a productive analytical approach by focusing on the individual *statements*, which can be found in the articles or in the discussions about the articles. Latour notes that not all statements seem equally factual, and this inspires him to develop a 5-grade scale of "facticity."

Type 5 statements

A number of statements are so well-known and generally accepted that they have faded into the background as a form of "tacit knowledge" shared by all participants. This knowledge only becomes explicit when participants need to explain themselves to outsiders. Type 5 statements can also be found in materialized form. As noted in Latour's description, the many inscription devices used in the laboratory incorporate a significant amount of generally accepted knowledge from neuroendocrinology and other scientific fields.

Type 4 statements

Science textbooks contain a large number of statements of the following type: "A has a particular relationship to B." Like type 5 statements, such type 4 statements appear to be incontrovertible facts. But by contrast to the tacit or materially incorporated type 5 statements, the type 4 statements are made explicit. Explicit statements like this, Latour observes, are a rare occurrence in the laboratory.

Type 3 statements

In those parts of their articles where scientists review the existing literature, Latour finds a large number of statements that he calls type 3. Like type 4, type 3 statements express a relationship ("A has a particular relationship to

B"); but in type 3, such relationships are contextually embedded or commented upon. For example: "*It is as yet unknown whether* A has a particular relationship to B" or "*Researcher X writes that* A has a particular relationship to B." Latour uses the term *modality* to designate the string of words in a statement that deliver the commentary or the contextualization (marked with italics in the two examples quoted earlier). Modalities are thus statements about other statements. Type 4 statements, Latour notes, can be transformed into type 3 by the addition of a modality – or from type 3 into type 4 by the removal of a modality. Such maneuvers have significant effects. For example, stating that "It has been reported that the structure of A is B" carries a very different meaning than merely stating that "The structure of A *is* B" (Latour & Woolgar 1986: 78).

Type 2 statements

Type 2 statements appear as claims rather than established facts. The modalities of type 2 statements refer to general conditions and circumstances that are relevant to the basic relation in question: "A number of studies indicate that A is B" or "Due to C, one must consider that it will remain difficult to determine whether A is B." Latour notes that type 2 statements are relatively common in the internal papers and drafts that constantly circulate within the laboratory.

Type 1 statements

This final – and least factual – type of statement assumes the form of vague speculations, assumptions and preliminary hypotheses. Such statements occur in private discussions and at the end of articles. Latour gives the following example: "It may also signify that not everything seen, said or reasoned about opiates may necessarily also be applicable for endorphins."

With this 5-grade scale in hand, Latour is now able to give a more satisfying account of what happens when researchers compare internal and external literature, both on their desks and in their articles. The internal writings are used to support, undermine or qualify the external texts. Certain research groups appear to be simply ignored in this process, and their statements remain pure speculations (type 1). However, the great majority of statements will stagnate in mid-air like a vast cloud of smog – neither finally proven nor disproven. In some rare cases, a statement is completely obliterated; in other cases, a statement is quickly taken up, used and re-used, until it is no longer disputed (type 5). According to Latour and Woolgar, this is exactly what a scientific fact is: a statement passed along by participants in a scientific field without any modalities.

To sum up, Latour and Woolgar depict the laboratory as a factory of literary inscriptions. Through chains of transformation processes, laboratory animals and chemical substances are turned into inscriptions that the laboratory may continue to operate upon, thereby either building up or undermining particular statements. In doing so, the laboratory becomes a participant in a battle with other laboratories. Scientific facts are those specific statements that no one attempts to disprove any longer. On the contrary, these statements become inscribed and distributed throughout an entire network of laboratories, textbooks, new inscription devices and so on. In actual practice, then, no one can dispute that water consists of one oxygen and two hydrogen atoms. This phenomenon exists within a network of laboratories, scientific articles, physics and chemistry teachings, generally accepted knowledge, illustrations, popular textbooks, etc. Scientific facts do exist "out there," if by this we mean outside of the minds of individual chemists, and outside of the laboratory. But a scientific fact exists only in and through specific networks – and these networks are precisely what we usually call "science."

Outside the laboratory walls: Machines, alliances and "machinations"

If a scientific fact is a kind of constructed order, and if the processes of construction take place within and between laboratories, then this leaves open the question of how facts come to be widely disseminated in the world at large. In other words, what exactly is the link between a few articles and statements accepted by a small domain of specialized scientists – and the enormous diversity of scientific knowledge and technological innovations that permeate the daily lives of a large part of the world's population?

In his book *Science in Action* (1987), Latour discusses these questions at length. He describes the question of dissemination as a battle between *fact-builders* attempting to spread a particular ordering on one side; and skeptics, dissidents and doubters refusing to go along with this ordering on the other. The challenges facing the fact-builders of this world are great – even insurmountable at times. But in a certain sense, the goal is the same whether we are dealing with laboratory work or the development of new technologies: In either case, the fact-builder will attempt to establish something that is so stable that recipients will accept it and carry it forward, rather than picking it to pieces. Such a stabilized set of relations is known as a "black box," a term Latour borrows from cybernetics. Cyberneticians draw black boxes in their diagrams whenever a piece of machinery or a set of commands is too complex to describe in complete detail. This simplification is only possible if the effect of the mechanism is well-known; that is to say, when the author as well as the readers know that a particular input will lead to a particular output.

In the following section, we take a closer look at this process of progressive ordering – or "black boxing" – with the help of an example often used by Latour: the story of the Diesel machine (Latour 1987: 104–107).

In 1887, Rudolf Diesel published a book in which he suggested the idea of a perfect machine, inspired by the French physicist Carnot's principles of thermodynamics. The idea is to generate combustion without an increase in temperature, and according to Diesel, this will be possible if one injects and burns the fuel in a novel way. In 1894, Diesel patents his innovative idea. From then on, a fact exists on paper, although it is still somewhat disputed, with some commentators arguing that it will never work in practice. Other colleagues, including the well-known physicist Lord Kelvin, declare themselves fully convinced.

The next step for Diesel is to construct a prototype of his machine. He enters into collaboration with MAN, a machine production company, and over the next four years, Diesel and the MAN engineers attempt to make just a single functioning prototype. MAN possesses the necessary machine tools and has more than 30 years of experience with pistons and valves, but in spite of this, the engineers run into numerous difficulties. For example, they face problems in creating just the right mixture of air and fuel, and for this reason alone, the machine design gets modified several times. Latour observes that the gradual realization of Diesel's idea implies that it is associated with a long list of other elements: MAN, prototypes, engineers, a new air-injection system and so on. He also notes that the original idea is significantly transformed throughout this process: Instead of constant temperature, the technical principle of the machine has now become one of maintaining constant pressure.

As the process of development continues, the machine undergoes further transformations; by 1897, Diesel presents his machine to the public. It is now possible for customers to buy licenses, accompanied by plans for how to construct their own Diesel machines. However, it turns out that these machines have a tendency to break down or stop working, and many license-holders demand their money back. By 1899, Diesel suffers a nervous breakdown and goes bankrupt. Latour comments that, at this point, the chain of elements associated with the original idea becomes shorter rather than longer. The machine becomes progressively less real.

In time, this chain of elements increases once again: The engineers at MAN continue to develop the machine single-handedly; as Diesel's patent expires, MAN decides to market the machine. Starting from around 1912, the machine begins to be stabilized, distributed and installed in industrial sites throughout the world. However, the question is: *What* exactly is being distributed? At a conference held in 1912, Diesel himself claims that it is simply his machine, which others have now developed. Other participants at the conference claim that, between Diesel's idea and the engine that finally worked – thanks to the efforts of hundreds of engineers – there is really only a vague resemblance. Diesel has merely given his name to the work carried out by many other actors. The following year, Diesel drowns during a sea voyage to England.

The story of Diesel is a vivid illustration of the fundamental dilemma faced by fact-builders. They have to inspire others to give a helping hand in making their ideas real, but they also have to prevent others from transforming their ideas beyond recognition (Latour 1987: 108). If others do not contribute, the idea will remain nothing but an idea on paper. On the other hand, if a fact-builder cannot prevent the collaborators from deforming the original idea, he may lose control with the entire process, and others will run away with all the money, credit, power and resources. According to Latour, the solution to this dilemma lies in certain strategies of *translation*.

Translation

Latour borrows the concept of translation from Michel Serres, who uses it to describe a specific kind of mediation that simultaneously transmits and distorts a signal. Translation involves movement and displacement. It thus creates a pattern of both order and disorder (Brown 2002). Up to this point, Latour's anthropological analyses of science already contain numerous examples of translation. Literary inscription translates a substance into a text. The adding of modalities to a statement passes the original statement on within a new text in a partially distorted form. Indeed, translation is a core concept in ANT, a body of work also known as the *sociology of translation*.

In the present context, where Latour aims to describe the challenges faced by fact-builders, translation designates the ways in which such actors interpret, construe and otherwise relate themselves to the interests of other participants in the fact-building process. Here, a whole range of possible strategies emerges.

One would be for the fact-builder to simply *attach himself to the projects of other actors*; Diesel, for instance, could have simply passed on his ideas to MAN. In this way, the fact-builder is almost certain to enroll others as part of the project, but at the same time, he will probably lose control of his own idea.

Another possibility is for the fact-builder to *ask others to participate in his project*; Diesel might have advertised for voluntary assistants, for instance. In this way, the fact-builder retains control over the project. The problem here lies in gaining and maintaining the interest of others.

The third and more ingenious possibility is for the fact-builder to portray the project as *only a small detour*. Hence, Diesel might have told MAN that it is in the best interest of the company to lend its engineers to Diesel's project for a few years, since the realization of the Diesel machine promises in the end to provide the company with better machines. This strategy neatly binds the interests of the two parties together. However, a central question remains: Who stands to earn the credit once the project is finalized? In addition, as one fact-builder among many, Diesel must compete with a host of other interesting projects that MAN might be invited into. Nothing stops MAN from pursuing its own goals by other means.

As a potential solution to these persistent problems, Latour sketches a fourth available strategy for the fact-builder: *to reorganize interests and goals*.

Potential collaborators may well have clearly articulated goals that point them in particular directions, and they might also believe that they have all the necessary means to reach these goals. But fact-builders can attempt to change these perceptions. MAN, for instance, is likely to believe that its own current research and development activities will fulfill its goal of creating better machines. Diesel, however, may claim that *his* machine will be far better than any other on the market, and that MAN will lose its customers if a competing manufacturer produces the Diesel machine first. With such an argument, Diesel may be able to influence MAN to change its goal, in a slight but significant way, from "better machines" to "the best machine" – that is, the one Diesel is going to provide.

In a further refinement of strategies, fact-builders may also attempt to redefine existing social groups, or create *new social groups* that have different goals for a particular technology. As an example of this strategy, Latour mentions the rather astonishing social reconfigurations that followed George Eastman's introduction of the Kodak camera. Prior to George Eastman, only professional photographers were interested in taking pictures themselves. This particular social group had high technical requirements, but they did not mind developing the photographic plates themselves in fairly expensive, semi-professional laboratories, which they often built in their own homes. With the invention of the Kodak camera, Eastman managed to define an entirely new social group: amateur photographers. This group was willing to accept different goals for the technology – technical quality, for instance, could be made slightly lower if, in return, the development of the photographs was to become an easy and fast service carried out by someone other than the (amateur) photographer.[3]

With reference to Diesel, Eastman, and a range of other lively innovation stories, Latour develops a whole catalogue of increasingly sophisticated strategies that fact-builders may use when attempting to enlist and control participants in their projects. We will not expand on the entire catalogue here,[4] but simply point attention to the most advanced strategy, which Latour calls the *machination of forces*. "Machination" here carries two connotations: One is to turn something into a machine-like device; and the other is to create a clever and cunning combination of otherwise divergent actors. This strategy further extends the initiatives employed by fact-builders to get collaborators interested in a project. When attempting this feat, there is always a risk that interest will disappear, and that participants will go off in different directions. The strategy of machination is thus designed to *hold together* interested parties, something that can be achieved if the fact-builder introduces more (and unexpected) allies.

Let us consider Diesel once again. He starts building a prototype along with the MAN engineers. To begin with, all the participants believe that they will be capable of building a machine that can burn any kind of fuel at constant temperatures, which would make it widely applicable and therefore an object of interest to a mass market. However, the fuel combustion does not work, and Diesel is forced to acknowledge that he cannot keep the project together. He must now choose between alliances. Does he want to make MAN interested? Does he want to target specific segments of the market rather than the entire market for engines? Will he limit himself to just one kind of fuel? The practical solution (which only later turns out to be unsuccessful) is to develop a high-pressure injection system that mixes petroleum and air. Such a design implies that only one kind of fuel can be used, and that the machine will turn out big and expensive. This limits its functionality and the potential market size. However, the advantage of this new injection system is that it joins together different forces in one unit: Air, petroleum, pressure and combustion are held in place, and the behavior of these elements becomes predictable. By implication, the behavior of MAN and the market also becomes more predictable. The injection system solves Diesel's problem because it literally holds together a number of elements and interests that are all necessary for the realization of his idea. The injection system is a *machine* in which certain forces are joined together, so that they work as one unit. The injection system is also a *machination* – an intrigue – that weaves together the interests of different actors.

Taken at face value, it may seem banal to state that engineers and inventors solve problems by building machines. Anyone knows that. However, the effect of Latour's focus on seemingly technical "details" as a part of an analysis of social interests and alliances is highly significant. Latour draws a parallel between his own analysis and the type of analysis associated with Machiavelli, the classical theorist of power *par excellence*. Machiavelli describes in detail how city-states and princes are built up through a series of strategic choices between alliances. The actors in Machiavelli's analyses constantly think about whom they can trust, whom they must abandon, who is a credible spokesperson, and how they can create new alliances. "But what did not occur to Machiavelli is that these alliances can cut across the boundaries between human beings and 'things'" (Latour 1987: 125). At exactly this point, techno-science becomes particularly interesting. Scientists and engineers create alliances like everyone else. But in contrast to many other actors, scientists and engineers are clever enough to include a broad repertoire of non-human resources in the construction of their alliances. By doing so, they achieve an enlarged margin for negotiation, which occasionally leads to the construction of amazingly strong alliances.

For science and technology studies (STS), this can be turned into a methodological point: Latour argues that researchers of science and technology must develop a cleverness and broadness of repertoire that can match the actors they study. The aim is to follow techno-scientific actors in all aspects of their attempts to create alliances, *no matter which* types of materials, artifacts or actors may become involved in the process.

Breaking with diffusion theory

In the previous section, we saw how Latour uses an apparently naïve anthropological description of laboratory work as a springboard for a radical break with the correspondence theory of epistemologists. A close enough look at laboratory work, he claims, will reveal that facts are indeed constructed: Nature is the result of work in the laboratory, not the precondition for this work. With his analysis of alliances, machines and *machinations*, Latour prepares the ground for yet another break with a dominant epistemological idea. In this case, the "opponent" is not correspondence theory, but instead *diffusion theory*.

Diffusion theory is Latour's common term for a range of well-known ways of describing technology.[5] Basically, diffusion theory describes technological development as the result of a number of brilliant inventions, created by outstanding individuals and then spread – with some delay – to the rest of society. Latour finds several aspects of this diffusion model unrealistic, idealistic and otherwise problematic. First, diffusion theory assumes that facts move by way of some built-in inertia; according to Latour, this approach thus overlooks the multitude of actors who contribute to the realization and dissemination of technological and scientific devices like the Diesel machine. Second, diffusion theory assumes that facts retain their *original form* as they spread; to this, Latour objects that facts and technologies are constructed entities that gradually change form during the entirety of this process. Third, Latour is highly critical of the decisive role that *inventors* play in the diffusion model. Genius inventors are depicted as mythological figures who did all the work "in abstract" or "in theory," despite that these actors only did a very small part of all the work that eventually constructed a workable black box. The concept of *ideas* plays an important role here. In the diffusion model, the basic story of Diesel would be that he had a brilliant idea, which then spread through its own force out into the world. Latour's version of the story is that Diesel further developed Carnot's thermodynamics; that he did not work alone; that his machine design was continuously modified; and that the machine was only distributed due to a multitude of other actors.

The further question is how we might explain the significant delay in the building and dissemination of a technology like the Diesel machine. In Latour's translation model, the explanation is quite obvious: Facts are only realized and distributed because increasing numbers of actors become interested and involved in stable alliances. This takes time. By contrast, proponents of diffusion theory need to explain what has *obstructed* the otherwise natural process, whereby "good" ideas spread through their own force. From this perspective, the explanation lies with *society*: Some social groups resist, while others allow ideas to flow. Thus, society is seen as a medium through which ideas travel. Latour is strongly critical of this point, since just about anything can be explained using this model: If the machine is disseminated, this is explained as a natural course of events; if the machine is *not* disseminated, this is said to be due to resistance from some social groups. With this explanatory tool in hand, diffusion theorists introduce a kind of analytical *asymmetry* – when things go wrong, social factors are brought in to provide an explanation; when things work out for the inventor, the diffusionists assume that this is simply due to the inherent brilliance of the idea. Latour suggests – drawing on the work of sociologist of science David Bloor – that one needs to maintain a principle of analytical symmetry. The *same* types of factors should be used to explain both success and failure, realization and non-realization, dissemination and breakdown. Indeed, Latour's translation model attempts just such a symmetrical analysis.[6]

As we have seen, Latour's analysis of machines and *machinations* is a continuation of his laboratory studies. In these, Latour examines how literary inscriptions are constructed with inscription devices, how statements are painstakingly established as facts, and how these facts become incorporated into the laboratory in the form of new inscription devices. In his analysis of Diesel (and several other cases), Latour examines how new technological machinations are meticulously realized through the struggle to attract and maintain the interest of a number of human and non-human allies.

As already noted, Latour is consistently pursuing an anti-epistemological project. The notion of Nature as something external and pre-given (correspondence theory), and the notion of ideas possessive of immanent force (diffusion theory) is challenged and replaced by a detailed analysis of construction and translation processes. In doing so, Latour consciously and continuously fuses knowledge, truth, effectiveness and power. Uniting allies and keeping them together is just like establishing facts or constructing effective machines. Latour is able to use the same Machiavellian war-like metaphors in each of these cases; it is simply the types of allies and strategies that differ. To highlight these essential similarities between science and technology – their hybrid materiality, their dependence on alliances and their hard-won stabilities – Latour frequently uses the term *techno-science*[7] to cover both endeavors.

Worldwide techno-science

The analytical program that Latour initiates with his laboratory studies and continues with analyses of machines is expanded with yet another topic: Not only does techno-science construct facts and machines, it also produces worldwide networks.

In the early 1980s, Latour and some of his colleagues start taking an interest in how, throughout history, Western techno-science has come to be spread around the globe. The challenge is to understand how successful fact-builders construct stable, loyal and trustworthy "delegates," and how this may develop into techno-scientific centers that can profit in various ways from the vast flow of delegates that circulate back and forth between the center itself and several locations outside of its immediate reach.[8]

In *The Pasteurization of France* (1988b [1984]), Latour presents a large-scale analysis of one of the great heroes of French scientific history: Louis Pasteur (1822–1895), the man credited with having originated the theory of how microbes cause diseases. Pasteur developed vaccines that have proven significant for public health, and he invented the method (*pasteurization*) used in production to kill pathogenic microbes – for example, those naturally found in milk and wine. The dominant narrative of Pasteur's work is *hagiographic*: Due to his great intelligence and scientific methods, Pasteur developed ingenious ideas and solutions, which then came to be spread to the rest of society. Latour, not surprisingly, is critical of such a diffusionist explanation. Instead, he focuses on the arduous process of alliance-building on the part of Pasteur, which was necessary for him to establish durable connections between one central laboratory and a range of other participants in the "Pasteurization of France." Among these participants were skeptical members of the medical profession, researchers holding other theories about the causes of illness, and members of the so-called hygiene movement, a diverse group of health administrators, city planners and "lifestyle advisors." Together, these hygiene-movement actors were in possession of some (mostly) untested ideas about the sources of dangerous infection, and how to avoid them. Other notable actors include scientific instruments, experiments and – of course – the microbes themselves, behaving differently under a variety of conditions. Latour describes Pasteur's eventual success as the effect of a series of translations, which builds and stabilizes a network between these heterogeneous actors.

One crucial event takes place at a farm in the small town of Pouilly-le-Fort, where Pasteur demonstrates his vaccine in front of the public: In a fenced-off area, sheep are given feed contaminated with anthrax spores; half the flock is provided with the vaccine. A few days later, the vaccinated sheep are running around and healthy, whereas the unvaccinated sheep are lying dead on the field. A diffusionist interpretation of this episode would be that the same essential law of nature that was uncovered under laboratory conditions has now been proven in the field. Latour, however, explains the episode as a result of an extension, expansion and translation of the laboratory network. First, bacteria from the farm have been brought back to the laboratory, bacterial strains have been weakened, and the vaccine has been developed and tested on animals in the laboratory. Then, the farm is rearranged as an extension of the laboratory, with animals divided into a group of experimental subjects and a control group. The animals are carefully monitored, both by Pasteur's staff and by a crowd of journalists and politicians, who have been specially invited and transported to the farm. Results are recorded, and the remarkable success of the Pasteur laboratory is communicated to the outside world. In sum, a wide-ranging network thus assures that laboratory results can be translated to new actors positioned on a far-away farm, and that credit for the ensuing results can be attributed to the central laboratory. The "magical" results on the field at Pouilly-le-Fort were then a consequence of logistics rather than logic.

The overarching point of Latour's book is that "the Pasteurization of France" cannot be explained by way of individual genius, but rather by way of translations. Although Pasteur and his workers were indeed centrally involved in the staging, they achieved their results due to a range of co-actors, who were mobilized and persuaded to contribute to the further expansion of the network. In the concluding sections, Latour describes how "Pasteur" (the network) not only expanded throughout France, but also – via tropical medicine – formed connections with the colonial ambitions of France as a nation.

Latour's book on Pasteur is a single-case historical analysis of how "Pasteur" becomes the center of a national (and later global) network. However, in the final chapter of *Science in Action* (1987, chapter 6) and in an important follow-up article (1990), Latour articulates a more general explanation as to why, in many cases, Western techno-science has managed to establish durable, global networks. He returns here once again to his interest in *inscriptions*.

Latour raises the deceptively simple question: When two parties are in conflict about statement S, who will win? His general answer is that the winner will be whoever can amass, on the spot, the largest number of disciplined and loyal allies (Latour 1990). However, the more specific answer is that *inscriptions* will often serve as a physical device used by one party in an effort to convince the opponent. Imagine how many discussions get settled by throwing a photograph, a report or a paper filled with numbers on the table. This way of settling discussions is perceived as obvious and natural for modern Westerners, but it has a very long and interesting history. Latour describes a series of techno-scientific innovations that have made it possible to establish more durable connections between inscriptions and phenomena.

The development of *perspective drawing* in the Renaissance established a clear correlation between a three-dimensional object and its depiction on a flat surface (Latour 1990: 27–31). Hence, allies who could be summoned with the help of such a drawing became significantly more credible.

The invention of the *printing press* made it possible to (re)produce texts in larger numbers. This had a number of decisive effects. First, inscriptions now became a medium by which statements could be spread to many others, thus accelerating the power and range of inscriptions. Second, the accurate reproduction of texts made possible by the printing press also meant that errors were reproduced faithfully. When a reader found an error – for example, in an astronomical table – a correction could (in principle) be sent back to the author. It was then possible to construct inscriptions that incorporated these corrections, and hence over time accumulate knowledge and precision from many sources. This would increase the authority of any specific inscription, simply because it could summon more allies.[9]

Latour also highlights the significance of so-called *metrology* – the establishment of stable measurement standards. Metrology is not just a matter of setting precise definitions; it also involves the materialization of these definitions in a network of instruments. Without standardized units of measurement, it would be almost impossible to construct inscriptions that were trustworthy allies for specific statements – and the same would be true if measuring instruments were not manufactured, calibrated and maintained so that they would constantly meet these standards.

Let us imagine a situation where the use of various instruments, drawing conventions, the printing press, stable measurement standards and many other practical innovations have generated a stream of trustworthy inscriptions. Latour calls such inscriptions *immutable and combinable mobiles*. Let us also imagine that this stream of inscriptions all flow back to a specific location, which Latour calls a *center of calculation*. One example would be a meteorological institute, which gathers inscriptions about the weather from international collaborators, satellites and thousands of land-based measuring stations every day. As inscriptions flow into the meteorological institute, it becomes possible to focus on paperwork rather than "the weather" as such. According to Latour, this has several advantages:

- First, inscriptions can be moved around – for example, from one department to another. As we know, the weather itself cannot.
- Second, inscriptions hold their shape constant; they are neither changeable, nor will they disappear between the fingers of employees.
- Third, inscriptions are flat, making it possible to "dominate" them; people can, for instance, hold them in their hands, lean over them or point to parts of them.
- Fourth, inscriptions can be scale-modified; hence, the contours of a low-pressure weather system can be plotted on standard paper or enlarged onto a larger piece of paper without modifying the internal proportions of the initial plotting.
- Fifth, inscriptions may be reproduced and distributed inexpensively.
- Sixth, inscriptions can be combined with other inscriptions; for example, rainfall measurements for this year can be plotted alongside the rainfall of last year.
- Seventh, inscriptions can be drawn onto each other; rainfall can be plotted on a map showing height variations, crop types, gross national product or any other variable of possible interest in relation to rainfall.
- Eighth, inscriptions can be made part of written texts, and such text can comment directly on the inscriptions it contains. Thus, the meteorological institute can participate in the types of activity that Latour describes in relation to laboratory studies. The institute may compile its own and others' inscriptions, and it may use these configurations to operate on the "facticity" of statements about the weather.
- According to Latour, the ninth (and largest) advantage is that two-dimensional inscriptions provide opportunities to connect up with geometry. Dots on an inscription can be counted, and the length of a curve can be measured with a ruler. In both cases, a *numerical figure* is achieved. This number can be combined with other numbers, and a new cascade of possibilities for inscription and combination opens up.[10]

Anthropology of science 45

By analyzing immutable mobiles and centers of calculation, Latour contributes to the description of how techno-science is able to establish and disseminate specific orderings – in this case, worldwide orderings. Needless to say, Latour discusses not only meteorological institutes, but also a wide range of examples, such as the Versailles court of Louis the 16th, Tycho Brahe's observatory at Oranenbourg, and the contemporary New York Stock Exchange. In all cases, Latour highlights how techno-scientific centers of calculation summarize and condense inscriptions in increasingly sophisticated "cascades." This allows for such centers to keep still more allies together, to become increasingly persuasive, and to achieve ever greater opportunities to dominate the network in which they act as central nodes.

As we have seen before, a showdown with epistemologists and cognitive explanatory models is never far away for Latour. However, the question remains whether epistemologists will win this time around. The history of techno-science diffusion – the epistemologists might well maintain – can hardly be anything but the history of the *superiority* of Western scientific, theoretical and abstract thinking in relation to other "mentalities."

This is obviously not Latour's interpretation. The overarching point in the analysis of the centers of calculation is that any form of abstraction is a practical, concrete and tangible achievement. There is every reason to be impressed by the powers mobilized by Western techno-science, but the secret behind this power lies in all the practical innovations that make it possible to summon and combine allies in one single location. Scientists and engineers will tend to be interested in any novel device that may contribute to this project:

> New photographs, new dyes to color more cell cultures, new reactive paper, a more sensitive physiograph, a new indexing system for librarians, a new notation for algebraic function, a new heating system to keep specimens longer. History of science is the history of these innovations.
> (Latour 1990: 20)

Latour thus rejects the notion that we would need to look further than such numerous tangible innovations to explain the dominant status of Western techno-science. Even so-called "theoretical" work – "abstractions" and "formalisms," which many would regard as uniquely epistemological themes – is explained by Latour as a matter of practical combinations and the mobilizing of allies. A formalism (or a theory) is just another cascade that combines, juxtaposes or otherwise draws together earlier inscriptions. If a theory can hold many inscriptions together in a single statement, on a single piece of paper, we call it effective or strong – which is precisely a description of the theory's ability to bring many allies together in one place.

For Latour, there is nothing mysterious about theory. Theories may be described in exactly the same terms as any other activity that attempts to hold allies together. By the same token, Latour accuses epistemologists of making things mysterious by introducing the adjective *theoretical*, as contrasted with the term *empirical*. Through such terms, epistemologists conjure up the image of a separate universe of theories, which may be understood independently of what they are theories about. In Latour's view, this is just as absurd as imagining a history of hammers that does not take nails, planks, carpenters and houses into consideration; or a history of checks that pays no attention to the banking system (Latour 1987: 242).

Latour's description of theories, formalisms and abstractions – and their tangible basis in immutable mobiles and centers of calculation – provides a distinctive account of what knowledge is. This account differs significantly from many standard perceptions.[11]

The most obvious contrast is to correspondence theory (as previously mentioned). Proponents of this position believe that knowledge is true if it mirrors a naturally given reality. If not, then the theory is false. In sharp contrast to this type of *scientific realism*, Latour describes how truth (and realism) is laboriously constructed, step by step. By implication, truth and realism come in degrees, according to Latour. A theory is constituted by the particular set of allies that it can hold together at a given time – and over time, this set of allies may be strengthened or undermined.

Postmodernism is another position from which Latour strongly dissociates himself. Postmodernists argue that knowledge is to be regarded as texts, and as a result of the changing rhetorical practices of human storytellers. By contrast, Latour describes knowledge as a material–semiotic struggle rather than a conversation, and he stresses how non-human elements play crucial roles in determining which "story" wins.

Finally, Latour distinguishes himself from *social constructivism*. Social constructivists view knowledge as a result of the social interaction and organization of human groups or communities. From this position, reality is seen as a social and symbolic process of meaning creation. In Latour's account, however, we are not dealing with "social" elements adding layers of meaning on top of "natural" elements. The inscriptions and calculation processes described by Latour consist of cascades of relations and associations that constantly mix human ("social") and non-human ("natural") elements.

In short, Latour is neither a scientific realist, nor a postmodernist, nor a social constructivist. Instead, *constructivism* seems the best available label to describe the position that Latour develops in his anthropology of science work. Incidentally, constructivism is also his own preferred term; this was clearly indicated when Latour and Woolgar reissued *Laboratory Life* in 1986. The original edition of this book (from 1979) was published with the subtitle *The Social Construction of Scientific Facts*. By the time of the second edition in 1986, the word "social" had been removed, and the subtitle became simply *The Construction of Scientific Facts*. As we will see later, constructivism continues to be Latour's preferred term of theoretical self-description throughout his later works – although the meanings and implications of this term evolve and expand in new contexts (see especially Chapter 4).

Actor-network theory

In this chapter, we have discussed central components of Latour's work in the anthropology of science: namely, the construction of scientific facts, machines and centers of calculation. We have also seen how, embedded in this work, Latour develops something that could be called an anti-epistemological genre. He accounts for techno-science in a manner that avoids the usual epistemological assumptions and forms of description; correspondence theory, diffusion theory and the notion of a separate "theoretical" universe are all rejected with great conviction and consistency.

Latour's construction stories produce a particular effect that is perhaps best described as an effect of presence or tangibility: There is no objective pre-given nature *out there*, independent of the inscription devices of scientific laboratories. Moreover, there are no immutable *underlying* ideas that would somehow flow into society and materialize themselves in functioning machines. And finally, there is no theoretical universe *up there*, separate from the practical handling of inscriptions. To the contrary, Latour draws all forms of existence into a middle realm where everything is simultaneously a part of the action – where engineers and scientists mobilize whatever they can to interest and retain allies; and where anthropologists of science and technology must develop an equally broad empirical sensitivity if they want to understand why certain constructions attain relative stability while others perish.

Latour's work in the anthropology of science is clearly inspired by a number of thinkers: We have mentioned Machiavelli, Serres and the anthropologist Marc Augé, together with several other important sources of inspiration, including the semiotics of Algirdas Greimas. But the most remarkable aspect of Latour's constructivist work in the anthropology of science (and the genre he develops) is that it has gradually come to be transformed into a distinct theoretical tradition – a stabilized fact or machine, one might say. Over time, this relatively stable construction has become known as *actor-network theory* (ANT).

ANT is usually defined as a material semiotics grounded in the sociology of science and technology. It was developed by Bruno Latour, Michel Callon and John Law, who were colleagues in Paris (at the *Centre de Sociology d'Innovation, Ecole de Mines de Paris*) in the early 1980s. We will not attempt here to unravel the construction story of ANT, which would be a complicated project in itself. And, bearing in mind the story of Diesel and the MAN engineers, we refrain from trying to distribute credit for ANT between Latour and the other participants. But we do want to outline some key concepts and principles of ANT,[12] because ANT, in many contexts, has emerged as a kind of summary or codification of the anti-epistemological genre that Latour develops in his analyses of techno-science.

We begin with the element that is most vividly illustrated in Latour's analyses: ANT deals with *translations*.[13] Latour analyzes how fact-builders inside and outside of the laboratory try to link allies to their projects by transforming or translating their interests. Similarly, other actor-network theorists focus on the wide variety of strategies, technologies, texts and materials that are used to interest, mobilize and retain allies (see Callon 1986, 1998; Law 1986, 1994, 2002; Elgaard Jensen 2008).

ANT not only examines "social" actors or relations – ANT is interested in any element and any relation that helps to stabilize, or destabilize, a network. This broad analytical scope is also reflected in Latour's work: He is not simply interested in laboratory scientists, but also in their inscriptions and inscription devices; he is not solely interested in Diesel, but also in patents, customers and injection systems. In ANT, this analytical breadth is codified by means of the semiotic concept of an *actor*, which is sometimes called an *actant* (a concept derived from Greimas' version of semiotics). A semiotic actor, or actant, is any entity that plays a role in a narrative; that is, an entity that other actants in the network recognize, take account of, or are influenced by. Rudolf Diesel, a laboratory rat or a low-pressure weather system may each qualify as an actant.

The term actant thus also serves as a kind of provocation to those parts of social science that insist that only humans act, and that everything else is merely materials or tools for human action. By contrast, ANT claims that actants (actors) have a "variable geometry"; it cannot be determined in advance which network of elements will end up creating an "agency effect." ANT illustrates this by highlighting how human and non-human actants are constantly related and folded into one another through processes of translation. Effects are generated by *heterogeneous* networks, and not by (purely) social actors. The vaccine is not due to the person Pasteur, but due to the network "Pasteur." By extending this deliberately open approach to actants – their character and their relationships – ANT articulates the so-called *generalized principle of symmetry*.[14] This principle acts as a kind of methodological rule-of-thumb, requiring analysts to follow *any* relation or connection that is established by participants in the project, case or controversy under study. Any explanation for the outcome of projects is to be found in such specific relations; the analyst should refrain from introducing explanations taken from outside the project itself. Therefore, to practice ANT is to renounce the opportunity to claim that Nature or Society was the cause, or that either of these were there in advance and determined the outcome (Callon 1986; Law 1994).

ANT evidently breaks with any hagiographic description of technoscience: It is not brilliant people, but heterogeneous networks that are given credit when a techno-scientific project succeeds, or blamed when things go wrong. Despite this, certain feminist writers have criticized ANT for its so-called "managerialism" – a tendency to see things from the point of view of the powerful manager, entrepreneur or fact-builder (Star 1991; Haraway

1994). The American sociologist Susan Leigh Star has used her personal encounter with the McDonald's fast-food chain to illustrate the alleged managerialism of ANT. McDonald's, as we all know, produces entirely standardized burgers at high speeds. Star, however, is allergic to onions, but if she decides to order a burger without onions, she will have to wait half an hour for it to be prepared. In practice, this means that she will order a standard burger and use a plastic fork to scrape off the onions herself. This small anecdote is meant to illustrate that what seems to be an effective and stable network from one perspective (McDonald's, the fact-builder) can be a source of great distress when seen from a different perspective (Star, the customer). The story shows how effective standards may need to be "paid for" with a great deal of hidden work – and sometimes hidden pain – that is suffered by relatively invisible, marginalized existences. Star criticizes ANT for unilaterally allying itself with the fact-builder's perspective.

Latour's response to this criticism takes two different directions. First, he argues that the strong focus on fact-builders was a matter of priorities. In the 1970s, there was still very little sociological analysis available on the controversies and disputes within the practical work of science. Therefore, a focus on the struggles to stabilize techno-scientific "black boxes" was necessary and useful in order to establish STS as a field of study (Crease et al. 2003). Second, Latour seems in practice to have partially taken the criticism to heart, in that he has gradually changed his preferred political metaphor from that of war to "experimental democracy" (see Chapter 4). The response among other actor-network theorists has been similarly mixed.[15]

Regardless of the specific analytical perspective and possible biases herein, we may summarize by saying that ANT defines a specific *ontology* using the concepts of actor, network and translation. This is a thoroughly *relational* ontology: ANT claims that any actant is entirely defined by its network relations. There is nothing but networks: no essences, no underlying factors, no contexts. ANT thus describes the world as a multitude of points and connections (and nothing else). This results in an unusual topology:

> Instead of surfaces, one has threads (or the rhizomes of Deleuze). (. . .) Instead of thinking in surfaces – two dimensions – or spheres – three dimensions – one is required to think in points that have as many dimensions as they have connections. [Modern societies] cannot be described without recognizing them as having a fibrous, thread-like, wiry, stringy, ropy, capillary character that is never captured by the notions of levels, layers, territories, spheres, categories, structures, systems.
>
> (Latour 1996b: 370)

By way of this distinctive topology, and by introducing the core concepts of ANT, we now have a satisfactory outline of what this theory is all about. We also have a possible way to summarize Latour's work in the anthropology of science: Latour gives us an account of how actants, through a variety of translation processes, are able to build and stabilize the kinds of networks we call facts, machines and theories. At the same time, Latour traces important parts of the extensive and heterogeneous materialities that constitute these phenomena.

Summing up: A new origin story

At the beginning of this chapter, we told the background story of *Laboratory Life*, based on Latour's own account in the postscript of the book (Latour & Woolgar 1986). During his stay in West Africa, Latour became skeptical of the cognitive explanations of comparative anthropology at the time. Latour's intuition was that practical and material circumstances were sufficient to explain why African students would fail in certain situations, in relation to the goals set by the French technologists. There was no reason to introduce an epistemological explanation, and to argue that failures resulted from a particular African mentality. Subsequently, Latour and Augé articulated the question that Latour would later pursue in California: What would happen to the Great Divide between scientific and pre-scientific thinking if the field-study methods employed to study farmers in the Ivory Coast were also used on first-rate scientists?

We now know the answer: The sharp divide between scientific and pre-scientific thinking *evaporates*. Solid facts, efficient machines and strong theories are not due to epistemological distinctions, but to extensive heterogeneous networks, strategic translation processes, and the construction of laboratories and centers of calculation. There *are* indeed vast differences between the West and "the rest" – the difference is that the West has constructed longer and more extensive actor-networks.

Put in these terms, we arrive at an almost-too-neat summary of that phase, or professional identity, that we call Latour's anthropology of science. Taking a clear question from Africa, Latour found a clear answer in California. However, in a recent speech delivered in Frankfurt, Latour has suggested an additional source of inspiration for his anthropology of science (Latour 2008a): He now refers to his doctoral thesis in Biblical exegesis, based on his studies in Dijon, but finished while in the Ivory Coast. In the thesis, Latour engages the work of German theologian Rudolf Bultmann, well known for his systematic attempts to de-mythologize the Christian Gospels. Bultmann aimed to identify the few authentic sentences actually spoken by Jesus, and to separate those original truths from the bewildering array of repetitions and interpretations found in the Gospels. Latour might have considered Bultmann's analysis an elaborate deconstruction of the entire Catholic faith – including his own – but instead, he develops an entirely opposite reading of Bultmann. Latour argues that the interpretations should not be seen as "noise"; on the contrary it is precisely the numerous interpretations that produce the "truth effect" of the Gospels. For such effects to happen, however, the interpretations need to be "in the right key" – they cannot be mere repetition, and the original intention must somehow be carried forward. Bultmann's version of Biblical exegesis, Latour now states, was "my first translation network – something that had a decisive influence on my thinking" (Latour 2010a).

Latour further explains:

> What Bultmann did for me [. . .], was that, when I entered the biological laboratory in California [. . .], I was primed to detect its exegetic dimension in the immense complexity of scientific practice. Hence, my fascination for the literary aspects of science, for the visualizing tools, for the collective work of interpretation around barely distinguishable traces, for what I called *inscriptions*. Here too, exactly as in the work of biblical exegesis, truth could be obtained not by *decreasing* the number of intermediary steps, but by *increasing* the number of mediations.
> (Latour 2010a)

Religion and science are obviously not the same; on the contrary, Latour stresses that any "regime of enunciation" has its own struggles over what is necessary and sufficient for some translation to contribute to the creation of truth effects.[16] But the fact remains that Latour's "analytical approach" – which, of course, gets reproduced, translated and carried forward in many interesting ways – emerges from a specific discussion about Biblical exegesis.

In Latour's anthropology of science, we may therefore identify a fundamental *question* that contains an echo of Latour's encounter with Africa and anthropology; we may also identify a fundamental *approach* to this question that contains an echo of his religious studies in France. But first and foremost, Latour's anthropology of science takes us on a journey through heterogeneous and wide-ranging techno-scientific translation networks that are rooted in the world of Western modernity.

3 Philosophy of modernity

As we saw in Chapter 2, nothing would be more misleading than to consider Latour's interest in science to be narrowly local or "micro-ethnographic." Since the beginning of his career, Latour has been a man on the hunt for big intellectual agendas. He is not simply curious about how life unfolds in a single research laboratory; his interest is driven by much larger questions about the relationship between Western and non-Western rationality. By implication, his analysis of specific scientific practices is continuously linked to discussions about the general character of scientific facts, how they are dispersed, and how they are involved in building centers of calculation and other global projects. As a kind of culmination of his work in the anthropology of science, Latour (along with Callon and Law) develops actor-network theory (ANT), which – in texts such as *Irreductions* (Latour 1988b) – manifests itself as a coherent and full-blown philosophical program.

This chapter takes a close look at Latour's *next* big agenda, which he initiates with the book *We Have Never Been Modern* (1993).[1] This book is yet another attempt to draw philosophical implications from the basic insights of science studies; in this case, Latour starts to grapple with the concept of *modernity*.

What makes our society *modern*? And what makes us modern humans? The most common answers to these questions – among historians, sociologists and other social scientists – is that we are modern because our regime of government consists of a well-established representative democracy, rather than some random brutality. Also, that we rely upon scientific principles, rather than faith and superstition. And that we live in an industrialized society, and we recognize the rights of individuals. Moreover, most people associate modernity with a kind of hope and faith in progress: We can rise above brutality and arbitrariness. We can increase our understanding of objective nature. We can create order for the good of all.

Needless to say, more critical analysts and commentators have denied such an altogether positive interpretation of modernity. Modernity has heralded much more than simply progress – it has brought the colonization and exploitation of the Third World; world wars and weapons of mass destruction; pollution and the destruction of nature on a scale never before imagined. Depending on the standpoint, modernity can thus be viewed as either a blessing or a disaster; or commentators will articulate one of a wide range of middle positions, such as cautious optimism ("we will probably be alright") or moderate concern ("if we do not act soon, then . . . ").

A common note in this choir of voices is the implicit assumption that modernity is something that *exists*. One can certainly discuss when the modern began and whether it will persist, but right here and right now – in democratic, industrialized, scientific, high-tech Western societies – there can be no doubt whatsoever that we are *in* modernity.

Latour, however, disagrees completely. As the title of his book suggests, he argues that we have simply *never* been modern. Modernity is like "the good old days" and "childhood summers"; it is an anachronistic[2] view of our own culture that has never been accurate, and that now more than ever needs to be updated.

In this chapter, we review Latour's philosophy of modernity, which contains at least two major contributions. First, Latour uses insights from his anthropology of science, and the wider history of science, to develop a particular definition of modernity. Modernity, he claims, stems from a *separation* between Nature and Society, which began to be established in the 1600s. Natural science is one – but not the only – essential building block of this separation. The second contribution of Latour's book is his attempt to outline what he sees as a more realistic and constructive view of our present scientific, technological and political culture. In this context, Latour presents a vision, both concerned and optimistic, of how we ought to respond to some major problems in the contemporary world. In sum, we are dealing with a work in the philosophy of modernity, which also contains a diagnosis of our times; Latour's project is to examine the present-day troubles of "modern" culture by means of a philosophical ilucidation of the root of all evil: our ingrained but erroneous belief that we are modern.

The method of the book: Anthropology, constitutional metaphor and thought experiment

We Have Never Been Modern raises some very comprehensive questions: What mental landscape do modern people find themselves in? How do we understand nature? How do we understand society? What is the relationship between science and politics? To get a grip on these questions, Latour draws inspiration from anthropology, which he notes, has been "pretty good at tackling everything at once" (Latour 1993: 14). In their descriptions of far-away cultures, anthropologists are capable of linking a wide variety of different elements. As an example, Latour quotes from the anthropologist Philippe Descola's description of the Achuar tribe in the Amazon region. Like any good anthropologist, Latour notes, Descola speaks in one single section about "the definition of the forces in play; the distribution of powers among human beings, gods, and nonhumans; the procedures for reaching agreements; the connections between religion and power; ancestors; cosmology; property rights; plant and animal taxonomies" (Latour 1993: 14).

Latour's ambition is to do something similar: He wants to define modernity by talking about many different things at the same time. According to Latour, any collective mobilizes heaven and earth, body and soul, property and law, gods and ancestors, etc. (Latour 1993: 107). We all operate within the same ancient anthropological matrix, but all collectives do this differently. The question is: What characterizes the moderns?

To answer this question, Latour introduces a thought experiment, or a metaphor, that he uses throughout *We Have Never Been Modern*. He makes the assumption that it will be possible to discover or assemble a *constitution* that establishes the rules of modern thought and action. Latour imagines that this modern Constitution will resemble a political constitution. It acts as a kind of common law, prescribing certain divisions of power, rights and guarantees. But the modern Constitution is not just about politics – it defines our entire vision of nature, science, religion and much more. *We Have Never Been Modern* is an attempt to uncover, write up and assemble a Constitution for the moderns, just as Descola (without using this metaphor) assembled the constitution underlying the life of the Achuar tribe. Latour's project is dizzyingly ambitious; he attempts to summarize how *everything* (politics, religion, science, etc.) has been configured throughout the whole of the Western world in the entire period from the mid-1600s until the present. Therefore, it should come as no surprise that Latour bases his analysis on an extensive selection of ideas and theories, and that he articulates his characterization of modernity in quite abstract terms.

On the trail of the modern Constitution

If one is writing about "everything," then where does one start? Where should one look to get a glimpse of a constitution that underlies modernity? In an initial attempt, Latour delves into a copy of a contemporary French newspaper. Reading through the pages, it strikes him that one story after another reveals a remarkable web of complexly interwoven events.

For instance, in reading a story about holes in the ozone layer, one learns first of atmospheric chemists and the measurements they conducted in the air above the Earth's poles. You then hear about decisions made in the management offices of large multinational corporations. The story evolves through factories attempting to change their production processes, and one reads about chemical substances, freezers, types of gases and patterns of consumption. Discussions among heads of state enter the story a little later, along with international agreements, the rights of future generations and environmental-movement protests. In the very same newspaper article, Latour comments, one finds a mix of chemical reactions and political reactions. A single thread links the most esoteric sciences and the most sordid politics, the most distant sky and some factory in the Lyon suburbs, dangers on a global scale and the impending local elections or the next board meeting.

(Latour 1993: 1)

What exactly is the interesting aspect of this newspaper article? Latour suggests that stories such as this reveal a remarkable paradox. On one hand, there is one contemporary issue after another that weaves together all sorts of elements and actors. As further examples of such interwoven or hybrid phenomena, Latour mentions AIDS, computer chips, frozen embryos and the burning of Amazonian forests. On the other hand, we have a well-established tradition for categorizing the world in a completely different ways: We tend to think that we must distinguish between knowledge and interests, between justice and power, and between the social and the natural. In other words, we have a tendency to believe that the world can and must be divided into such clear-cut categories. The paradox, however, is that one phenomenon after another mixes up all of the things that we believe should be kept separate.

Latour believes that we are on to something here, which he calls *the modern Constitution*. We – the moderns – are a type of people who maintain a belief in the existence of pure categories, such as the scientific, the economic, the political, the cultural, the local, the global, etc. And this happens *despite* the fact that we surround ourselves with ever-more extensive and unruly hybrids that churn up all of culture and all of nature on a daily basis. Latour illustrates the modern practice with Figure 3.1.

The figure outlines two different sets of practices; at the bottom of the figure is the so-called *work of translation*. This corresponds to the practices that create mixtures and new types of entities; that is, hybrids between nature and culture. Science studies have helped to shed light on this work of translation, and the results that stem from the work of translation are registered in the steady stream of hybrids appearing in newspaper articles. At the top of Latour's figure is the so-called *work of purification*. This work consists of the continual practical and discursive efforts to separate nature and culture into two distinct ontological zones.

Latour's figure is neither readily understandable nor intuitive; in fact, there are many possible ways of misinterpreting it. One might, for instance, get the idea that translation is the real engine of modernity, while purification is a kind of epiphenomenon, perhaps even an expression of "false consciousness." This, however, would be an incorrect impression. Latour's view is that the secret of the moderns – and the real cause of the extraordinary dynamism of modern society – lies in a kind of synergy, or mutual reinforcement, between purification and translation. The evident paradox – between purified ontological zones on one hand, and the production of hybrids that merge these zones together on the other – is thus a *productive* paradox.

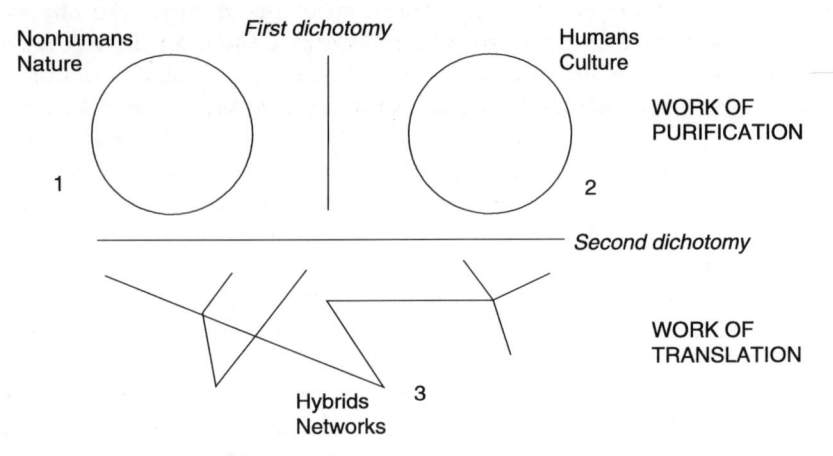

Figure 3.1. Purification and translation.
Source: Latour 1993: 11; Figure 1.1.

In order to better understand this entire paradoxical and productive modern arrangement, we turn to Latour's discussion of how the modern Constitution was gradually established along with the emerging natural sciences of 17th-century Europe.

Hobbes v. Boyle: Origins of the modern Constitution

In 1985, two historians of science, Steve Shapin and Simon Schaffer, published a book called *Leviathan and the Air-Pump: Hobbes, Boyle, and the Experimental Life*. This book is a sociological analysis of a conflict that occurred between Thomas Hobbes and Robert Boyle in the mid-1600s. Since then, Hobbes has come to be regarded as a political philosopher and Boyle as a natural scientist. But one of the main points of the book is that Boyle was *also* a political philosopher, and Hobbes was *also* a philosopher of nature. At the time of their vigorous disputes, nature and culture had not yet been defined as two distinct ontological zones and academic domains. This separation only occurred later, in large part due to the procedures, arguments and practical arrangements generated by Hobbes, Boyle and their mutual conflict. This, at least, is Latour's interpretation of *Leviathan and the Air-Pump*. He reads the book as an account of how the nature/culture distinction was invented; to him, Shapin and Shaffer's book is an origin story of the modern Constitution, and Hobbes and Boyle play the roles of constitutional fathers.

In Latour's terms, one might say that Hobbes and Boyle each provide their own take on how the anthropological matrix is to be configured. They each have their own comprehensive view on how to position nature, culture, religion, government and a range of other elements in relation to one another.

Hobbes is famous for his notion that the state of nature – the war of all against all – must be replaced by a social contract and a Leviathan (a sovereign) that speaks on behalf of all citizens.[3] The context for this view is that England has been plagued by civil wars for decades, and Hobbes is therefore strongly pre-occupied with the concept of *unity* (Latour 1993: 18–20). For Hobbes, the sovereign should be an overriding and powerful incarnation of the unity of society, "authored" by the citizens themselves. This idea carries implications on several fronts. Above all, it means that the role of religion in society will be reduced: All citizens must submit to a mortal god; that is, the sovereign. At the same time, Hobbes's vision has implications for the question of how to establish true knowledge; again, the purpose is to avoid the splintering of the social unity, and the dilemma is how to control all the self-proclaimed knowledge authorities who constantly make their appearance. For Hobbes, the only proper solution to this dilemma is the mathematical demonstration. He argues that such a demonstration is, by its very nature, rational and logical, and it should therefore be immediately convincing to everyone. Like the sovereign, mathematical demonstrations are compelling forces that everyone must obey.

Robert Boyle, the other protagonist of this story, has a distinctly different view of how to establish authority and authoritative knowledge. In science history and introductory-level physics textbooks, Boyle is mostly famous for his experiments on gas pressure and his demonstration of the air vacuum. In the 1660s, however, the most interesting quality of these experiments is that Boyle does *not* use mathematical demonstration as the main vehicle for producing knowledge. Instead, Boyle establishes knowledge by means of a range of other elements: He uses extremely costly and advanced equipment (by the standards of the time), including an air pump; he establishes a laboratory for his experiments; and he invites members of The Royal Society – a prestigious gentlemen's club in London – to witness his experiments. In his laboratory, Boyle carefully separates the recording of what actually happens (so-called "matters of fact") from various interpretations of the phenomena under study ("matters of opinion"). In doing so, Boyle attempts to defer any personal interests and religious pre-conceptions of his witnesses to the world outside of the laboratory. The world inside the laboratory, then, becomes devoted to pure, objective observations.

Hobbes was not particularly fond of Boyle's elaborate arrangements. In fact, he was furious and indignant! Hobbes' vision of security and lasting peace, based on unity, required that all citizens stop appealing to all sorts of authorities, such as ghosts, souls or self-styled religious leaders, who claimed to possess some special access to knowledge and truth. In Hobbes' view, Boyle and his laboratory were yet another dangerous attempt to create a dubious, self-appointed authority. Boyle's closed circle of gentlemen and his extravagant instruments would create an exclusive space within which he would be free to fabricate his own facts, rather than submitting to the requirement that knowledge should take the form of a mathematical demonstration. If it was to become generally accepted that Boyle could produce authoritative knowledge in *his* own way, then the door would be open for an entire flood of self-appointed authorities – and the splintering of the fragile, hard-won political unity would be unavoidable.

Who is right in this dispute? Most contemporaries would say that history granted victory to Boyle: His way of producing facts has since become widely accepted, and Boyle is now commonly regarded as the father of experimental science. According to Latour, however, the most interesting part of the story, or the conflict, is that together, Boyle and Hobbes invent a set of linguistic and practical arrangements that were to become fundamental to modern culture. The key word is *representation*. For his part, Boyle invents a procedure and a set-up that allows scientists to speak on behalf of nature: Given the right instruments, the right laboratory, the right kinds of witnesses and the proper distinction between "matters of fact" and "matters of opinion," the scientist will emerge as the authoritative spokesperson for nature. Hobbes, in turn, invents a terminology that describes how citizens, by way of the proper social contract, may have their interests represented in an authoritative political "body." Scientific representation and political representation. Latour points out that the inventions of Boyle and Hobbes should not be considered separately: What we are witnessing here is a division of power and a basic separation of nature and politics, which together contribute to one and the same modern Constitution. Boyle may claim to represent nature (and nothing else) because his notion of "matters of fact" presumably allows him keep anything political outside his laboratory walls. Hobbes may claim to hold the recipe for political representation (and nothing else) because his notions of social contract, interests and power are all about human subjects. The division is clear and sharp: nature on one side; the social and the political on the other.

However, what Hobbes and Boyle say is one thing; what they do is another. Latour points out that if we continue our modern habits of thinking of nature and politics as two separate spheres, then it is quite obvious that both Hobbes and Boyle produce strange hybrids – just like those creatures that inhabit a newspaper article about holes in the ozone layer. Boyle does not position himself within an *already given field* of nature. Rather, he constructs procedures, concepts and instruments that together actively try to *create a boundary* between what he defines as nature (and places inside the laboratory), and what he defines as politics, attitudes, opinions and culture (and places outside the laboratory).

In a similar vein, Hobbes' Leviathan, Latour argues, does not simply seize a phenomenon – society – that is already constituted. The representation of the interests of all citizens in and through a sovereign requires an extensive mobilization of a range of elements and resources. We might call this "the state apparatus," in a broad sense. However, this elaborate mixture of social, material, technological and bureaucratic elements, which together will allow the Hobbesian sovereign to act as a representative of society, is scarcely mentioned in Shapin and Schaffer's book. According to Latour, this sin of omission is a consequence of the two authors' sociological point of departure, which leads them to assume that society is an always already-existing entity, rather than to explore how it is constructed.[4]

For his part, however, Latour insists that representations of "pure" nature and representations of "pure" society both constitute the results of a laborious work of construction. Paradoxically, this work of construction involves an extensive mixing, joining or hybridizing of human and non-human entities.

All of the previously mentioned elements of the modern Constitution are now in place. With Boyle, we get a procedure for how nature can be purified as a particular and separate domain. With Hobbes, we get the basic concepts of how individual interests may be joined together to form a society. With both Hobbes and Boyle, countless new nature–culture hybrids come into being, but they are kept separate from the purified representations of nature and society.

The dynamism of the modern Constitution

The crucial question now becomes: What *advantages* do the moderns gain by separating the representation of nature from the representation of society (even though, in practice, they produce hybrids)? It remains obvious, after all, that the moderns have enjoyed considerable success in spreading their way of life. Latour seeks the answer by way of a comparison with so-called *pre-modern* cultures. Based on anthropological studies, Latour argues that pre-modern cultures tend to take an intense interest in hybrids that mix the natural, the social and the divine. This obsessive attention leads to a constant concern with possible disruptions of the established order, and thus to extreme caution in dealing with the world. The moderns, by contrast, have thoroughly put aside this caution. When Boyle mobilizes his strange hybrids in the laboratory, he does not perceive this as a potentially risky endeavor. Boyle and his many modern successors simply believe that scientists in their laboratories discover "pure" nature – nothing more, and nothing less. The modern Constitution guarantees that pure Nature and pure Society can be articulated and represented *separately*, and this act of purification makes the moderns incapable of imagining that hybrids would threaten to interrupt the natural or social order. Latour's line of argument, then, is that cultures that make hybrids clearly visible to themselves will also show restraint. Conversely, cultures that conceal the hybrids (and make only purifications visible) allow themselves a sense of freedom and a carefree attitude, which in practice makes it possible to produce and mobilize an ever-increasing number of hybrids.

To follow Latour's argument, we must keep in mind an important point that emerged from his anthropology of science: Modern laboratories make it possible to experiment with any imaginable combination of natural, technical and social entities in order to construct stable orders and effects (through things like immutable mobiles). Further, laboratories operate in increasingly extensive networks (including centers of calculation) in which their hybrid constructions are distributed and translated. Such extensive networks develop in close connection with the kinds of nation-building projects theorized by Hobbes, and which have proven willing to incorporate and employ almost any techno-scientific construction. The moderns have thus, on one hand, produced self-confident spokespersons for nature who freely experiment in their laboratories without regard to given social orders; and on the other hand, a society unafraid to accommodate new techno-scientific constructions because it is fully convinced that it shapes its own destiny. The *combination* of these two, Latour argues, is the source of the uncontrollable dynamics that we recognize as modernity. The key to understanding the dynamism of modernity – and its associated ideas, rights and forms of productivity – is thus the establishment of scientific laboratories within a collective that is ready to incorporate a steady stream of techno-scientific products.[5]

The exercise of modern critique

The hyperactive production of hybrids is not the only comparative advantage rendered by the modern Constitution. Latour argues that it also establishes an unprecedented, broad spectrum of opportunities for the exercise of *critique*. Generally speaking, criticism is possible to the extent that one actor can define and apply a point of reference to which the counterpart – the one criticized – does not live up. The purification of Nature here provides an evident first source of modern criticism: From this point of reference, one may criticize, expose and condemn any form of knowledge or practice that threatens to confuse the pure causality of things with human prejudices and projections. This, according to Latour, is the major critical force embedded in the so-called "First Enlightenment" beginning in the 17th century. However, a quite opposite form of purification – the purification of society – provides further sources of criticism. By referring to established knowledge about the laws of society (like sociology and economics), it becomes possible to criticize ideological distortions of any kind, including those ideological distortions that may affect natural science. This critical impulse corresponds to the so-called "Second Enlightenment" of the 1800s.

So far, so good. The moderns can now appeal to both natural realism and sociological realism. But the possibilities extend further: The moderns may argue that people themselves shape society, which means that the moderns are not subject to the laws of society after all. Similarly, the moderns may claim that they, through science and technology, are capable of manipulating nature, which means that the moderns are not subjected to the laws of nature either. Such "social constructivist" positions are fully possible within the discursive space set up by the modern Constitution.[6] At one point, Nature and Society are *transcendent*: They are absent, external forces that we may criticize others for not seeing clearly. The next moment, however, Nature and Society may be described as *immanent*: They are forces that we ourselves shape, and which we may once again criticize others for overlooking or underestimating. To complete the picture, Latour claims that something comparable applies to modern conceptions of *God*: In this domain as well, one may claim that God is both absent (transcendent and remote) and, at the same time, supremely present (immanent) in that He speaks directly to the heart of each person.

With this array of apparently solid reference points – where Nature, Society and God can be alternately depicted as immanent and transcendent – the moderns possess so many options for critique and so many possibilities to switch from one position to its very opposite that, according to Latour, they would inevitably feel almost invincible. At the very least, they have to feel quite superior to all the cultures that did not have possession of such critical resources. Latour drily remarks that Native Americans were fully correct when they accused the white men of speaking with forked tongues! But this did not prevent the moderns from continuing their critical endeavors.

And yet we have never been modern, Latour claims; in reality, the world has never functioned according to the precepts of the modern Constitution.

We have never been modern

To understand how Latour can claim that we have never been modern, it is useful to take a closer look at another of his sources of inspiration, the French historian François Furet. Furet is an expert in the French Revolution, and his work has radically re-opened a discussion of how to interpret this Revolution (Betros 1999). Whereas previously, scholars – and Marxists, in particular – have interpreted the French Revolution as an obvious result of the shift in the mode of production, Furet argues that a sharp distinction must be made between the revolution as a process, and the revolution as a modality of historical action. The French revolutionaries used the concept of revolution to make sense of the events in which they participated – "revolution" was their own definition of what was happening. Incidentally, this definition was also performative, in the sense that it instilled in them a courage and an optimism that they would otherwise not have had.

However, Furet argues that it would be a serious mistake if historians simply adopted the interpretive schemes held by the leading participants in historical events. Historians ought to distance themselves to a certain extent, and should at least remain open to alternative interpretations. Furet demonstrates this attitude, for instance, in analyses where he shows that there was no discernible "bourgeoisie" that confronted and defeated a fundamentally feudal ruling class in 1789, contrary to what the Marxists assume (Betros 1999). For Latour, there is an obvious parallel to the moderns. What we need to understand is how the moderns acquired certain expanded opportunities because they believed themselves to be modern. This is what Latour attempts

62 Philosophy of modernity

when he analyzes how the modern Constitution allows the moderns to mobilize hybrids on a massive scale, and how it provides them with countless sources of critique. Yet it would be a mistake to simply adopt the self-understanding of the moderns. Instead, we need to examine events, practices and theories that shape the world in ways that diverge from the moderns (as in the following section). By looking at such competing modes of ordering, we might begin to explain why the modern order – which at one point seemed invincible – now appears seriously weakened. Just like Furet can pronounce that "the French Revolution is over" (Furet 1981: 1)– because the revolution has lost its status as a self-evident fact now that we can view it as one interpretation among others – Latour declares that we have never been modern, because it is now increasingly clear that there are – and have always been – significant alternatives to modernity.

According to Latour, the alternatives to the modern Constitution emerge, and become visible, in a variety of different ways. First and foremost, he highlights his own field of *science studies*. When anthropologists of science and others explore how practice unfolds in scientific laboratories, they describe the creation of networks that continually weave together, and hybridize, human and non-human elements. The anthropologists' stubborn analytical focus on the actual material practice of science has made the work of hybridizing visible. These stories do not fit with the official, purified, modernist version, which claims that laboratories simply discover Nature, and that Society is only found outside the laboratory walls. Constructivist descriptions of science therefore threaten the moderns' strongly held belief that the "recipe" for progress is an increasingly clean separation of Nature and Society.

Instead, network analyses lead to the conclusion that it is precisely the ongoing hybridization that makes the construction of scientific facts and technical artifacts possible. According to Latour, the small field of science studies is a non-modernist practice because it makes visible those hybrids that the modern Constitution renders *in*visible. After three decades of anthropological studies of science, it is increasingly difficult for the moderns to claim that pure Nature is a transcendent condition that is simply discovered by laboratories.

In Latour's view, a second important contribution to the weakening of the modernist self-understanding is the *sociology of criticism* developed by Luc Boltanski and Laurent Thévenot (see Boltanski & Thévenot 2006[1991]; Latour 1993: 43–45). As noted, the modern Constitution provides a range of opportunities for the exercise of critique. For instance, the moderns may use their purified representation of the laws of Nature and Society to reveal and criticize the obscure mixtures and illusions of the "pre-moderns." Many social scientists would see it as their main mission to participate in these modern critical efforts, but Boltanski and Thévenot raise an entirely different question. Boltanski and Thévenot analyze critique as a competence exercised by participants in particular contexts, based on a range of historically received moral vocabularies called *regimes of justification*.[7] They show that, in practice, participants always have a variety of different options for justifying their own actions, and for criticizing the actions of others. If, for instance, a person gives a free blood donation, he may justify this as an act of compassion (based on a civic logic), whereas a critic may accuse the blood donor of being naïve (on the basis of a market logic). If the first person had chosen to sell his blood instead, he would be able to justify this action as realistic (from a market perspective), whereas a critic in this case could easily accuse him of being greedy (from a civic perspective) (Jagd 2007).[8]

The thing to note here is that the flexible sources of critique and justification, which are readily available to the blood donor and his critic, are similar to the range of critical resources that the moderns have in their power, according to Latour. Indeed, Latour makes no attempt to hide that his analysis of critique is strongly inspired by Boltanski and Thévenot. The crucial importance of their analyses, according to Latour, is that their rich empirical studies make it blatantly apparent that a wide range of regimes for criticism and justification are available to the participants at almost any point. In effect, by making this wealth of critical resources visible, Boltanski and Thévenot undermine the self-assured modernist assumption that critique is the surefire way to have the final word. According to Latour, this once again demonstrates that the modern Constitution is merely one particular attempt to organize the world, rather than a precise or complete description of what is actually happening in practice.

As a third and final strike against the modern Constitution, Latour argues that the clearest expression of the successes of the moderns – the massive emergence of hybrids – is now, paradoxically, beginning to undermine its own project. We return here to the example of a contemporary newspaper reader who is confronted by one story after another that churns up nature and culture. Latour claims that the situation was entirely different at the time when it was "only" a matter of Boyle and few laboratories. At that point, it was possible to keep the representations of nature and society fairly separate. Today, however, we stand in the midst of a veritable invasion: "frozen embryos, expert systems, digital machines, sensor-equipped robots, hybrid corn, data banks, psychotropic drugs, whales outfitted with radio-sounding devices, gene synthesizers, audience analyzers, and so on" (Latour 1993: 49–50). All of these monsters, as Latour calls them, are difficult to classify as either Nature or Culture. "It is as if there were no longer enough judges and critics to partition the hybrids. The purification system has become as clogged as our judicial system" (Latour 1993: 50).

This state of clogging weakens the modern Constitution for two reasons: First, it becomes increasingly difficult to share the modern belief that we should, we can and we will eventually separate everything into pure nature and pure culture. One might say that the accumulation and visibility of hybrids becomes an ontological challenge; the world looks less and less purified, in spite of the expectations of the moderns to the contrary. Second, it becomes increasingly difficult to maintain the modern belief that the pro-

64 *Philosophy of modernity*

duction and proliferation of hybrids in laboratories should be no cause for concern. As noted, this lack of concern stems from the assumption that laboratories merely discover nature, whereas people – and only people – create society. With the flood of hybrids, it is increasingly difficult to maintain a notion of a "social order" in which hybrids play no active role. On this basis, Latour argues that the hyperactive production of hybrids that was made possible by the modern Constitution is slowly but steadily undermining its own foundations.

Radical consequences

So here we are, Latour seems to say, with a modern Constitution that has never given us an adequate account of our practice, and that is now becoming more and more unacceptable. What consequences should we draw? In principle, the answer is simple: We need to make room for the hybrids; we need to be able to talk about them, to register them, to respond to them and to see their relation to the work of purification. The problem we face, however, is that the *in*visibility of hybrids is deeply embedded in our modern ways of thinking. If the hybrids are to be acknowledged, there will be radical consequences for the entire mental landscape of modernity. Later in this chapter, we examine these radical consequences in greater detail, particularly Latour's attempt to transform how the moderns understand time, and how they understand the difference between modern and pre-modern cultures. But first, we need to take a closer look at Latour's thoughts on how hybrids can be mapped.

As a framework for the mapping of hybrids, Latour introduces the a diagram, in which he plots five different versions of the vacuum constructed by Boyle in his laboratory (Figure 3.2).

At the top of the figure, a horizontal axis runs from the "Nature pole" to the "Subject/Society pole." This corresponds to the purified dichotomy that the modern Constitution attempts to establish. At the center of the diagram, a vertical axis runs from "Essence" to "Existence." This axis registers varying degrees of stability: the more stable an entity, the closer it moves toward the "Essence" pole. The construction and stabilization of scientific facts (as discussed in Chapter 2) exemplifies such an upward movement toward "Essence." But upward-directional, stabilizing movements may also produce other "essences," such as a society or a subject.

By following Boyle's vacuum through the points of this diagram (A to E), we notice that the vacuum gains stability – it moves upward. At the same time, it moves erratically from right to left (and back) on the axis of Nature and Subject/Society. As with any mapping exercise, Latour's goal is to create clarity where there once was confusion. Confusion arises when only the horizontal axis is considered (which is the mistake of the moderns). This limited focus will only give rise to the question of whether the vacuum is a phenomenon of nature or of society. From this point of view, it seems alternately one and then the other: one moment, it is a naturally given fact; the next moment,

Philosophy of modernity 65

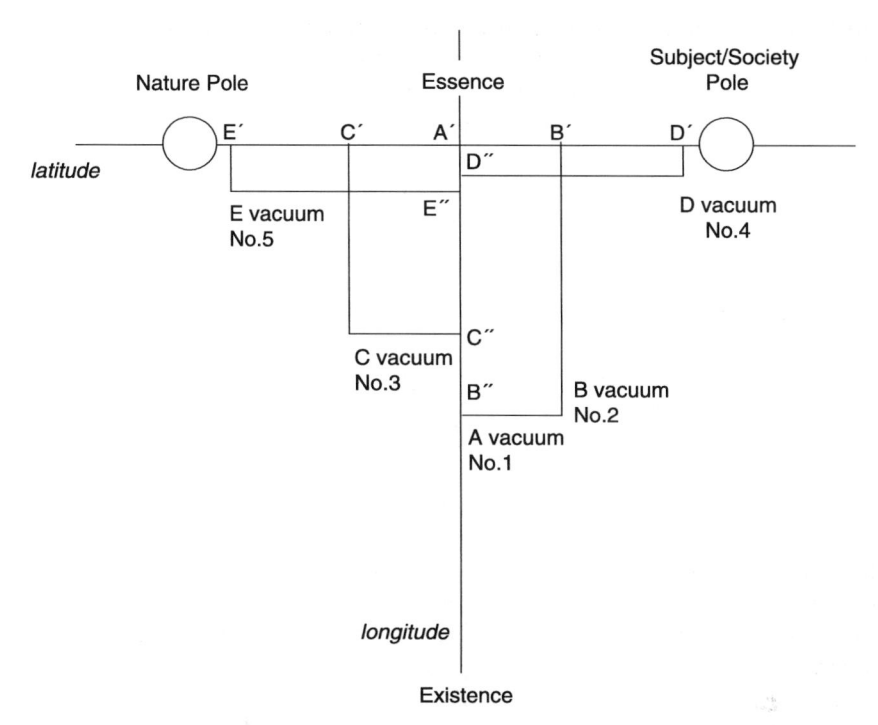

Figure 3.2 The modern Constitution and its practice.
Source: Latour 1993: 86; Figure 3.4.

it is socially constructed; later on, it may be seen as half natural, half social. According to Latour, clarification comes with the addition of the vertical axis, which makes it apparent that rather than *being* something specific, the vacuum is in a process of *becoming*.

The vacuum is a growing hybrid that mobilizes a number of elements whereby it gradually achieves stability. In short, the vacuum has a history. To understand the hybrid vacuum, we should not simply plot a point on the Nature–Society axis, as the moderns would do. Rather, we should plot the trajectory that becomes apparent when the Essence–Existence dimension, and thus the work of hybridization, is included. This trajectory is the unique signature of the vacuum. Latour emphasizes, once again, that the vacuum is not given in or by nature. On the contrary, the trajectory of the vacuum in the diagram illustrates that the opposite is true: Nature is the late result of the work of stabilization, provided by the practices of hybridization.

Latour's mapping diagram is not an empirical tool in any specific sense. Rather, it represents a kind of summary of his ontological assumptions. The most striking assumption is that the vacuum has its own history. Modernists (and epistemological realists) would claim that the vacuum exists outside of history; that it is given as a natural reality or possibility. The historical question is when and how people discover and make use of the vacuum, but not a question of what the vacuum *is*. Latour's assertion that the vacuum *itself* has a history breaks radically with traditional modernist views.

With this point, Latour draws inspiration from the French philosopher Michel Serres, who strongly criticizes the prevalent modernist perception of time. According to Serres, the modern concept of time is based on the notion that time is something that *passes*, which implies that everything within a given historical epoch gets left behind at an earlier stage as we move forward and upward onto the next stage. Serres and Latour argue, however, that in practice, time does not function in this way. Every event is a mixture of different epochs or times. As Serres notes, a supposedly *brand-new* car model is in fact an aggregation of technical and scientific solutions that date back to a number of different time periods: some components are decades old, and others are from previous centuries; the wheels are from the Neolithic era. When a car appears to be new, current or "contemporary," then this is simply a result of the way it has been designed, assembled and marketed (Serres & Latour 1995: 45). In a more humorous vein, Latour notes that no one will consider him an ethnographic curiosity just because he is capable of using both hammers (dating back 5,000 years) and electric drills (invented 35 years ago) (Latour 1993: 75). In a similar fashion, any other situation can be viewed as a compilation of elements stemming from a range of different times.

If every single event is a hybrid of times, then it should come as no surprise that these temporal hybrids – like all other types of hybrids – would be ill-treated by the representational framework of the modern Constitution. The modern Constitution aims to divide up any hybrid: On one side, we get society as created by people in a continuous historical process; and on the other, we get nature as given, transcendent and thus existing outside of history. The question then becomes: How do the moderns deal with those frequent situations in which hybrid practices produce or compose some new condition or phenomenon? How do they position themselves when Boyle, after numerous experiments and translations in his laboratory, manages to produce a fairly stable hybrid called "the vacuum" – consisting of a somewhat capricious air-pump, tubes, flasks, experimental procedures, polemics with Hobbes, invited witnesses, observational protocols, assistants and much more? According to Latour, the moderns possess only one answer: Since they cannot represent the hybrids, and they cannot imagine that hybrids have a history, new phenomena (like the vacuum) must be seen as suddenly springing forth, in a completed state, as an "unconstructed" discovery or a sudden invention created in a moment of genius. The vacuum must have been there all along, outside of time – but only now, at this very moment, did it reveal itself to us. By implication, the history of the moderns assumes the shape of a revolution that constantly starts over. An entirely new world emerges – and a whole new stage is reached – following the discovery of the vacuum, electricity, the invention of the computer, etc. In this way, the moderns construct history as a continuing series of jumps, revolutions and epistemological breaks, all serving to separate them from their past (Latour 1993: 70–72).[9]

As a radical and rather poetic alternative to this modernist perception of time, Latour imagines time as a kind of whirlwind or spiraling movement. Within this metaphor, there is still a past and a future, as we move forward in the loop of time. But the past is not bygone. Rather, it is "revisited, repeated, surrounded, protected, recombined, reinterpreted and reshuffled" (Latour 1993: 75). Using this image, two elements may be far from each other on the course of the spiral, but they can still be situated on two loops that are close to each other. Conversely, two elements that are close to each other on the spiral's course may appear to be entirely separate if they are positioned on different "spokes," to use Latour's metaphor of a bicycle wheel (Latour 1993: 75).

As depicted earlier (in figure 3.2), Latour argues that the modern dichotomy between Nature and Society should instead be seen as a continuum, and that a second axis needs to be added in order to register how hybrids move from unstable existence to stable essence. With this mapping tool, the in-between work of hybridization becomes visible. It becomes evident that "pure nature" and "pure society" should be regarded as eventual results of such processes, and that they simply represent projections on the horizontal axis. It also becomes clear that all things – that is to say, hybrids – have a continuous history. This perspective implies that Latour cannot ground his explanations, or his criticisms, in any notion of transcendent natural or social laws that determine the creation of the hybrids. Nature and society, Latour emphasizes, are *not* like two urns from which to pull up elements, and from which one may then compose the world. Any explanation needs to work in the opposite direction: From within the realm of hybrids, and through gradual processes of stabilization, the predictable essences known as nature and society will sometimes emerge. Such a reversal of the direction of explanation is yet another radical consequence of making hybrids visible. The exact meaning of this reversal, and what it implies for the practical analysis of "nature" and "society," is discussed further in Chapters 4 and 5 of this book.

In this chapter, we focus instead on a final radical blow dealt to the modern Constitution by Latour's embrace of the hybrids. This concerns the relationship between the modern and the non-modern world or, in popular terms, between "the West and the rest." Latour begins by listing a number of ways that modern anthropologists have viewed the non-modern world. Some anthropologists consider each culture as a delimited entity, which is qualitatively different from all the others. This perspective implies that cultures are mutually incommensurable and cannot be arranged in any form of hierarchy. Nothing is said here about nature. Latour calls this position *absolute relativism*. Other anthropologists assume the existence of a universal nature, of which each individual culture has a more or less refined understanding. This perspective of *cultural relativism* implies that it is possible to rank cultures based on the degree of precision contained in their understanding of nature. Finally, Latour marks out a position that he calls *particular universalism*, which is attributable to, among others, the famous anthropologist Claude Lévi-Strauss. Like cultural relativists, particular universalists believe that nature is universal – there is only one nature common to all cultures. On top of this, they add the notion that, among the diverse cultures of the world, only one – our own Western, modern culture – enjoys a privileged access to nature by way of the natural sciences. According to these particular universalists, this special access (mocked by Latour as "miraculous") institutes a decisive epistemological break between "us" and "them": *We* see nature as it actually is, while *their* understanding of nature is really a projection of their own social categories.

Latour disagrees with all these positions for reasons that follow from the parts of his analysis of modernity that we have already covered. First and foremost, Latour maintains that the construction of nature and society needs to be seen as two sides of the same coin (cf. the Hobbes–Boyle discussion). Any given *collective* – Latour prefers this term to "culture" – constructs both nature and society, alongside a whole range of other elements.

> No one has ever heard of a collective that did not mobilize heaven and earth in its composition, along with bodies and souls, property and law, gods and ancestors, powers and beliefs, beasts and fictional beings ... Such is the ancient anthropological matrix, the one we have never abandoned.
>
> (Latour 1993: 107)

On this basis, Latour considers it a fundamental lack in absolute relativism that this position simply ignores nature. For the same reason, he disagrees with cultural relativism, which also tends to ignore nature because it simply assumes that universal nature exists "out there."

The third position – that of Lévi-Strauss and the particular universalists – cannot be accused of overlooking nature or the role the natural sciences. But the key problem with this position, according to Latour, is that it lacks any sense of how the modern collective, and other collectives, *construct* nature. Particular universalists uncritically accept the transcendent Nature of the moderns – the late purified result of hybrid translation processes. By doing so, they once again render hybrids invisible, even though these are the precondition for the construction of nature "out there." Latour insists that *all* collectives hybridize nature and culture. The difference is simply that some collectives – that is, the moderns – simultaneously render this practice invisible. Latour therefore agrees entirely with Lévi-Strauss when he writes that non-modern cultures mix cultural categories into their understanding of nature; but Lévi-Strauss is wrong to suggest that a similar mixing is not also occurring in the everyday work of a modern scientific laboratory. The potential difference between "them" and "us" is therefore not a matter of hybridization. Instead, Latour suggests, we should find the basis for a comparative anthropology of collectives, or nature–cultures, in the varieties of *types* and *scopes* of hybridization.

To compare collectives, we first need to recognize that every collective

Philosophy of modernity   69

produces countless "species" of entities; things get divided up and assigned specific characteristics. It becomes acceptable to mobilize certain things instead of others. Taken together, such divisions create numerous small divides that make the nature–cultures of this world mutually different. In this context, the modern collective is simply one version among many: We, the moderns, are "as different to the Achuar as they are from the Tapirapè or the Arapesh" (Latour 1993: 107). We are not dealing with one great divide between modern and pre-modern collectives, but rather with multiple small differences between collectives. From this point of view, Latour may be said to come close to some version of cultural relativism: Collectives are all incommensurable in a qualitative sense.

However, Latour goes on to argue that quantitative differences also play a crucial role; some collectives mobilize comparatively few entities, whereas others mobilize enormous masses. Based on such differences, some collectives grow significantly stronger than others and will have more opportunities to dominate others. Thus, Latour in no way shares the cultural relativists' tendency to ignore power struggles between collectives, or the immense quantitative differences in their effects.

Latour points out that a mechanism of mutual reinforcement also seems to affect the dynamics of mobilization: When collectives need to keep a greater number of subjects together, it becomes necessary to mobilize still more objects; and when the collective has produced more objectivity, more subjectivity will be needed (Latour 1993: 108). Latour again uses the image of a spiral to describe such progressive processes. Expanding collectives build new loops. New rounds of objects – like atomic power stations, maps of the human genome, or a satellite network – create a new type of collective, with new types of subjective, social and societal entities (Latour 1993: 108). To Latour, the remarkable thing about modern science is *not* that it gives the moderns some privileged access to nature. The natural sciences are remarkable because they have managed to create and mobilize an ever-expanding range of hybrids, and this has led to a continuous reconfiguration and extension of the modern collective.

As noted, Latour's interpretation of relations between "the West" and "the rest" is yet another of those radical reshufflings of the modern mental landscape that follows from making the hybrids visible. If we acknowledge that representations of nature in any collective will be based on hybridization, then this eliminates the basis for claiming the existence of one great qualitative and epistemological divide between modern and non-modern collectives. If we simultaneously acknowledge that the type and scope of hybridization may vary greatly between collectives, then, Latour claims, we will have a much better chance of explaining why some collectives have been capable of dominating others. Basically, we may thus characterize Latour as a philosopher of continuity, in the sense that – despite all the relative differences – the moderns are not fundamentally set apart from the non-moderns (see Finnemann 1996). "The collectives are all similar, except for their size, like the successive helixes of a single spiral" (Latour 1993: 108). This point about continuity parallels Latour's philosophy of time, as already mentioned. Even though we are moving further away from the past, we never break with it entirely. The past is always reworked, repeated and reinterpreted (Latour 1993: 75).

We are now able to pinpoint the radical consequence drawn by Latour when making hybrids visible: He re-inscribes continuity in all the places where the modern Constitution prescribes a rupture. The rupture from the past becomes the spiraling motion of time. The rupture with the non-modern world becomes an all-encompassing practice of hybridization. And the rupture between nature and society turns into one collective of human and non-human actants.

The parliament of things – Proceeding with caution

As a final facet of his diagnosis of modernity, Latour attempts to articulate a non-modern constitution (Latour 1993: 138–42). Latour imagines this non-modern constitution as a more appropriate set of rules for a collective that has never been modern, and which is finally beginning to face this fact – with a helping hand from science studies, the sociology of criticism and an ever-more unruly proliferation of hybrids.

In his non-modern constitution, Latour attempts to combine the best of the moderns, the pre-moderns and the post-moderns. Rather than describing all the details of the non-modern constitution, we will simply highlight its most significant feature, which is Latour's attempt to solve the following dilemma: How might we simultaneously start to make hybrids visible, and retain some of the capacities of the modern sciences, in order to create extensive networks that contribute to a larger collective? Or to put it differently: How might we strike a balance between the "full speed ahead" of the moderns, where the production of nature is not seen in relation to the production of society; and the "slow motion" of the pre-moderns, where minute changes to the natural order generate anxieties over the consequences for the social order (and vice versa)? According to Latour, the best solution is to turn the production of hybrids into a collective and explicit affair (like the pre-moderns), but at the same time to let go of the obligation to always connect social and natural orders (like the moderns). Hybrids should be seen as entities that may eventually enrich our collective with both "nature" and objects, as well as with "citizens" who will be capable of freely creating "society."

In fact, Latour argues that we ought to view the simultaneous promotion and production of objective nature and liberal societies as something of an ethical obligation. Thinking about the collective in these terms, Latour claims, provides a foundation for extending democracy. Where Hobbes and his successors have long been preoccupied with how to represent *citizens*, Latour's non-modern constitution focuses on how to represent *hybrids*. The question then – and one that Latour leaves mostly hanging in the air – is how to give voice to strange hybrids like the holes in the ozone layer, and how to use this voice in the internal and external negotiations of the collective? How might one establish a new type of collective assembly, which Latour now calls the *parliament of things*? On this point, as noted, Latour fails to get very specific. But a decade later, he returns to "the parliament of things" in his book *Politics of Nature* (2004d), which we discuss in Chapter 4. For the moment, we simply want to emphasize the basic moral significance that Latour attaches to the question of an extended democracy that includes hybrids. If democracy is to be expanded, this must somehow entail an increase in the number of "checks and balances," together with more extensive forms of involvement of a broader range of representatives, in the negotiations of the collective. As a result of this, a certain degree of deceleration, moderation and regulation is both probable, reasonable and – at the end of the day – morally desirable (Latour 1993: 141). The onward journey of the collective that has never been modern should not happen in slow motion, nor should it proceed full speed ahead.

Summary and discussion

As mentioned at the beginning of this chapter, *We Have Never Been Modern* is an incredibly ambitious project. To attempt to work on the whole of modernity is one thing. But to attempt to explain modernity using an underlying 400-year-old constitution is in some sense sheer lunacy. If nothing else, it must be considered an extremely brave and highly abstract thought experiment.

As we have outlined, Latour develops his notion of the modern Constitution through discussions with a large number of authors. In this context, we have focused in particular on Latour's use of Shapin and Schaffer, Boltanski and Thévenot, Furet and Serres. This selection is not an exhaustive list of Latour's extensive network of references and arguments. Indeed, three important omissions in our presentation come to mind:

1   Latour interprets the ideas of a number of well-respected modernist philosophers – such as Kant, Hegel, the phenomenologists and Habermas – as a progressive series of still more unsuccessful attempts to grapple with the impossible distinction between nature and subject/society.
2   Latour depicts postmodernism as the most recent, and the least successful, attempt to deal with the Nature/Society distinction; and throughout the book, Latour talks about this line of thinking in distinctly negative terms: "I have not found words ugly enough to designate this intellectual movement – or rather, this intellectual immobility" (Latour 1993: 61).
3   Latour's engagement with ideas of God and religion are more extensive than the impression given by our cursory remarks on the subject.

But despite these omissions, we have given sufficient details to trace the direction that Latour has taken since his work in the anthropology of science. Or, to use an image he would probably prefer, we are now able to describe how Latour has added yet another loop to his spiral – we can trace the rewriting, revisiting and reinterpretation of his earlier work.

First, we should note the rather obvious fact that science studies have now been positioned in relation to a much larger set of discussions than before. Already with ANT, an entire philosophical program was articulated (see Chapter 2). What we have seen in this chapter, however, is a new interpretation of what science studies do, and what they make visible. Along with the sociology of criticism and the explosion of hybrids, science studies are presented here as the last straw that threatens to break the back of the modernist camel. Modernity (as defined and analyzed by Latour) is challenged, even shaken to the core, by the material produced by science studies – to such an extent that the existing (philosophical) order can no longer be maintained. According to Latour, this should compel us to re-inscribe a number of long-abandoned continuities; and in doing so, we will alter our entire mental landscape. We can no longer believe in the existence of a great epistemological divide, separating us from our past or from the pre-moderns. We can no longer think of time as something that passes behind us; and we can no longer depict the world as consisting of two basic ontological spheres (nature and subject/society). Such habits of thought are all undermined by the hybrids swarming out of science studies' descriptions – and from other contexts. Evidently, this interpretation is both original and radical. Prior to Latour, no one had attempted to assign such a decisive role to science studies and hybrids in the analysis of modernity. And we would argue that this key point in his analysis should, to a certain extent, be allowed to overshadow some of the "easiest" possible rejections – such as the argument that others before him have announced the current fatigue of modernity, or noted that the trust in science is waning, or predicted that our opportunities for exporting problems to the Third World are quickly running out.

How, then, should we evaluate such a radical thesis about the ontological constitution of the world and the new collective visibility of hybrids? This is not an easy task, and it is indeed something of a project in its own right. As a first approximation, it is worth noting that there is clearly something in Latour's depiction of modernism and hybrids that continues to strike a chord with contemporary readers of European newspapers. While we were writing this chapter, a global debate on bio-fuels was raging. This invention promises to replace parts of the conventional fuel used in cars with byproducts from crops, thus alleviating some of our environmental crises. Chances are, however, that the cultivation of crops for fuel might also unleash a global food crisis. It is hard to imagine a more vivid example of an unruly hybrid.

Or, to pick a different newspaper example, this time taken from our native Danish context: During the early months of 2008, a debate arose about the future of the Danish Council of Ethics, which has existed for just over 20 years. One article related that the Council was established in 1987 because the government needed a "lightning rod" to defuse a potentially unpleasant and heated public debate about the new possibilities afforded by technologies of artificial insemination.[10] The established political system, it seems, was unable to deal with the interwoven political, scientific and ethical aspects of this case. One is tempted to suggest that ethics councils, such as the Danish one, can be seen as experimental institutions similar to the Latourian "parliaments of things." Further on, we learned from the article that the Danish Council of Ethics was originally designed as a temporary invention, to be dissolved once the case of artificial insemination was settled. But as it happened, a whole series of other controversial technologies emerged on the agenda (such as fetal diagnosis, egg donation, surrogacy, etc.). The Council thus still exists, and many commentators even argue that we need to establish more ethics councils, in order to deal with further technological domains, such as the environment and climate change. With Latour's philosophy of modernity, we could easily interpret this as a case of an uncontrollable accumulation of hybrids, together with a "clogging" of our "purification system": Our existing political and scientific institutions can no longer manage everything.

Clearly, we would not claim that hand-picked examples such as these *prove* Latour's analysis correct. What they do prove, however, is that Latour's analysis of modernity functions as a network, capable of mobilizing further allies with relative ease. If we are inclined to do so, it is entirely possible to move around in the contemporary world and observe how the modern order seems under pressure – and how it is, at times, replaced by something apparently more non-modern. Those who choose to do so may also note that there is very little evidence to suggest that the modern order will break down or disappear in a single moment. The camel's back does not break. Instead, non-modern orderings seem gradually, and unevenly, to be gaining ground in certain specific contexts – while in other contexts, modernist imaginations and ordering processes seem almost unshakeable.

This brings us to what we consider the most fruitful and adequate reading of Latour's diagnosis of modernity. *We Have Never Been Modern* should be read as an attempt to establish an alternative mode of ordering. The book draws resources together in order to induce specific and directed effects: It attempts to moderate the recklessness of the moderns by challenging the risky notion that science simply discovers transcendent nature outside of any relation to – and any need for – considering society.

At the end of the day, Latour's non-modern constitution is an active attempt to create something new; that is to say, it reads as a manifesto. It is an interpretation of current events meant to inspire us to act differently – by throwing ourselves even more boldly into the conduct of science studies, for instance. *We Have Never Been Modern* is thus simultaneously a description and a proposal. The meaning and effect of this proposal depends on the responses of future readers, as well as how it "interferes" with other ordering processes.

To some interpreters, Latour seems to stimulate nothing but well-known modernist ordering processes. In this respect, the following rhetorical question, posed to Latour by one (Danish) philosopher, is illustrative: "How is the collective able to construct neurotransmitters, if the thought processes that form the prerequisite for such constructive activity are only possible as a result of the causal effectiveness of these very neurotransmitters?" (Collin 1996: 80–81). With questions such as this, the notion of a pre-existing Nature is smuggled back with notions of "causal effectiveness" – a Nature supposedly existing outside of, and unaffected by, the hard and ongoing work of construction undertaken by the collective.

Other interpreters have shown more willingness to follow Latour's description of the world, while still raising concerns about the shortcomings and challenges of his project. Some philosophers, for instance, have pointed out that the modern "a-historical" maximization of mobility and control also entails an amplification of the "historicity" of the situation. The fact that certain specific European societies, and certain specific actors, initiated processes of modernization at some well-defined point in history has come to carry far-reaching consequences all around the world. For this reason, we may well need a more extensive analysis of the historical circumstances of modernity than what Latour wants to deliver.

Likewise, sociologist of science Mark Elam points out that Latour's analysis of modernity focuses on certain "Great Divides" at the expense of others. For Elam, it is striking that both gender and national differences are entirely absent in Latour's analysis. Furthermore, Elam notes that Latour's analysis of modernity bears a significant resemblance to dominant discourses of international politics. Whereas the Cold War period was characterized by notions of a bi-polar world, technological competition has since come to been seen as the main driving force of the international system. In such a situation, the surveillance of a multitude of techno-scientific centers and hybrids becomes a key activity. Elam thus suggests that we need to further examine the ways in which Latour might implicitly have allied his diagnosis of modernity to the continuation of Western hegemony in the world (Elam 1999).

The reception of Latour's analysis of modernity should be seen as an open game, and one might say that the game has only expanded in recent years: *We Have Never Been Modern* has been translated into numerous different languages, and the book has achieved status not simply as Latour's most significant work, but also as a substantial and profound diagnosis of our contemporary world in its own right. And Latour himself participates in this ongoing game – as we see in the next two chapters of this book, where we examine his political ecology and his sociology of associations, both closely associated with the philosophy of modernity.

We Have Never Been Modern is thus one performative description in continual interaction with others. One possible conclusion, then, is that we have *neither* been modern *nor* a-modern. But we have been ordering, and continue to order, the world in both ways.

4 Political ecology

> *We do not know what is interconnected and woven together. We are feeling our way, experimenting, trying things out. Nobody knows of what an environment is capable.*
>
> (Latour 1998c: 233)

Introduction: Toward a new political ecology

"What is to be done with political ecology? Nothing. What is to be done? Political ecology!" With these words, Latour commences *Politics of Nature* (2004d: 1). This book focuses on a political issue of particular significance to the contemporary world: our shared – and seemingly endangered – nature, environment and ecology. It is worth noting that Latour's opening line is typical of his general rhetorical attitude: Problems are always to be found buried deep in the many interpretive layers of words. As noted in the introduction to this book, most of Latour's analyses are ultimately attempts to alter our familiar and well-known interpretive categories through detailed re-descriptions (and a number of neologisms) of science, technology, modernity, society, nature, etc. We have already seen many examples of this, and in *Politics of Nature*, Latour turns his attention to the part of the modern Constitution that concerns Nature as a supposedly transcendent, non-human, ontologically separate domain in the world (see Chapter 3). This entire book (along with a major part of Latour's political–philosophical thinking in general) is all about his showdown with the concept of Nature with a capital N – that is, transcendent Nature. For this reason, readers do not have to go far into the book before experiencing the first of many shocks (Latour 2004d: 5): Political ecology, Latour tells us, has nothing to do with any notion of nature! Either there is nature, or there is democracy. Once again, Latour presents us with a crossroads: We must choose between continuing the techno-scientific modernization of the past 300 to 400 years, or to begin "ecologizing" our collective life. In this context, Latour playfully paraphrases William Shakespeare's immortal words: "To modernize or to ecologize – that is the question" (1998c).

In this chapter, we look more closely at what Latour means by ecologization, and how he reaches this crossroads in the first place. We also outline his attempted answer, which assumes the shape of a new democratic procedure for dealing with our non-human and ecological fellow-beings. In other words, we delve deeper into Latourian political philosophy, which is really to a great extent an eco-political philosophy. Latour envisages ecological threats as a defining element of our contemporary world, and this point of view inspires him to (almost) adopt – from his German colleague, sociologist Ulrich Beck – the well-known and far-reaching diagnosis of the "risk society" (see Latour 2003b). Indeed, environmental risks are exactly hybrids that transgress the boundaries between nature and culture; and the sciences come to be deeply implicated in all aspects of the numerous controversies surrounding ecological issues. As such, environmental risks represent an important litmus test for Latour's non-modern political thinking.

According to Latour, the greatest challenge of political philosophy is not simply how people may come to be represented in political institutions. The simultaneous challenge is to specify how nature, science and non-human actants may become the objects of communal discussion and decision-making. In this respect, science too is a matter of *re*-presentation – of establishing chains of translation that enable humans to speak on behalf of nature. So far, however, the modern Constitution has prohibited us, in the Western world, from merging these two types of representation: the political and the scientific. Latour believes that such a distinction, between the spokespersons of humans and the spokespersons of non-humans, is becoming increasingly untenable, alongside the explosion of new nature–culture hybrids made visible by the ecological crisis. Hence, in *Politics of Nature*, Latour revisits the project that he began with *We Have Never Been Modern*: the creation of a "parliament of things" in which humans and (quasi-)objects may come to be represented *simultaneously*. In 1991, this notion remained a rough sketch (see Chapter 3); but 10 years later, in *Politics of Nature*, Latour produces a much more detailed draft of such a new, non-modern constitution – as a novel set of institutional guarantees for a democratically legitimate assembly of our heterogeneous collective. As such, political ecology provides Latour with an opportunity to engage still more fundamental questions, and indeed to reshuffle (in an affirmative sense) our mental landscape of subjects and objects, values and facts, politics and science. To Latour, political ecology is an exercise in "political epistemology" – because nothing could be more political than our dealings with science and nature (2004d: 28).

By implication, and in mirroring Latour's own political–philosophical thinking, this chapter works simultaneously on two different levels – levels which may at first seem very different, but which must nonetheless be linked in order to understand the Latourian argument. One level is relatively abstract and concerns the question of representation, which necessitates a rethinking of basic philosophical categories – particularly, the categories of facts and values. This is where we start our exploration, by also invoking

Pandora's Hope (1999b), a book that may well be seen as the philosophy of science forerunner, or counterpart, to *Politics of Nature*.[1]

The other level appears to be more concrete. It concerns the numerous environmental risks, hybrids and ecological quasi-objects that are well-known from the mass media, and which clearly represent one of the greatest political challenges of our times. Throughout this chapter, we aim to illustrate just how and why Latour considers his political–philosophical ideas to form a constructive contribution to various environmentalist struggles for the "ecologization" of society. This is also to say that Latour is quite explicit about his own political position: He engages in political ecology because he considers this movement a vital opportunity to reformulate a progressive historical struggle for liberation and democracy (see Latour 1998a). We end this chapter by critically discussing Latour's argument, both at the level of political philosophy, and as it is relevant to the eco-political project with which he seeks to link himself.

Political epistemology and the double representation

With the discussion of the philosophy of modernity (see Chapter 3), it becomes clear that, in the Latourian theoretical perspective, our so-called modern era is characterized primarily by one basic dichotomy: the division of collective life into Nature and Society, science and politics. In the mental universe of the moderns, there can be no greater crime than the deliberate mixing of these two ontological and social spheres – or even the blurring of their mutual boundaries. On one hand, the modern philosophy of science (with its normative epistemology) may be considered a sustained attempt to cleanse science of those disruptive, irrational and interest-driven factors that could potentially obscure scientific purity, truth and enlightenment. In the post-World War II era, Nazi racial doctrines and the "Lysenkoism"[2] of the Soviet Union are often highlighted as some of the most shocking examples of just how wrong things can go when science is forced to comply with political considerations and ideologies.

On the other hand, German social theory in particular has tended to cast a vigilant eye on the social and political alienation that may result from excessive forms of "scientification" and "technocratization" of society.[3] Although the two forms of criticism (the transgression of science by society versus the transgression of society by science) may well seem diametrically opposed, Latour's point is that they are both made possible – and even reinforced – by the modern Constitution (see Chapter 3). Every time the mixing of science and politics becomes apparent, an army of agitated critics is aroused. Such critics take it upon themselves to bring things back into order. The most recent example of such a modernist and constitutionally sanctioned reaction is precisely the so-called "science wars," which Latour presents and interprets in *Pandora's Hope* (1999b).

From Latour's perspective as an anthropologist of science, it is impossible not to view such debates as somewhat surreal, since they all rest on the same fundamentally *unrealistic* assumptions; assumptions that Latour has spent his entire intellectual effort rebelling against. For more than 35 years, and through a large number of meticulous case studies, Latour – and the rest of science studies – has attempted to empirically demonstrate that scientific laboratory practices are closely interwoven with their historical, social, cultural and political contexts (see Chapter 2).

Along a more theoretical and philosophical track (see Chapter 3), Latour argues that our contemporary world is characterized by a dramatic increase in the number of hybrids that transgress the boundaries between nature and society, and hence also the boundaries separating scientific and political forms of representation. As long as we stick to the modern Constitution, this work of hybridization remains concealed – but the *effects* of hybridization are still felt. Contemporary ecological crises constitute the clearest and most omnipresent illustration of the expansion in new hybrids; an increase that may even challenge and threaten our entire collective life. Thus, in Latour's view, the challenge is to ask how, as a political collective, we may turn the work of hybridization into something *explicit* and *legitimate*. Borrowing a concept from American pragmatist philosopher John Dewey, Latour states that the new politics of hybrids needs to follow "due process" – that is, an appropriate democratic procedure.

The challenge, then, is to rethink the entire relationship between our two main mechanisms of representation – the scientific and the political – in order to arrive at one integrated, collective and "experimentally metaphysical" process of ordering the collective life of humans and non-humans. Instead of the two entirely separate "chambers" of the modern Constitution – one for Nature, one for Society – Latour advocates a parliament of things, arranged so that nature–society hybrids can be treated as one and the same collective, experimental and democratic process. We present the details of how Latour imagines the organization of such parliaments of things later in this chapter. For now, we focus on two basic characteristics of the entire endeavor. First, we should note that, with his parliament of things, Latour is balancing on a razor's edge of political philosophy. He needs to constantly demonstrate that his attempt at combining science and politics results neither in the "politicization of science" so dreaded by the moderns, nor in the equally loathsome "scientization of politics." This is indeed where the whole challenge lies for Latour – because to bring home his point, he must instigate a radical break with core modernist dichotomies, especially the divide between facts and values.

The second characteristic of Latour's endeavor is that the radical nature of his showdown with modernist patterns of thinking puts his eco-political writings in a somewhat ambivalent position when it comes to their relation to any easily recognizable empirical world. On one hand, it is obvious that Latour discusses a number of well-known problems regarding relations among science, society and the environment – and that he illustrates his points via stylized empirical examples. On the other hand, it is hard to deny that the Latourian parliament of things can have the appearance of an abstract, future-oriented utopia (or, perhaps, dystopia). The parliament of things does not exist "out there" – in that sense, it remains Latour's own construction. Nonetheless, Latour obviously wants to claim that the contemporary world is, in any case, working toward a realization of his visions.

Latour seems to find much of the inspiration for his radical and abstract analytical approach in the work of his mentor, Michel Serres – and, in particular, from Serres' work on political ecology, *The Natural Contract* (1995b). According to Serres' misanthropic vision, humanity is in the midst of a "parasitical" war with its surrounding environments, rooted in the way techno-scientific "progress" has made humanity the master of "earth, matter, life, time and history, humanity, good and evil" (cited in Whiteside 2002: 125). By implication, the fundamental question for Serres is whether humankind will manage to enter into a new "contract" with nature and move beyond the notion of techno-scientific supremacy.[4] Latour comments that, with *Politics of Nature*, he attempts to further develop Serres' idea as to the contractual – and thus politically constitutional – role of science in contemporary society (2004d: 251, note 1). However, while Latour clearly takes environmental risks seriously, in contrast to Serres, his work does not seem driven by any acute sense of an impending ecological Armageddon.[5]

Politics of Nature carries the subtitle "How to Bring the Sciences into Democracy" – a phrase that sets the tone for Latour's argument in political philosophy. The phrase more than indicates that, up until now, and under the modern Constitution, the sciences have held a powerful and paradoxical position. On one hand, the sciences have been considered to be a-political; on the other, they have tacitly provided the vast majority of significant ingredients in the collective life of society, in the form of new techno-scientific hybrids.

In order to legitimize such power privileges, Science (with a capital S) seeks the help of philosophers, in the form of an epistemology deeply committed to transcendental notions of Science, Truth and Nature. This epistemology claims that science, and only science, enjoys access to the truth of nature. In Latour's view, this epistemology is not nearly as innocent and self-evident as it appears. On the contrary, such an epistemology is deeply and *inherently* political because its very notion of a "natural order" is employed in order to short-circuit, in quite illegitimate ways, the political and democratic decision-making processes of society. In this context, Latour speaks disdainfully of the "epistemology police," a position embodied by certain philosophers of science. Without acknowledging their own political implications, these epistemology police summarily dismiss, and thus keep at bay, any discussion of the *intimate* connection between nature and society, science and politics, truth and power (2004d: 18ff).

In stark opposition to this current situation, Latour wishes to practice "political epistemology," understood as an *explicit* reflection on the distribution and balance of power in-between science and politics. Political epistemology may also be dubbed "cosmopolitics," a term Latour borrows from his close colleague, Isabelle Stengers. According to Latour's new political epistemology, there is politics *in* nature – in the sense of a politics dealing with the composition of our common and heterogeneous "cosmos." The fundamental "cosmopolitical" question, then, is how to create a *good common world* that takes both people and things into consideration: fishermen as well as their fish; industry and consumers alongside the ozone layer and the global climate. As Latour remarks with reference to climate change: Today, people have once again begun to worry about the cosmos; to worry that the sky may be falling on our heads! (See Latour 2003b.)

It should be clear from this short overview of Latour's eco-political engagement that it brings many elements into play at once: It is not "simply" about reshuffling the basic organizing principles of the modern Constitution, but potentially also a matter of rearranging the future of our entire cosmos. The antithesis of cosmos is chaos; and "chaos" – in the form of ecological meltdowns, technocratic tyrannies or violent conflicts between collectives – lurks in the background of Latour's political philosophy, as symbolized by his invocation of Carl Schmitt's famous notion of "the enemy" as an existential threat (see Latour 2002d). With regard to eco-politics, however, Latour's tone is more optimistic: The environmental movements, he argues, constitute the only social forces that stand to benefit from the new "knowledge politics" that can be derived from his (and others') science studies. As we have already emphasized, this knowledge politics is not to be considered "anti-scientific." Rather, it marks a transition from Science to "research," understood as an open, continual, collective and uncertain process of inquiry (see Latour 1998b). Latour's main message is that, only by assuming the shape of such open and experimental research will the sciences be capable of integrating into political democracy. Likewise, this is the only route by which political ecology may hope to gather support for its cosmopolitics (Latour 1998c).

The main challenge to be solved in the formation of the parliament of things, then, is to find out exactly how this collective experimental process may be organized in such a way that it simultaneously respects the strengths and particularities of both the sciences *and* politics. Once again, this is a matter of maintaining a certain balance, and Latour remarks that his own primary qualification in this respect is that, personally speaking, he respects political activity just as much as he respects the scientific (2004d: 6f).[6] The notion of politics that Latour respects, however, is rather different from the usual focus on power, sovereignty and interests found in political theory. In addition to seeking to democratize the sciences, inspired by Dewey, Latour also aims to make political democracy (more) experimental: We, the public, should constantly ask ourselves what elements comprise our collective life, and how these elements will be best organized.

The representation of hybrids – from climate change to genetically modified foods; from HIV to mad cow disease – thus constitutes an ongoing challenge, a political project without any end in sight. Or, as Latour puts it in his "manifesto" for a renewal of left-wing politics (1998a): "The only thing we can be sure of is [. . .] that whatever topic we chose to focus on, from ecology to genetics, from ethics to law, the future will be even more entangled than the past." We should therefore abandon the idea of "modernizing the modernization" – and instead choose the non-modern path of "ecologization," where uncertainty, precaution and collective ignorance will be the order of the day. For this to happen, however, a number of preparatory steps are demanded, in order to bring us out of the de-politicized politics of Nature and Science.

From epistemology to articulation: Circulating facts

We have previously characterized Latour as an "anti-epistemologist" and demonstrated how, throughout his work, he has consistently adopted a highly critical stance in relation to the traditional, normative philosophy of science – most recently dubbed the "epistemology police." The thrust of science studies (Latourian and otherwise) is usually to show how every attempt to demarcate – in an absolute and final way – *the* true scientific method from various false and non-scientific "ideologies" is destined to continuously fail.

Seen in relation to the interpretive categories of the modern Constitution, it would be easy to assume that Latour's approach basically amounts to an *attack* on all scientific reason. As we noted in the introductory chapter, Latour's name is sometimes (incorrectly) associated with the term "postmodernism," and thereby also with notions of epistemic anarchy – usually summed up by Paul Feyerabend's famous slogan that "anything goes" in the world of science (see Tucker 2007).[7] In all fairness, Latour *has* arguably toyed with this tarnished label at times, especially in the articulation of his early studies in the anthropology of science, where science tends to be portrayed as a kind of politics, or war, "by other means" (see Chapter 2).

Attempting to understand Latourian political ecology through such a lens would give the impression that his basic endeavor is to entirely obliterate the world of science, at the expense of some enlarged political power game. This would be nothing but a crude caricature, however, in that it overlooks the crucial fact that, along the way, Latour is simultaneously *redefining* the meaning of both science and politics. In this section, we thus describe how Latour, in tandem with his political ecology, attempts to define his philosophy of science – in the shape of a new normative criterion for distinguishing between *good* and *bad* (scientific) knowledge. Next, we describe how Latour redefines the meaning of politics by using the German-sounding neologism *Dingpolitik*. With these re-descriptions at hand, the contours of his political ecology – and the parliament of things – stand out more sharply.

One appropriate starting point for this discussion of Latour's more normative philosophy of science is the concept of "circulating references," which he put forward in *Pandora's Hope* in relation to an empirical study into biological field research. In brief, the analytical point here is still – in continuation of his earlier science studies – that "facts" are circulating entities that flow through complex networks of semiotic and material connections. Biological facts are created through long chains of translations: from savannah to fenced-off plots of land; onto carefully collected samples of earth, which are coded, standardized and sent off to the laboratory; then into comparisons, models and tables; and, finally, making their way into the published article and its conclusions (see Latour 1999b: chapter 2). Up to this point, the picture is a familiar one in the Latourian universe.

However, compared to his earlier anthropology of science, Latour now adds one more crucial element, this time more philosophical in nature: He spells out why this analysis of circulating references breaks completely with traditional epistemology as built on the notion of an *abyss-like chasm* between the world (Nature, Object) on one side, and language (Society, Subject) on the other. In this traditional epistemology, science is a matter of creating correspondence between world and language; and hence, a matter of creating linguistic representations that in some sense make visible the objects that exist "out there." Not surprisingly, Latour argues that such a modernist and visual metaphor should be entirely rejected – and replaced by an approach that relativizes the divide between language and the world, given that the two are intimately connected inside scientific practice. This is precisely the point, then, of the term *circulating reference*: The semiotic (language) and the material (world) are so seamlessly joined and concretely intertwined that no ontological divide is perceivable. Instead of one great ontological divide, what we encounter is a multitude of relative *differences*: differences in research instruments, theories, data, alliances, public relations, etc.[8] What is interesting about solidly constructed facts is precisely the way they allow for movements in both directions along such chains of translation.

With the concept of circulating references, it should now be apparent that Latour moves close to an entirely *realistic* understanding of scientific knowledge; in fact, his theory might even be labeled as "hyper-realistic." *Every* difference in scientific modes of circulation – apparatuses, theories, concepts, relations to political interests and so on – needs to be considered whenever the aim is to evaluate whether or not we are dealing with good and interesting science. Only in certain specific cases (and through painstaking, conscientious work) may some branch of science achieve its desired goal – that is, to make its particular object of study relevant for our collective linguistic statements about it. To put this differently: Under favorable conditions, things *can* actually be "incorporated" into human language, but this demands extreme attention to nuances, dislocations and translations into still new contexts. At the same time, this process demands that one does not strictly separate scientific from non-scientific linguistic registers, but rather allows for a kind of cross-fertilization between the two.

As one way of illustrating this theoretical point, Latour draws on his long-time collaboration with primatologist Shirley Strum, in order to frame a discussion about the relationship of primatology to ideas stemming from feminism and popular culture (see Latour 2000a). According to traditional epistemology, feminist perceptions of gender would have to be seen as so many "filters," distorting the true, objective and scientific recognition of the behavior of large primates. Latour's point is the exact opposite: Rather than filters, interpretive categories such as gender – alongside popular animal documentaries and Japanese biological theories – should instead be seen as "bridges" that facilitate and *allow* for a gradually more nuanced understanding of primate lives. The more interpretive offers we make available to primates, the more visible they become in all their complexity. Hence, when asked directly, Latour replies that it is the primates *themselves* that have forced us to revaluate our perception of them since the 1960s – in close collaboration, of course, with hard-working primatologists (ibid.: 360).

Developing a point made by Isabelle Stengers,[9] Latour adopts the Whitehead-inspired notion of "proposition" to talk about such interpretive offers, which continuously connect us to the surrounding world. Propositions represent possibilities of relating to the world in new, specific and – at times – surprising ways (Latour 2000a: 372). As such, propositions are not merely linguistic statements since they consist in a number of heterogeneous elements, brought together and connected in a network. By implication, propositions are not *true* or *false*, in the traditional epistemological sense of these words – that is, as a matter of correspondence. As an alternative to correspondence, and as the crux of his normative theory of science, Latour suggests that propositions may be more or less *well-articulated*. In this context, articulation is a question of recognizing, in the course of time, some still finer distinctions, increasingly subtle nuances and growing numbers of active connections in the world and its objects.

To illustrate this point, Latour refers to a rather peculiar and certainly non-scientific career: At the perfume counters of large department stores, shop assistants need to gradually train their bodies (and, more specifically, their noses) to recognize still more subtle nuances in perfume scents (see Latour 2004a). During this process, the scent of perfumes becomes increasingly well-articulated, as assistants learn to improve the sensitivity of their noses. Latour claims that, in quite similar ways, scientific articulations possess their own rhythms, colors and tempos, and only highly experienced researchers are capable of dealing with such intricate aspects in a sophisticated manner (2000a: 375).

Put differently, and by way of summing up: When it comes to evaluating the quality and authority of a certain proposition (or interpretive offer) within public political life, it is no longer sufficient that the proposition stems from a scientific institution. It is similarly important to ask whether the proposition is *well or poorly* articulated – that is, does it allow for a richer, more interesting and more nuanced understanding? Furthermore, an interpretive offer is no longer disqualified simply because it originates from outside the recognized scientific establishment. On the contrary, Latour's point is that a whole range of significant insights – or "relative certainties" (1999b: 12) –

84 *Political ecology*

may be accumulated from outside, or partially outside, the ranks of institutionalized science. By way of illustration, he points to projects of community-based nature conservation taking place around the world and particularly in developing countries, where local populations become involved in decisions regarding such things as the management of elephant populations in agricultural regions of Africa (Latour 2000a: 377).[10]

This then brings us back to political ecology, the clarification of which remains the goal of this entire excursion into the philosophy of science. The central point is this: Whenever Latour speaks of "political epistemology" and "cosmopolitics" in his political ecology, he does *not* mean to imply that knowledge and science should be considered mere instruments in the exercise of power. On the contrary, the aim of the Latourian parliament of things is exactly to strive toward the best possible articulation of our contemporary hybrids – the ecological as well as the non-ecological. This kind of articulation will ensure that collective decisions are based on a nuanced and experimentally solid foundation. As we see later, this requires a range of different skills – scientific, political, moral and diplomatic – to be applied to the *same* set of issues. Before we go on to discuss the parliament of things in more detail, however, we take a closer look at how exactly Latour interprets the political issues we face by using his original and German-inspired concept of *Dingpolitik*.

From *Realpolitik* to *Dingpolitik*: Object-oriented democracy

By now, it should come as no surprise to readers that Latour chooses to create yet another neologism in relation to his political philosophy – nor that this neologism is designed to conjure up numerous connotations at the same time. Along with the terms *political ecology*, *political epistemology* and *cosmopolitics*, Latour thus describes his political–philosophical project in terms of *Dingpolitik* – a qualitatively new type of politics, named after a German word that means both "thing" and "assembly" (see Latour 2005a). In one respect, the meaning of this "politics of things" is straightforward: The Latourian universe always teems with material objects – from technoscientific measuring instruments to biological organisms, ecosystems, the climate and the ozone layer. As such, it seems reasonable that these hybrid objects deserve their own politics. In this sense, the parliament of things is precisely a matter of *Dingpolitik*, given that, according to Latour's basic political–philosophical diagnosis, the twin representation of humans and things, of nature–culture hybrids, constitutes the greatest political challenge of our times. The parliament of things, and thus the politics of things, is all about making things – quasi-objects, hybrids, material objects – the center of political discussion, conflict and compromise.

But at the same time, it is important to emphasize that Latourian *Dingpolitik* is meant as a more general alternative to another type of politics that may be summed up by a better-known German-inspired concept: *Realpolitik*. In

Latour's view, *Realpolitik* is synonymous with the kind of organized politics that we all know from the mass media: an economistic, factual and prosaic way of dealing with clearly defined interests and power relations between various social groupings. This type of *Realpolitik* usually plays itself out in parliaments that are organized around political parties. It tends to celebrate progress and liberty, and it orients itself around time-honored ideologies on a scale running from "left" to "right." According to Latour, it is now high time to realize that this kind of politics has become completely outdated – particularly since the end of the Cold War – and thus also that the time is ripe for a complete reformulation of what would constitute a progressive political project (Latour 1998a).

Dingpolitik is Latour's proposal for such a new collective project, fit for the contemporary world. Environmental politics is clearly central to this project, but the analysis applies much more broadly than to just ecology in a narrow sense. Latour's own illustrations of the politics of things cover such diverse topics as Islamic headscarves, genetically modified foods, architecture, financial markets and the tragic demise of the space shuttle *Columbia*. Not to mention the notorious speech – delivered by former U.S. Secretary of State Colin Powell to the United Nations Security Council in 2003, during the run-up to the American invasion of Iraq – regarding (alleged) Iraqi weapons of mass destruction (Latour 2005a: 18f).

In all of these cases, material objects, both techno-scientific and mundane, are placed at the center of heated societal debates. Moreover, the character, locations and lines of conflict drawn up by such debates cannot be understood through the filters of *Realpolitik*. In the specific case involving weapons of mass destruction, Powell's blurry photos achieved nothing more than a worsening of the conflict. Latour believes that this case allows us to draw an important, general lesson: An object-oriented democracy calls for the establishment of *both* a legitimate assembly of representatives (e.g., nation-state diplomats) *and* a procedure that ensures that facts and objects are represented for the public in a legitimate manner. According to Latour, this latter procedure was simply lacking in the case of Colin Powell.

The concept of *Dingpolitik* has still further levels of meaning, since Latour plays with the etymological and philosophical traditions embedded in the concept of the "thing." In both respects, a direct (if perhaps slightly ironic) reference extends to someone who is perhaps the best-known German philosopher of the 20th century, Martin Heidegger, and his work on *das Ding* (the thing). In this work, Heidegger celebrates the artistic skills that go into the careful crafting of things, as epitomized in the famous example of a handmade mug (see Latour 2004c: 233).

In his *Dingpolitik*, Latour wants to retain the association of a highly skilled and meticulous fabrication of things – but compared to Heidegger, his interest encompasses more diverse "things," in particular the objects of techno-science.[11] Latour's main point here is that, like the mug, the objects of techno-science are also skillfully fabricated. As such, they cease to be *objective*, in the standard sense that a scientific fact ("matters of fact") is supposed to reflect, in unmediated and direct ways, some hard, unambiguous and compelling reality "out there" in Nature. Latour argues that scientific facts may indeed, over time and under the right conditions, become hard and inevitable. Nevertheless, it is highly problematic to associate objectivity as such with the unconstructed, non-political and naturally given. To Latour, such a description of facts amounts to an illegitimate short-circuiting of political ecology (Latour 1998c).

Within his *Dingpolitik*, Latour portrays the objectivity of things in a different light: Things are presented as "matters of concern." Matters of concern possess all of the qualities that "naturally given" facts *do not*: They are rich, complex, uncertain, surprising and artificially constructed. At the same time, this artificial fabrication serves only to make them more real – and, in this sense, more objective (Latour 2004c). Fundamentally, matters of concern, or hybrid quasi-objects, possess an open and uncertain character that makes them *inherently* political: As opposed to "naturally given" facts, their place in the future collective world is never completely settled. On the contrary, different points of view, different life-forms and different political practices will gather around the things in ever-changing ways, thus creating a string of occasional public forums where their future will be negotiated and influenced.

When Latour talks about a parliament of things, this should be seen as a kind of rough outline, the practical organization of which will be constantly re-negotiated, depending on the nature of the conflict that plays itself out around some specific matter of concern. Despite his use of the singular form, then, Latour does not envisage one *single* parliament of things – in the way *Realpolitik*, for all its diversity, has tended to converge around one physical assembly of elected representatives. Instead, Latour imagines the establishment of a series of parliaments of things – or "hybrid political forums"[12] – adapted to the specific circumstances of the objects around which political conflicts revolve.

Throughout the 1990s, for instance, Latour engaged in studies of what he calls "water parliaments"[13] in France: local political forums in which biologists, engineers, farmers, anglers and local citizens met to discuss how to ensure the sustainability of rivers, waterways and local ecosystems (Latour 1998c). Similarly, Latour depicts the United Nations-sponsored Intergovernmental Panel on Climate Change (IPCC) and the negotiations surrounding the Kyoto climate summit in 1997, as another example of an (at least partially) functional parliament of things – this time, on a global level (Latour 2004d: 56f). The crucial point is that both local water issues and global climatic concerns call for new political institutions where a whole range of spokespersons – across the divides of science and politics – meet around the same table, because they are all engaged in the same collective experiment.

To briefly summarize, then, we might say that Latourian political philosophy pursues a symmetrical strategy in which he seeks to redefine the meanings of both science and politics in two different directions – with the goal of creating a common meeting-point in the parliament of things. In this respect, Latour argues that science and politics should not be perceived as two essentially different and ontologically separate activities, as was dictated by the modern Constitution. But neither should they be seen as completely overlapping, as is the case when science is conceptualized as "politics by other means." Instead, Latour wants to conjure up an image of science and politics as complementary, and *mutually enriching*, forms of practice that aim to explore the same problems – the same matters of concern – but using very different means and resources.

The principal duty of the sciences in the new experimental ecological democracy should be to explore and articulate – via gradually more refined methods – the range of non-human actants that currently intrude on the collective. This task of articulation is not the *sole* duty of the sciences, but Latour notes that the sciences are particularly well-equipped for this purpose. The task of politics is to design a democratically legitimate process for dealing with such hybrid matters of concern – a process that should result in the resolution of conflicts. Once again, this is not the sole burden of politicians; it is a common challenge in the parliament of things.

To modernize or to ecologize?

As mentioned in the introduction to this chapter, Latour's philosophical discussion of the parliament of things, and the wider question of representation, is closely linked to his more concrete interest in ecological issues. Latour commences his exploration of the past few decades of environmental politics by noting that the environmental movement and the Green political parties, both in France and elsewhere in Europe, face an apparent and serious paradox (Latour 1998c). On one hand, these environmentalists endlessly claim to be speaking on behalf of the greatest of all entities: Earth and all of its inhabitants – humans as well as animals, plants and organisms; present as well as future generations. In this sense, political ecology seems destined to become synonymous with *all* politics. On the other hand, despite the sporadic success stories of the environmental movement, political ecology has remained a fairly marginal program in the traditional political scenes around the world. In France, *Les Verts*, the largest Green political party, obtains only around 5 percent of the vote in local and national elections; even in Germany, where *Die Grünen* has been comparatively successful, this environmental–political party seldom surpasses the 10 percent barrier (see Burchell 2002).

The question, of course, is how to understand and mitigate this ecopolitical paradox – the paradox of present marginalization versus a requirement for future totality. Latour suggests that the basic parameters of this paradox stem from a problematic understanding of totality that thrives in the self-perception and rhetoric of environmentalists. Based on his *Dingpolitik*, Latour claims that environmental movements, despite their obvious importance, have sadly misunderstood both their own politics and their own ecology! In fact, Latour goes so far as to claim that *true* political ecology has not even started yet (2004d: 3).

According to Latour, two trends in particular account for the paradoxical situation of politics faced by environmentalists. First, one may observe how ecological issues are progressively *normalized* in societal life – partly through government policy and regulatory constraints, and partly in the practices and self-conceptions of everyday life. Administrative networks of scientific environmental monitoring, environmental law, limit values, etc., have gradually been established in most parts of the (Western) world. As such, the environment is subjected to the standard tradition of de-politicization through bureaucratic administration – an obvious example of a predominant characteristic of modernity, as described by Max Weber, father of sociology (Weber 1978).[14] Gradually, the environment becomes simply one among several political "sectors," and environmental movements and Green parties are likely to fade away, as ecology becomes internalized into standard political–economic practices.[15] If this should occur, Latour argues, we must admit that, after all, there was nothing new and innovative in political ecology: The movement simply contributes to a modernization of modernization.[16]

To explicate this possible normalization of ecological concern, Latour once again refers us back to his French counterparts, Luc Boltanski and Laurent Thévenot, and their sociological theory of "justificatory regimes" in the modern, Euro–American world (see Chapter 3). In brief, what Latour argues is that all previous political ecology might, on the whole, be interpreted within the frameworks of already existing moral practices. For instance, most initiatives of nature conservation may reasonably be understood in the context of romantic (and often nationalist) notions, according to which nature forms a constitutive part of "the domestic world." Similarly, the explosive growth in the number of green and organic consumer products illustrates how ecology, in many respects, has become integral to "the market regime" (Latour 1998c: 224ff). Unless environmentalists manage to articulate a fresh set of normative coordinates, they risk seeing the specific value of their interventions gradually vanish from politics.

In parallel to this normalization, however, another (and partially related) trend is similarly in effect: the tendency toward a radical *professionalization* of environmental politics, whereby responsibility for the future of the planet is potentially placed in the hands of a small group of powerful ecological experts. This kind of professionalization likewise extends a well-established modernist tradition: As the Latourian philosophy of modernity shows, the "chamber" of Nature has been entrusted to spokespersons of science ever since the 1600s. In the extreme, one may imagine an environmental politics that functions like a completely de-politicized global thermostat, where experts adjust human activities depending on the limits and needs of Nature (or Gaia). Latour, however, is highly skeptical of such a "technocracy of brains," which is not only undemocratic – because any connection to ordinary citizens and politicians is quickly lost – but also bases itself on scientifically unsound and potentially "anti-human" notions of totality (Latour 1998c: 222). In this context, Latour urges environmentalists to not blindly copy the misleading modernist concept of science – with its hard, unambiguous and so-called "realistic" facts – in an effort to achieve quick gains. Instead, eco-advocates ought to learn from the new knowledge politics of constructivist science studies (Latour 2003c). Ecological politics needs to acknowledge that ecological crises are not simply crises in nature, but also a *crisis of objectivity*: By definition, its objects are uncertain, controversial and shape-shifting hybrids; or, to use the term just introduced, matters of concern (Latour 2004d: 18ff).

What, then, would constitute an "ecologization" of political activism capable of bringing some much-needed renewal to the environmental movement? Conveniently enough, Latour need not look very far for an answer: In *practice*, environmentalists have always been engaged in an unconventional type of politics that is far better than their official self-conception! Officially, environmental movements claim to protect nature against all human intervention – but in practice, political activism is always orientated toward complicated imbroglios of numerous beings; some human, others not. Hence, it is never Nature as such, but always *this* species of bird, *this* branch of the river, *these* stranded whales or *this* land-use plan that becomes the matter of human concern, protection, criticism and scientific controversy (Latour 1998c: 222f). Political ecology is not about nature rescued from human influence, but about a redistribution of agency, roles and power relations that, in practice, breaks down the boundaries between the human and the non-human; society and nature.

One need only to think of debates about climate change: Here, a long chain of complex connections is frequently articulated, interrelating businesses, political regulations, scientific equipment, consumption habits, atmospheric chemistry, coral reefs, polar bears, melting glaciers, low-lying island states, poverty, the future movements of refugees and much more. Nobody seems to imagine that anthropogenic climate change can be avoided altogether. But the entire debate is about how to reorganize and manage these (and other) connections, in ways that avoid irreversible damage, even in a situation where the precise effects of this damage remain scientifically controversial and uncertain. In this process, no one – and certainly no environmental movement – is capable of ranking all of the implicated factors into a simple hierarchy, either scientifically or morally. Even the smallest of organisms may turn out to be more vital than the largest of companies!

According to Latour, we need to recognize that we now involuntarily find ourselves in the middle of a political–scientific experiment – where no one can determine with any certainty what is essential, what values should be prioritized and how we may live together. This entire situation is exactly "ecological" (Latour 2004d: 20ff). In Latourian political philosophy, then, ecology clearly implies a lot more than what we traditionally understand as environmental and nature-conservation problems. Rather, ecology is the name of a movement that has, in political practice, served to reopen basic modernist questions of non-human nature, scientific objectivity and the complex relations among human and non-human actants. Latour expresses his ecological point in strong rhetoric (1998c: 231): "What would a human be without elephants, plants, lions, cereals, oceans, ozone or plankton?" This also makes it clear why political ecology requires a rethinking of the relationship between facts and values: Non-human entities can no longer be unequivocally understood as facts – and humans are no longer the sole sources of intrinsic value, as Kant's famous moral maxim claimed.[17] This is not to imply that political ecology is simply about a shift from "anthropocentric" to "eco-centric" values as imagined by, for instance, Arne Næss, the Norwegian deep ecologist (1989). In this context, Latour's political and moral point is rather that neither "purely natural" nor "purely human" values exist. Instead, like everything else, such values should be viewed as intimately related within specific networks (see Whiteside 2002: 134ff). Hence, the move is not from anthropocentrism to eco-centrism, but "from being anthropocentric to becoming *decentered*" (Latour cited in Whiteside 2002: 136). Uncertainty, precaution and gradual experimentation are the new priorities of Latourian political ecology – both when it comes to "facts" and when it comes to "values."

A few examples may serve to flesh out, and further specify, these somewhat abstract thoughts on ecologization. First, Latour's political ecology may reasonably be juxtaposed with the ongoing "personification" or "humanization" of animals, which is often articulated in terms of animal welfare and rights (see Teubner 2006). Among animal-rights activists in particular, emphasis is typically on the "inherent" value of animals, regardless of their value for human (economic) purposes. Especially when it comes to "charismatic" animals, such as whales, elephants and pandas, this thinking carries significant legal–political power on a global scale (see Blok 2007a). The attribution of rights to animals is consistent with Latour's call to rethink the relationship between means and ends (Latour 2002c): These animals are no longer seen simply as resources for human activity, but also partly as ends in themselves. At the same time, however, we need to acknowledge the implications of the aforementioned de-centering: In Latour's political ecology, animals (and other forms of "nature") are not posited as carrying *absolute* value in themselves, but rather by virtue of their constitutive relations to people and other non-human actants.[18] Latour is basically advocating a "relational ethics" (see Whatmore 1997) where, for instance, the rights of elephants should be seen in the context of their specific "ecology" of connections. The point is that such relations are fundamentally uncertain, requiring mutual adaptation and thorough exploration to arrive at a *well-ordered* local common world, where poor Kenyans may co-exist with elephants, cows, crops and safari tourists (Latour 2004d: 170).

The next example we provide clarifies why this type of ecologizing – where the moral–political relationship between ends and means is redrawn – is correctly depicted by Latour as the diametrical opposite of modernization. As noted, Latour has been engaged in empirical studies of local water politics in France. In this respect, he has listened to the way biologists and engineers nowadays talk about the mistakes made during the 1950s and 1960s, in the name of modernization, agricultural productivity and "progress." Back then, the engineers relate, rivers were straightened out, dammed up and otherwise calibrated to the free-reigning desires of techno-science (see Latour 2007). Today, local planners across the board condemn such practices, not only because the projects were expensive to implement, but mostly because the rivers back then were not treated with sufficient *humility*. As a consequence, the rivers have now taken their "revenge," in the form of soil erosion, loss of aquatic biodiversity, the cleansing of nitrogen from agriculture and so on (Latour 1998c: 232ff). Anglers, bird watchers and nature-conservation groups are now pushing to restore the rivers, and thereby show a higher degree of respect for the inclinations of the water itself. It is hard to imagine a more striking illustration of the Latourian eco-political diagnosis: Where previously we modernized, we must now ecologize; where previously we interrupted the flow of water for purely human purposes, we must now show greater respect for the water's own *finality*.[19]

To sum up on this note, it should be clear why Latour perceives his science studies, as well as his political philosophy of *Dingpolitik*, as both highly relevant to the practical political issues facing contemporary environmental movements and Green political parties. What Latour is offering is nothing less than a new self-conception – or a new language for self-description – of the self-declared political ecology of environmental activists. Without such a novel self-conception, Latour claims, environmentalists will never be able to register, order and gain *Real-political* advantages from their many scattered and successful cases of political-activist practice. It is certainly debatable whether Latour is here presenting us with a fully convincing argument – both when it comes to the underlying empirical diagnosis, and to the more normative message for eco-political reformism. One might argue, for instance, that Latour's exposition lacks full recognition of the rather obvious power struggles and conflicts of interest that structure much of the political battle over the environment. Such battles often have more to do with ideology and material interests than with scientific and other uncertainties (see Lahsen 2005). However, such critique should not deny that the Latourian analysis focuses on a range of *specific* features of contemporary ecological risks, which gives political ecology some qualitatively new dimensions. We return to this discussion in the chapter summary. Next, we outline more accurately how Latour imagines the translation of ecologization into innovative political–institutional procedures, assembled under the concept of the parliament of things.

The non-modern Constitution: The good common world

So far in this chapter, we have seen how Latour employs political ecology as an opportunity to reconsider a number of basic issues that all relate to the divisions between science and politics, objects and subjects, and facts and values, as set up by the modern Constitution. In this respect, *ecologization* designates a collective movement that searches for a fundamentally different model for the organization of human and non-human collective life, their common cosmos. Practical experiments in political ecology – from animal rights to the restoration of river flows – constitute valuable steps in this direction. But Latour's claim is that environmentalists have so far failed to reflect deeply on their implicit political and epistemological ideals. With *Politics of Nature*, Latour seems to appoint himself as the chief eco-political ideologue and constitution builder: His (quite immodest) aim is to establish the contours of a new, non-modern, "ecological" Constitution in the form of an expanded outline of the parliament of things. The overall purpose is clearly articulated in classic liberal-utopian terms: At stake is the freeing of people and things from the false necessities implied by the notion of a transcendent Nature (Latour 2004d: 51f). It is now easier to understand why political ecology, in Latour's view, should have nothing to do with "nature." Beyond an all-encompassing Nature, all things – air, water, animals, technologies – should have their historicity, activity and specificity restored, and thereby their rights to be heard on their own terms in collective life (see Lash 1999: 314 ff). At the same time, people should be freed from the obligation to always justify their liberty through notions of a fixed and unchanging Nature, including ideas pertaining to "human nature" (see Fraser 2006: 55). Hence, the question that concerns Latour in *Politics of Nature* is: How might we organize the new *Dingpolitik*, so that this twin liberation project is best promoted – and protected against potential enemies?

By asking this question, Latour "the monist" willingly assumes a task that requires the creation of new political–ontological boundaries. He must now outline the institutional procedures that guarantee not only a democratic, but also a sensible and realistic, way of dealing with the many ecological hybrids of the non-modern world. In other words, when it comes to political philosophy, Latour is neither an anarchist nor a deconstructivist; rather, he strives to reconstruct a liberal, representative and "deliberative" democracy where *things* (and their representatives) will *also* be subjected to demands of public debate and negotiation.[20]

As noted, Latour obtains a great deal of inspiration in this endeavor from American pragmatist John Dewey, for whom the question of "volatile" political publics and their changing concerns was central to the effort of creating a liberal, but also inclusive and responsive, democracy (Dewey 1927). With the parliament of things, Latour undertakes to heed Dewey's call for an open and experimental political life. The main tenet here is that, as members of public life, we need to constantly be on the lookout for new considerations, new actors and new interests that require us to reconsider the overall composition of the collective. In Latour's case, this essentially means that we must stay alert to new techno-scientific hybrids – from the ozone layer to genetically modified crops – that seek out a place in the collective. If the hybrids are to be seen as part of an experimental democracy, it is obviously crucial that they are not treated as pre-given objects. Rather, they should be treated as matters of concern; that is, as controversial and uncertain things around which divergent spokespersons gather in conflict, discussion and negotiation.

At the same time, Latour believes that such experimental political processes demand a relatively well-defined division into new competences, powers and guarantees – similar to the way that the modern Constitution functioned (in spite of everything). What we need is not an *abolition* of representative democracy, but rather a *redefinition* of its two-chamber system. To define such new guarantees, Latour needs to first introduce a fresh vocabulary to replace the distinction between "facts" (objects, science) and "values" (subjects, politics) made by the old Constitution. In the following section, we outline this updated vocabulary by taking a tour around the parliament of things and its new two-chamber system.[21]

Touring the construction site of the parliament of things

When seen in relation to the question of what makes up a good common world, the interesting thing about Latour's outline of a parliament of things is that he explicitly seeks to avoid the conclusion that everything should be "mixed together" in chaotic struggles of power and interest. Rather, Latour seeks to clarify, order and redistribute the conflicting considerations that have so far been hidden within the concepts of "facts" and "values" – and thereby, in the end, to create a more *realistic* process for political ecology.

Basically, Latour imagines a new two-chamber system, where the Upper House decides which hybrids may become part of the collective, and where the Lower House decides how all of the incorporated hybrids will co-exist. More specifically, Latour imagines that the two chambers (the Upper and Lower Houses) should each solve two specific tasks, which means that each hybrid needs to undergo four phases (or trials) before its possible inclusion in the collective (see Figure 4.1). Hence, to fulfill its function, the first (Upper) chamber manages the tasks of "perplexity" and "consultation": *Perplexity* concerns the active search for new and potentially risky entities in the surrounding world of the collective (external reality); *consultation* is about allowing as many spokespersons as possible to articulate these new propositions and their relevance to the collective.

When compared to the modern Constitution, perplexity belongs to the world of facts, and consultation belongs to the world of values – thus, perplexity has traditionally been associated with the sciences, whereas consultation is thought of in relation to politics. However, Latour's point is precisely that both tasks should be solved as part of the *same* experimental political

94 Political ecology

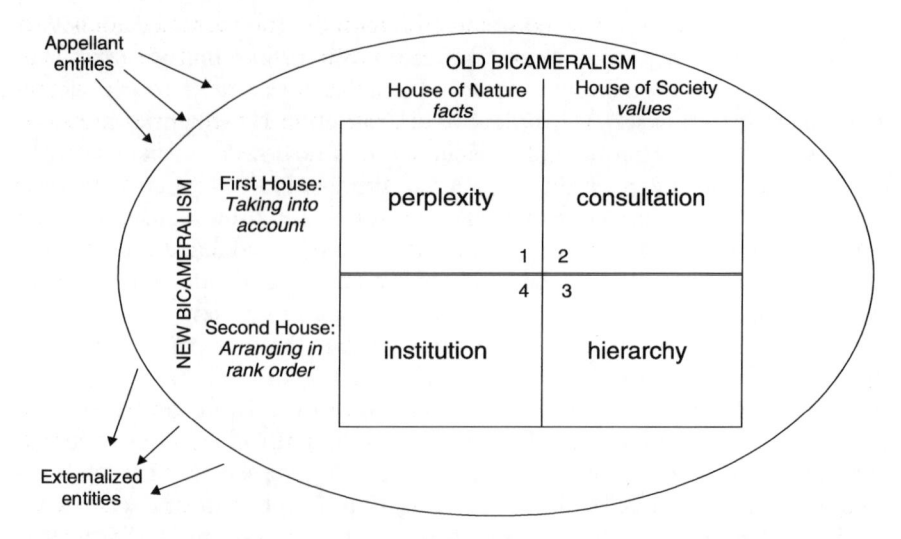

Figure 4.1 The four collective tasks in Latour's new parliament of things.
Source: Demeritt 2006 (after Latour 2004d; Figures 3.1 and 3.2).

endeavor – namely, the attempts of the collective to actively explore, accommodate and otherwise react to new hybrids that arise in its surroundings.

Similarly, the second (Lower) chamber should solve the tasks of "hierarchy" and "institution" – in step with the hybrids working their way through the first chamber, and thus coming to appear as well-articulated, faceted and (network-)connected as possible. *Hierarchy* denotes the process whereby the different spokespersons of the collective publicly discuss and negotiate the effects that the new, articulated hybrid will have on existing orders of power and value. The course of these debates is then finally concluded through the *institution* of the hybrid in a new order – or, alternatively, with the chamber rejecting the relevance of the hybrid in question, in which case it is excluded from the collective altogether. As an illustration of such an "externalized" hybrid, Latour mentions the 8,000 people who die every year in France as the result of car-related traffic accidents. In practical politics, it has come to be "decided" that these people simply do not count, since the interests of smooth traffic flows prevail (2004d: 124). But in the parliament of things, one crucial point is that such excluded entities always possess options for having their claim to existence and recognition re-evaluated.

As with the first chamber, the second chamber carries out two tasks that were traditionally kept separate on opposite sides of the fact/value divide: Hierarchy is regarded the domain of moralists or moral experts; and institution is often left to the economists and their powerful tools, calculating their way to "the common good" (see Demeritt 2006). Again, Latour's main point is that these tasks and skills must be brought together if the inclusion of eco-political hybrids is to happen in accordance with democratic procedures. Just as Nature and its scientific spokespersons exhibit an unfortunate tendency to short-circuit political consultation, Latour holds the view that the economists and their Market Order show a similarly unfortunate tendency to short-circuit normative discussion about the good common life (see Latour 2004d: 131ff). In the new parliament of things, both of these risks to democracy are finally avoided, because there is no longer any one profession that enjoys a monopoly on solving the problems of the collective. On the other hand, the parliament ensures that four major considerations in collective life are met: external reality; relevance; public visibility; and the legitimate closure of debates.[22]

One of the core arguments in this Latourian political ecology, then, is that the only way of making the parliament of things act both democratically legitimate and eco-politically sensible is to bring together carriers of the aforementioned skills – the skills of scientists, politicians, moralists and economists. In other words, the basic idea is that these four professions – science, politics, morality and economics – should *all* contribute to the solution of each of the four tasks of the collective. In this sense, perplexity, consultation, hierarchy and institution are indeed *collective* challenges, to which each profession may bring its own historically rooted experience, skills and tools.

For our purposes here, it would lead too far astray to go through the entire list Latour sets up to clarify the respective properties of these professions. By way of illustration, let us focus on the moral profession – such as we might find it represented in a council of ethics.[23] In relation to the task of perplexity, Latour believes that the moral profession contributes a sort of permanent "ethical alert" that forces the collective to actively search for invisible or excluded hybrids. Concerning the task of consultation, the moral profession contributes by defending the rights of these hybrids to each be heard on their own terms. As for hierarchy, the intervention of the moral profession is largely responsible for the fact that the collective finds itself forced to search for a single order of value, as opposed to several disjointed orders. Finally, it is largely due to the moral sensitivity of these specialists, regarding issues of exclusion, that rejected hybrids are granted the right to appeal their cases.

If one compares this outline to contemporary debates about biotechnology or climate change, Latour's main point is that moral considerations are relevant to *all* parts of these debates – including those parts typically seen as technical, scientific, political or economic. On the other hand, the same applies to the other professions: Scientific considerations cannot suddenly be ignored just because a specific debate on climate change moves into global politics, market economics or ethical aspects. In brief, Latour imagines our public political life reorganized in such a way that scientists, moralists and other "world builders" are brought together in hybrid forums to jointly discuss collective issues – especially the many ecological risks of our times (Fraser 2006).

96 Political ecology

As already noted, it is difficult to assess the extent to which this Latourian outline of a parliament of things bases itself upon empirical observations of political ecology, or the degree to which it remains a utopian and idiosyncratic thought experiment. In Latour's self-conception, the former is obviously the case: In his characteristically polemical style, Latour claims that his non-modern constitution simply expresses a new "common sense" that has long been anticipated in eco-political practice (2004d:7). His empirical illustrations, however, are somewhat sparse. In this context, he particularly emphasizes the UN's Intergovernmental Panel on Climate Change (IPCC) as an example of a hybrid forum, in which all spokespersons meet under the same roof: the oil-industry lobby, coral-reef experts, Indonesian forest people, American political economists, landscape ecologists, etc. (ibid: 65). A more in-depth example concerns prions, the infectious particles that were under suspicion for destroying cow brains and causing mad cow disease (or BSE, *bovine spongiform encephalopathy*) (ibid: 111ff). Employing this case, Latour illustrates the perplexity among scientists ("what is the real source of infection?"); the attempts by politicians to find and consult relevant parties ("who is part of the problem, and who will be part of the solution?"); the many associated moral discussions ("will we accept that animals are fed their own species?"); and the institutionalization of specific solutions regarding feed and slaughter, which ultimately establishes a kind of co-existence between prions and the remaining collective. The point is that these voices – of biological scientists, European Union bureaucrats, breeders, veterinarians, consumers and ethicists – all need to be heard in the collective process of consultation and decision-making, which thus assumes the shape of a joint state of alert.

To sum up, it seems reasonable to conclude that – with his outline of a parliament of things – Latour undoubtedly contributes valuable insights and pointed formulations to one of the major political challenges of the contemporary world: the ever-denser interweaving of scientific and political issues of great importance for social institutions and citizens alike (see Demeritt 2006). This interweaving is especially evident in the domain of environmental risks, where science serves as an indispensable "sensory apparatus" in relation to otherwise invisible, global, complex and long-term collective problems. Nobody sees, smells or feels the presence of CO_2 pollution in the atmosphere – it is only through advanced techno-scientific mediation that we, as a collective, are capable of recognizing (and possibly reacting to) the threat of global warming. In this respect, the Latourian analysis is fully consistent with Ulrich Beck's diagnosis of the risk society: Ecological hybrids represent a fundamental challenge to the entire organization of our political and scientific lives (Latour 2003b). Compared to Beck, however, Latour is considerably more radical in the institutional reconstructions he proposes – in this sense, his parliament of things represents a general rethinking of all the major dimensions of modernity.

The Latourian approach has strengths and weaknesses. On one hand, he actually manages to present a political philosophy that radically breaks with the modernist divide between Nature and Society; on the other hand, one consequence seems to be that his argument appears somewhat abstract and debatable when put in relation to empirical observations (see Castree 2006; Bruun Jensen 2006). Latour's interpretation of the UN's IPCC as a full-fledged hybrid forum appears implausible: Although scientific, political, moral and economic concerns are indeed inextricably entangled in the climate debate, the IPCC is still organized according to some very "modernist" boundaries between science and politics (see Miller 2001). Based on such considerations, we might perhaps most fruitfully characterize the Latourian outline of a parliament of things as just that: a philosophical and political outline, the relevance of which will need to be discussed and negotiated in different contexts in the future. Like all other knowledge claims, Latour's own knowledge is subject to such performative conditions.

Conclusion: Between ecology, science and democracy

Political ecology designates the type of politics that arises from the crisis of modernity. Because of breakthroughs in techno-science, hybrids have now become so manifold as to threaten the very existence of our collective. The threats are symbolized by omnipresent environmental and health risks, with climate change as their most recent and iconic expression. For these reasons, we are now forced to choose our path ahead: either we attempt to modernize the modernization via increasingly frantic efforts to maintain our boundaries and control mechanisms; or we attempt to ecologize our collective life under uncertain, probing and experimental conditions.

This brief rendition of the main thrust of Latourian political philosophy indicates that the term *cosmopolitics* should be taken quite literally: In our contemporary world, the "cosmos" is once again a site of politics, in the sense of a gradual ordering of the good common world for humans, animals, plants – and gods. At this point, *nothing* may be excluded in advance when it comes to organizing common life. All actants, from the smallest organisms to the all-encompassing climate, will have to be provided with reliable spokespersons. Moreover, these spokespersons should be able to articulate – in the here and now, and in one single hybrid forum – the diverse consequences that such actants may represent for the future of the collective.

As such, political ecology marks the transition from the politics of *time* to the politics of *space*: Whereas the *Realpolitik* of modernity could be understood via concepts of "progress" and "development," the non-modern *Dingpolitik* is best understood via the notion of a cosmopolitics of "simultaneity." In *Dingpolitik*, everything is simultaneously involved in complex connections that transverse standard spatial divisions (Latour 2005a: 39f). Non-modern collectives will not resemble the national political assemblies that we have historically inherited from modern political revolutions. Hence, Latour argues, we will need to continually create new parliaments of things, in which the numerous contemporary matters of concern – from melting glaciers to the prions causing mad cow disease – can form the basis of an object-oriented democracy. In such parliaments, politicians, scientists, economists and moralists will have to meet around the same negotiation table: When "facts" and "values" can no longer be clearly differentiated, the two elements must be addressed using the *same* democratic process.

Throughout this book, we at times characterize Latour as an empirical philosopher – and this label seems particularly apt when it comes to his political ecology. At the same time, however, this term also highlights an area of tension in the argument, as stretched out between empirical and philosophical points of reference. Through his notion of a parliament of things, Latour is aiming to cover a field that seems almost impossibly wide: from the practical political struggles of environmentalists, right up to a range of metaphysical challenges related to the basic reorganization of science and politics in a non-modern collective.

Given this task of stretching such an apparent divide, much of Latour's argument is precisely about showing that there really *is* no dilemma here: If only we interpret them properly, Latour seems to say, environmental movements will be the true winners in his new politics of knowledge. This type of politics accentuates the uncertainties, unpredictability and mutual lines of connection between things – and, as such, it also emphasizes the necessity of collective experimentation and precaution in our handling of ecological risks. Not surprisingly, Latour suggests that science studies in general – and ANT in particular – are uniquely well-suited for such purposes. With his emphasis on far-reaching and mutable network connections among human and non-human actants, one might even say that Latourian thinking (as shown especially in ANT) has always manifested a certain "ecological" inclination (see Murdoch 2001). This is the ground on which to understand Latour's engagement with political ecology: In his view, there exists an *inherent* and positive connection between, on one hand, his preferred science and technology studies, and on the other, the practical political challenges faced by current-day environmentalists.

We should ask ourselves, however: Just how convincing is this Latourian claim about an inherent connection between science studies and the environmental movements – or indeed, between philosophical interpretations and empirical observations of political ecology? In doing so, it is worth recalling that Latour's thoughts on ecology articulate themselves into a political and intellectual context, in which a range of distinct but related ideas have already gained some degree of acceptance as guides for eco-political action. Hence, we have already emphasized how the Latourian argument of non-human actants as ends in themselves, enjoying their own finality rather than being simply means of fulfilling human needs, is quite reminiscent of the ongoing moral and legal discussion of animal rights (Teubner 2006). Similarly, one might argue that Latour's ecological politics of knowledge (as summarized here) in many respects articulates a version of the so-called *precautionary principle* that has gained ground in practical environmental politics since the 1990s, notably in the European Union. In popular terms, the precautionary principle dictates that, in cases of scientific uncertainty as to the potential adverse effects of new technological hybrids, decisions ought to favor (or at least take into account) the long-term interests of the environment, rather than abstaining from political action (Dratwa 2002).

In a more social-scientific context, we have already noted that Latour, to a large extent, adopts his eco-political worldview from sociologist Ulrich Beck and his notion of the risk society (Latour 2003b). In line with Beck's reasoning, Latour suggests that the current explosion of ecological hybrids, criss-crossing boundaries of nature and society, necessitates a rethinking of our entire societal organization – as well as the drafting of a new progressive political project. Latour and Beck also have their differences: In a normative political sense, Latour's proposal for a parliament of things is considerably more radical than Beck's notion of a "reflexive" science in dialogue with society (see Demeritt 2006). Generally speaking, however, Latour's interpretation of political ecology clearly resonates with Beck's, both in terms of eco-political practice and in terms of the social-scientific outlook. In this sense (and to the extent that the risk society is a credible narrative), there is clearly *some* degree of empirical grounding in Latour's empirical philosophy.

Meanwhile, we still need to acknowledge that the parliament of things has the appearance of a quite idiosyncratic and abstract thought experiment. This does not imply that the entire *direction* of Latourian political philosophy is idiosyncratic: On the contrary, it is fairly widely accepted that ecological issues necessitate some kind of democratization of scientific knowledge, in order for them to be used in political processes of decision-making (see Strand 2001; Jasanoff 2003). The notion that scientific expertise should be subjected to some form of public verification and discussion is rather widespread – and has even been institutionalized, for instance, in the so-called consensus conferences pioneered (and exported to other countries) by the Danish Board of Technology (see Blok 2007b; Bruun Jensen 2005). What is idiosyncratic about Latour's parliament of things is its *radical* character: In his projection, political ecology necessitates not simply a readjustment or containment of the sciences, but rather a full-blown revision of basic modernist distinctions between science and politics, object and subject, facts and values, nature and society. Perhaps it is not surprising that, when presented in such radical terms, it becomes difficult for Latour to provide empirical examples of parliaments of things that actually exist (see Castree 2006).

The radical aspect of Latourian political philosophy is most succinctly expressed in his complete reworking of the concept of nature. Latour considers his break with all traditional conceptions of nature to be a necessary step if political ecology is to be reconciled with democratic principles. His example of the elephants is indicative in this respect: On a global scale, severe political struggles are raging over these animals. Western conservationists and animal-rights groups are pitched against local African farmers, who view the elephants mostly as crop-destroying pests (see Thompson 2002). Latour suggests that, in this and similar situations, we need to recognize that not only do we live in a multicultural world, we also live in a world of "multi-naturalism" – one that consists of numerous divergent nature practices (Latour 2004d). The thrust of this argument is that we will need entirely new political maps, capable of showing the many lines of conflict constantly being drawn around issues of nature, environment and ecology. At the same time, harking back to political philosophy, Latour invites us to reinvent a respect for diplomacy: In cases of conflict among collectives with strongly divergent understandings of nature (and cosmos), the only way to avoid confrontations will be to seek out practical compromises. On all accounts, it would be misleading to view Latour's new parliamentarism as denying the fact of profound political conflict. To the contrary, it is precisely *because* we cannot take any "natural order" for granted that we need to experiment with the creation of new worlds.

To many analysts – and certainly to many environmental activists – Latour's break with traditional conceptions of nature (and the resulting democratization of scientific knowledge) likely appears to be a dangerous experiment. Such concerns are already articulated, in different but related ways. Certain skeptical commentators have emphasized that most environmental conflicts are not so much a matter of uncertainty and perplexity, but instead involve choices among fairly well-defined scenarios, interests and political factions (see Tucker 2007: 211). Latourian political ecology, such critics argue, demonstrates an insufficient understanding of political economy, power and conflicts of interest. Others have noted that, in the absence of an unequivocal scientific interpretation of such effects, it will become much more difficult to criticize actors for undertaking non-ecological and unsustainable practices (see Lahsen 2005). Hence, for instance, there is now little doubt that, for many years, the American oil industry and conservative think-tanks have attempted to obstruct debates on climate change by systematically creating and spreading suspicion as to the validity of the scientific recommendations made by the UN Intergovernmental Panel on Climate Change (IPCC) (see McCright & Dunlap 2003).

Evaluated in the light of a parliament of things, such "perplexity" might seem welcome – on the other hand, this would also appear to be a normatively untenable conclusion. In fact, Latour reflects explicitly on such questions in a (partially) self-critical article dealing with the current impasses of social critique – and in this context, Latour maintains quite bluntly that there is now no reason whatsoever to doubt the (constructed) facticity of climate change (Latour 2004c). From a Latourian perspective, the problematic aspect of "climate skepticism" may not so much be its science as its politics: the systematic attempt to distort, mislead and circumvent an open public debate as to the long-term consequences of their claims (see Demeritt 2006). By contrast, Latourian political philosophy hinges on a firm belief in the public use of reasoning; not in the form of purely scientific reason, but as a *common sense* of well- or poorly articulated propositions. Environmental activists ought to ally themselves with this common sense if they wish to gain public support for their cosmopolitics.

By way of concluding this chapter, we might reasonably say that Latour's extensive engagement with political ecology raises more questions than it answers. Fundamentally, his way of combining three of the most important challenges of our times – ecological risks, the end of modernity, and the crisis of scientific objectivity – is intellectually and politically sophisticated, radical and thought-provoking. With his outline of a new parliament of things, Latour succeeds in creating an original vision of an open and experimental object-oriented democracy. Whatever practical future this kind of democracy will enjoy is itself a topic worthy of critical and constructive discussion. Like all other knowledge claims, the parliament of things is subject to those performative conditions that the science studies of Latour (and others) have forcefully highlighted as a basic aspect of our thinking and behavior. The fate of facts, like that of democratic visions, is always in the hands of future users.

As such, the parliament of things may now join the long list of contemporary "ecological" uncertainties: The way that relations between science and politics develop in the future is certainly going to be a decisive factor in determining whether, as a collective, we are able to respond to the immense crises of climate change, biodiversity loss and ecological destruction. Latour's path through these crises may be idiosyncratic, but it rests on a simple intuition: Our challenges cannot simply be left to a narrow technocratic elite, as has been traditional in France and many other places (see Tucker 2007). Political ecology needs to be a shared matter of concern. Only together will we learn to recognize that, as humans, we are deeply connected to our non-human fellow beings.

5 Sociology of associations

> In the end, strangely enough, it's only the freshness of the results of social science that can guarantee its political relevance. [. . .] So the test for political interest is now slightly easier to pass: one must practice sociology in such a way that the ingredients making up the collective are regularly refreshed.
>
> (Latour 2005b: 261).

Introduction: Latour's sociological ambivalence

Latour has always had an uneasy relationship with sociology. In fact, he thinks everything was already horribly wrong for sociology at the end of the 1800s, when the entire discipline took a wrong turn. This may at first seem like only a peripheral problem, given that Latour's thinking in general – together with the field of science studies in which he positions himself – is intrinsically interdisciplinary. Nevertheless, throughout his entire career, Latour has been involved in a peculiar love/hate relationship with the discipline of sociology.

On one hand, from the beginning of his authorship, Latour has argued that his theories of science and technology are highly relevant to key sociological questions, especially when it comes to clarifying the so-called micro/macro problem (more on this later). At the same time – and as we mentioned in our introductory chapter – he has been teaching and supervising engineering students in this very discipline (sociology), based at a research center for the "sociology of innovation" in Paris.

On the other hand, Latour is often mockingly ironic when it comes to distancing himself from large parts of the sociological research establishment. He is particularly derisive of the branch of sociology that is typically known as "critical sociology," as embodied by, among others, Latour's slightly older and highly esteemed fellow countryman, Pierre Bourdieu. In much of Latour's work – and most notably in *We Have Never Been Modern* – Bourdieu serves as a kind of implicit scapegoat in Latour's orchestration of his showdown with modernist patterns of thought.[1]

When asked directly, however, Latour willingly admits that his "training in sociology is rather haphazard," and that his colleagues consider him more of a philosopher than a sociologist (Latour 1998d). At the same time, Latour would of course reject the notion that a choice needs to be made between these two disciplines: In his view, the whole challenge is to reunite sociology and metaphysics, and thereby to redefine the rules of sociological method (Latour 2002a).

Latour's ambivalent relationship with sociology forms one element in the development of his authorship that we highlighted in the introduction to this book: From a thematic starting point in science and technology, Latour has gradually become more preoccupied with developing a "general" and alternative theory of society, still under the banner of ANT. To be more specific, since the late 1990s, he has written books and texts on topics as diverse as French administrative law (2002b/2010b), religious icons (2005d), the economy (Latour & Lépinay 2009) and, of course, the politics of nature (2004d), as introduced in the previous chapter.

Up to this point, the pinnacle of such a "generalization" of the Latourian take on society occurred in 2005 with the publication of *Reassembling the Social*. In this book, Latour for the first time sketches, in one comprehensive presentation, his distinctive ideas on sociology, the social and "social explanations." As he states in the introduction: "After having done extensive work on the 'assemblages' of nature, I believe it's necessary to scrutinize more thoroughly the exact content of what is 'assembled' under the umbrella of a society" (2005b: 2). In a related fashion, and rather poetically, Latour declares that, having now done this work, he has finally discovered the conditions under which he "could be proud of being called a sociologist" (ibid.: p. x).

In *Reassembling the Social*, Latour distinguishes his own "sociology of associations" sharply from the entire "sociology of the social" that has developed and become dominant since the theories of Émile Durkheim around 1900. The sociology of the social concerns itself with social structures, social differentiation and, particularly, with social order – in short, it deals with "society" as an established domain of reality. Within this tradition, the social is considered a kind of material; we can speak of "social" stuff, just as we may speak of stuff that is "wooden" or "steely." Latour, on the other hand, adopts an entirely different starting point and an entirely different definition of the social. In the Latourian sociology of associations, there is no "social stuff." Rather, the social refers simply to that which is connected or associated. As such, sociology can only describe "the social" by tracing the constant movements (or translations) in the connections between heterogeneous elements.

According to Latour, the sociology of associations represents the lost path of the discipline, as symbolized by French sociologist (and psychologist) Gabriel Tarde, to whom Latour now points as his intellectual forebear (2005b: 13ff). By following this path, sociology will avoid the pitfall of getting lost in all the well-known and irresolvable dichotomies of the discipline, between micro and macro, actor and structure, technology and society, and – not least – between nature and culture. Instead, the sociologist will obtain new tools for mapping a hybrid social world in constant flux – as symbolized by fashionable buzzwords like *innovation, knowledge society* and *globalization*.

In this chapter, we follow Latour in his search for the lost path of sociology – starting with *Reassembling the Social*, but also employing a number of other texts from the late 1990s and onward. The Latourian sociology of associations may be seen as a comprehensive expansion upon – as well as continuation and reworking of – much of his earlier work. For this reason, *Reassembling the Social* contains a number of updated versions of previous arguments, points and examples. Hence, for instance, inspired by ethno-methodologist Harold Garfinkel, the Latourian methodological slogan is still to "follow the actors." But whereas actors used to mean "only" scientists, microbes, instruments, machines and centers of calculation, the cast-list is now expanded to include ecosystems, legal texts, practicing Catholics, classrooms, transportation systems and much more. In order to avoid repeating ourselves, we illustrate the sociology of associations using several of Latour's more recent examples and case studies; for instance, stemming from the worlds of law and religion. Further, we frame our presentation by asking what is specifically *sociological* about Latour's argument. Toward the end of this chapter, we take a brief look at some objections that have been raised against his sociology of associations, and against his attempt to reinvent the discipline from scratch.

From society to collective

In 1987, Margaret Thatcher, then Prime Minister of the United Kingdom and a conservative icon, became notorious and infamous for making a statement, in which she addressed the question of individual responsibility from a neo-liberal point of view: "There is no such thing as society." A little less than 20 years later, Latour provocatively reuses the same slogan for his sociology of associations – although he hastens to add that his motives are completely different from Thatcher's (2005b: 5). That is to say, Latour does not aim to fragment society into individual actors, but instead to replace "society" with "collective" – a familiar concept from Latour's philosophy of modernity (Chapter 3), and one that he further develops in his political ecology (Chapter 4). The concept of "society" may well have been useful at the dawn of the social sciences in the late 1800s, but Latour argues that it has now become superfluous – and may indeed work as a barrier against up-to-date and contemporary ways of practicing social science. As Latour writes, in reference to the aforementioned founders of French sociology, we "are witnessing, a century later, the revenge of Gabriel Tarde over Émile Durkheim: society explains nothing but has to be explained" (2000b: 113). In other words, the concept of "society" – and the whole notion of a stable social domain – is closely tied to that type of sociology for which the sociology of associations is meant to represent a clear alternative. With reference to his lifelong engagement in the anthropology of science, Latour thus writes that all is well in the social sciences, except for the concept of the social and the concept of science (2002a).[2]

Seen from the vantage point of the Latourian sociology of associations, we can pinpoint at least three serious defects in the concept of "society" – and these three defects may also serve to provide a preliminary (negative) encapsulation of his alternative sociology. First, the term "society" covers both too much and too little at the same time. Too much because, as Tarde had already noted, "everything is a society": We may speak of cellular societies, plant societies, societies of atoms and baboon societies. In this way, sociology might seem to be on the verge of assimilating all the other sciences! But the concept of "society" also describes too little because, throughout the 1800s, the term gradually became synonymous with only one, historically very specific, form of human community – namely, the nation state. The sociologists of the day, most notably Durkheim, were by no means innocent in this development. Hence, Latour approvingly refers to well-known Polish sociologist Zygmunt Bauman, who points out that, for much of the 20th century, social theory has been indistinguishable from "social engineering"; that is, sociology has played an active and political role in modernization drives led by nation states (2005b: 41). Throughout this process, the concept of "society" acquires strong connotations of order, continuity and (national) integration. This purification of society quite clearly forms a parallel to the purification of nature. According to Latour's philosophy of modernity, nature is "invented" as an independent domain by the natural sciences of the 1600s (see Chapter 3) – in the same way that society is, to a great extent, "invented" by the consolidation of nation states (and the social sciences) in the 1800s. "Society" thus forms part of the modern Constitution – and according to Latour, it should now be replaced by the non-modern concept of the collective (see Chapter 4).

The second problem is that the concept of "society" implies an all-too inflexible demarcation of spatial and geographic scales, and as such, severely restricts our possibilities for studying social distances. The techno-scientific actor-networks that Latour has been mapping for much of his career have never respected the boundaries of nation states – although, in the case of Pasteur, techno-science served to consolidate the power of the emerging French state (see Chapter 2). In fact, the techno-sciences are oftentimes global in their spatial distribution – and they may even be said to partially define what we mean by words like "global," "globe" and, of course, "globalization" (Latour 2004d: 450f). One obvious example here is the role played by cartography in the earlier phases of globalization, set in motion by voyages of exploration and European colonialism from the late 1400s onward (see also Law 1987). In general, one of the significant points of Latour's sociology of associations is that actor-networks – and, by implication, social collectives – do not possess fixed and unchangeable geographical boundaries. In this respect as well, the term "society" has an unfortunate tendency to mislead rather than to enlighten – and this is especially true in an age when information and communication technologies allow for rapid shifts in geographical scale. Latour himself provides the simplest of illustrations: "I can be one meter away from someone in the next telephone booth, and be nevertheless more closely connected to my mother 6,000 miles away" (1996b: 372). This type of everyday experience, as shared by increasing numbers of people, indicates that we need to think about social connections – and social distances – in ways that are quite different from what is allowed by the category of "society."

The third and final defect – and that which is most crucial to Latour – is that the term "society," in its narrowest sense, pretends to build communities that consist exclusively of humans. By contrast (and as we have noted several times throughout this book), Latour always thinks of his actor-networks in materially heterogeneous terms: They consist of both human and non-human actors; humans as well as machines, buildings, microbes and texts. This also applies to heterogeneous collectives, the mapping of which is the primary task of the sociology of associations. At this point, Latour's re-definition of the concept of "the social" – as compared to standard sociology – becomes pivotal. According to Latour, the social is not a term to designate human communities, and neither does it capture a stabilized domain, field or structure. To Latour, the social basically describes every connection, or association, between human and non-human actors. More specifically, it designates a trajectory of relations among heterogeneous and (from the outset) non-social elements – or, in other words, the movement or process whereby new types of connections are created.

There are at least two important – if still somewhat abstract – points to this. First, it obviously follows that sociology needs to include non-human actors in its domain of study. Whereas Durkheim encouraged sociology to "consider social facts as things," Latour now encourages his colleagues to "consider things as social facts" (1996c: 240). The second point (which has equally far-reaching consequences) is that the sociology of associations is always a matter of *new* connections – and, thereby, concerns a collective that is undergoing constant movement and change. Latour explicitly states (2005b: 11) that the sociology of associations becomes necessary whenever things accelerate; innovations proliferate; boundaries between groups are blurred; and the number of new entities in the collective multiply. Clearly, what Latour is implying here is that our present-day, science-dominated, high-tech society – with its rapid expansion of hybrids (see Chapter 3) – is marked precisely by just such an unstable state of movement and change.

It is important to emphasize this second point – i.e., that the social is in a constant process of transformation – partly because it refers back to a general characteristic of Latour's thinking: namely, his inspiration from the process philosophy of Whitehead (and his successors). Further, it also marks an opportunity to clarify the relationship between the Latourian sociology of

Sociology of associations 107

associations and the sociology of the social. Hence, Latour compares this relationship (quite ambitiously) to the impact exerted by the theory of relativity in physics. In most situations, the "pre-relativist" sociology of the social will be adequate, because society only changes at a slow pace. As Latour puts this (ibid.): It would be pedantic to completely ban the use of terms such as "IBM," "France" or "lower-middle class," despite the static nature of these concepts. On the other hand: In situations of rapid change – the restructuring of businesses, globalization, social mobility – such static concepts fall short, and sociology stands in need of the fully "relativist" sociology of associations.[3] With the sociology of associations, the aim is to "follow the actors themselves" as they restructure the heterogeneous collective. The logical implication of such an exclusive focus on restructurings is that, whenever a situation entails no movement and no change in social configurations, the sociology of associations – in contrast to the sociology of the social – will have nothing whatsoever to say: "No trace left, thus no information, thus no description, then no talk. *Don't fill it in*" (Latour 2005b: 150).

To sum up, we might say that the Latourian sociology of associations distinguishes itself in three basic respects from most (although not all) existing sociology. First, by focusing on the social connections of variable – and often global – spatial and geographic extensions; second, by focusing on the social as an ongoing process of transformation, in contrast to the focus on social order, structure and reproduction embedded in much of classic sociology since Durkheim; and third, by replacing the idea of a purely human society with the notion of a heterogeneous collective made up of both human and non-human actors. As noted in Chapter 2, this latter point is often expressed through the semiotic concept of "actants." Seen as a whole, Latour has thus reformulated most of the core questions of sociology as they are usually understood. Most importantly, Latour refuses to accord the question of "actors" and "structures" – that is, the human individual versus the collective order of society – any privileged role in his sociology of associations. In fact, he goes so far as to claim that sociologists ought to completely forget, or rather bypass, this traditional disciplinary "agency/structure" dualism. Instead, it is the relations among human and non-human actants – or, more generally, between society and nature – that emerge as a key concern of Latourian sociology.

"Society Explains Nothing But Has To Be Explained"

Latour often finds his discussion partners amongst sociologists of science and technology, who view their work as a question of providing "social explanations" for the particular ways in which specific scientific statements or technological artifacts have come to be developed. For instance, sociologists of technology may refer to gender roles and the competitive interests among groups of athletic young men when trying to explain why a particular "safety bike" – fitted with pneumatic tires of equal size – has replaced, since the late

108 *Sociology of associations*

1800s, the more demanding and dangerous wooden-frame velocipede, fitted with small rear and large front wheels (see Bijker 1997). Alternatively, when trying to explain the emergence of the indeterminist quantum theory in physics, sociologists of science may point to "macro-social" factors, such as the political and cultural climate of instability dominating the Weimar Republic of the interwar years (see Forman 1971). In the early laboratory studies of Latour and Woolgar (see Chapter 2), one may detect a certain tendency of the authors to introduce such social explanations – for instance, they use the concept of "cycles of credit" to explain how competitive researchers obtain recognition and funding.[4]

In his later work, however, Latour becomes increasingly skeptical toward the whole notion of explaining the techno-sciences in social terms.[5] This skepticism has led to lengthy critical dialogues between Latour and his colleagues in the sociology of science. In brief, Latour's objection is that science and technology are such key factors in the formation and development of the social (or "society") that it makes little sense to use some social context to explain these developments. In other words, to a large extent, the social context will itself be a product of the techno-sciences. In a nutshell, this is the point made by the title of one of Latour's earliest articles: "Give me a laboratory, and I will raise the world" (1983). It is also the point of his claim that France was *pasteurized* in the late 1800s: Pasteur, his microbes and his laboratories construct "France" just as much as – or perhaps more than – France constructs Pasteur.

Such ideas, stemming from Latour's work in science studies, form the backdrop against which one should understand his more general skepticism toward "social explanations" – and, by implication, his claim that "society explains nothing." By elaborating his sociology of associations, Latour seeks to draw as far-reaching and consistent sociological implications as possible from his negative lesson of science studies (Latour 2000b). Latour now points to a general and problematic characteristic of social explanations: As a rule, they aim to *replace* the object of explanation – science, art, fashion, law, economy, etc. – with some social force considered (by the sociologist) to be more basic than the object itself. Such social mechanisms may be norms, power and interests – or they can be "big" phenomena, such as capitalism, industrialization and globalization. Along such lines, sociologists will talk about "putting the economy into a social context," and thereby point to the importance of norms and power relations, for instance, in determining the way a market functions. According to Latour, these sociologists feel that they possess a better grasp of the actual forces that drive the economy than the economists or the economic actors themselves ever could. In fact, sociological explanations tend to deny and reject the understandings of actors themselves – and this is particularly true if the sociologist sees himself as a "critical sociologist." Latour mentions Bourdieu as a prime example of such a "critical" approach, which in effect replaces both the object of study and its traditional spokespersons (in this case, economists) with something considered to be more real, and more fundamental – i.e., "society" or "the social" (see Latour 2005b: 99ff).

In general, Latour is critical of all manner of ideas that lean toward social reductionism – for instance, the notion that just a few social forces, such as power and interests, should be enough to explain all kinds of heterogeneous social phenomena. As we have just described it, Latour is not entirely dismissive of the notion that prevailing forms of social explanation may have some limited validity in those cases where everyone already agrees on the existence and contours of a stable "society." Still, Latour detects numerous further problems in the free use of social explanations. One set of issues is the way social explanations tend to turn sociology into a kind of "super science," capable of explaining all of the social elements that it claims are lacking from other scientific disciplines – whether natural science, economics or law. The sociologist here commands a meta-language considered superior (at least by himself), thereby rendering him a "sociologist-king" (Latour 1996a: 167). Worse still, this meta-language and its social mechanisms tend to develop into standardized explanations, easily applicable to numerous situations but very difficult to test or evaluate. If, for instance, the sociologist invokes "individualization" to explain an increase in divorce rates, he is in a certain sense always correct – at the least, such a statement would prove near-impossible to refute.[6]

On the other hand, it proves remarkably difficult to figure out what exact effects something like "individualization" may have on any specific situation of divorce – not to mention whether the phenomenon (of individualization) actually exists. Latour regards this as a widespread flaw in the conventional sociology of the social. As he states in an unfriendly tone: The sociology of the social makes use of invisible substances – just like the ether of pre-relativist physics! (2005b: 191f)

According to Latour, such an invocation of social explanations generally used to work quite well, but only as long as sociologists studied "down" – that is, as long as they only studied groups with less power and prestige than themselves. Hence, no one was particularly concerned by the resistance of religious groups to being socially explained (away). However, this situation changes dramatically once sociologists begin to study the natural sciences up close – and this explains why Latour considers his small sub-field of science studies to be quite groundbreaking. As he puts this point, "It stirs a small scandal to deploy the British Empire in the physics of Lord Kelvin" (2000b: 111). Highly esteemed natural scientists are the first to have ever rebelled against being sociologically explained – in this way, objects and their spokespersons strike back. This is precisely the backdrop to the "science wars" of the 1990s. These wars primarily occurred in the United States as a battle between "social constructivist" humanists and "realists" of the natural sciences. As we showed in Chapter 4, Latour responded to this situation – via his philosophy of science in *Pandora's Hope* (1999b) – by basically considering it a misplaced war of the trenches.

110 Sociology of associations

In his more *sociological* response, Latour in some ways takes the critics from natural science more seriously: Natural scientists are right to resist being explained in social terms. Of course, this is not because science somehow constitutes a uniquely objective and "non-social" sphere (as classic realists might claim). The reason is that the "scandal" of social-constructivist science studies has revealed a general characteristic of the typical social explanations in sociology: Specifically, that they lose sight of *the object* of explanation – whether it is a scientific fact, a god or a work of art.

To sum up, Latour's main polemical point is that the sociology of the social has become too easy: It generates a great number of explanations based on underlying social mechanisms, but it does not engage in the necessary work of clarifying the existence, the content or the range of its mysterious social forces. Against this backdrop, the primary task of the sociology of associations is to establish an alternative to so-called "strong" social explanations. In this respect, Latour is greatly inspired by Garfinkel the ethnomethodologist – although, in the process, Garfinkel too is subjected to Latour's idiosyncratic version of semiotics.[7] The sociology of association slogan of "following the actors" thus acquires a twin meaning. On one hand, the task of the sociologist is to follow how the actors *themselves* create and order their social worlds, often in ways marked by mutual conflict. Here, it is the sociologist who learns about the social world from the "ethno-methods" of the actors – not the other way around. In fact, Latour even states that "our informants [. . .] do our sociology for us, and do it better than we could ever do it ourselves" (1996a: 10).

On the other hand, the Latourian sociology of associations is not a new version of symbolic interactionism – and this is where his semiotics enters the picture. The second meaning of "following the actors," then, is that sociology must trace the many connecting threads that create, and set the scene for, any particular interaction and any particular actor. An interaction or an actor is always shaped in concrete relation to other times, other places and other actants. Hence, for example, any interaction between teacher and pupils in a classroom will be shaped by the drawings made by architects 40 years earlier, by the annual coordination of timetables by the school administration, by the ancient forest and the wood that was felled to make the desks, by the grammatical rules of the language employed, and so on and so forth (Latour 2005b: 199ff). Once the sociologist begins to follow such connections, Latour notes, he will inevitably end up sketching a wide-reaching actor-network.

Put differently, the basic thrust of the Latourian sociology of associations is that the question of *what* makes up the social world is a fundamentally open – and metaphysical – question that neither can nor should be answered once and for all. For this reason, his sociology basically consists of various sources of uncertainty: which groups are formed; which agents act; how objects can be transformed; and what a text might accomplish. These are all open questions in the sociology of associations (ibid.: Part I). As such, Latour's theory is neither "strong" nor substantial. Rather, it is "weak" – it is not a meta-language but an "infra-language," as he calls it. The point is that only in this way will sociology become sufficiently abstract to be able to observe how the actors themselves pose – and respond to – such open, metaphysical questions in ongoing processes. In this sense, the sociology of associations is just as much method as it is theory; and to a large extent, Latour adopts an "empiricist" language. Good sociology, he tells us, can only be conducted by following the actors in concrete studies of social reality. On this note, we take a closer look at one of Latour's own empirical case studies, in order to see what the sociology of associations looks like in practice. The following section thus turns attention to Latour's book *Aramis* dealing with a (virtual) transportation system (1996a).

Latour-the-sociologist as techno-detective

Aramis is the name of a revolutionary system of urban transport: a fully automated system of individually controlled carriages that run on train tracks; a high-tech prestige object that was under development in and around Paris from about 1970 until 1988. Aramis is also synonymous with an innovation project that failed spectacularly: The new system was never realized, and present-day Parisians still make do with the familiar Metro. Latour writes his account of this unsuccessful technological project as a kind of detective novel. The recurring question throughout the book is articulated in terms of a mystery murder: *Who killed Aramis?* (1996a).

The two detectives who must solve the mystery are Norbert – an aging sociologist who bears a striking resemblance to Latour – and his assistant, a young engineering student. The parallel thus drawn between sociology and the detective genre is not just a stylistic effect for Latour; it also demonstrates a general point of his sociology of associations. In this context, the act of searching for sociological explanations in some series of events may well be compared to the work of a private detective: You follow leads, try out different hypotheses, interview ("interrogate") various actors ("suspects"), etc. All of this is hard work, and the main point is that there are indeed no easy explanations to be found – neither for a private detective nor for the sociologist of associations (see Austrin & Farnsworth 2005).

The study of the Aramis project is a paradigmatic example of Latourian sociology: no meta-theorizing is found here; no grandiose social explanations; and no "pure" human relations that are not already closely interwoven with esoteric, technological details. Instead, the book contains a series of reflections on practical ethnographic work, and how best to trace the concrete – but also changeable – relations among engineers, industrial companies, local politicians, world exhibitions, motors, infrared signals and other significant actants. As is characteristic of the sociology of associations, Latour thus adopts a contextualized approach: *Aramis* is a case-study account of one particular innovation project, located in time and space with great precision. Throughout the book, Latour (in the guise of Norbert) continually rejects the attempts of his assistant to explain the fate of the project by invoking general social structures and dynamics, such as "technological necessities," "global political constellations," "the workings of market forces" and the like. Not that technology, politics and economics are irrelevant factors – quite the contrary. The point is that such factors should be studied in their tangible specifics. As Latour writes, with reference to "market forces": "Who decides about the economic profitability of Aramis? Eight people, all identifiable and to be interviewed" (1996a: 134). To Latour, the market is not a context, but an actor-network; as such, its connections and channels of influence should be mapped out in detail, not taken for granted.

The main task of the sociologist of associations is to follow, to the best of his or her abilities, the many trajectories and detours taken by the actors. Sociology is primarily a matter of conducting many interviews, Latour suggests in an only partly joking tone (1996a: 52) – and he cannot resist the temptation of mentioning the mound of taxi receipts left behind by the sociologist as he drags himself around in the spatially far-flung networks under description. Another important source of information to the sociologist is the piles of documentation written on the progress of the project, as produced by research institutions, companies and political authorities. Such piles of documents reveal that actors themselves are in a constant process of reflecting upon, coordinating – and thereby reformulating – the very basics of the project: its temporal structure (when will it be finished?); its spatial positioning (where should the tracks be laid out?); its relative size (the whole of Paris or a single suburb?); and the degree to which it even exists (is it technologically feasible?). Only by tracing and reconstructing these myriad translations and subtle alterations will the sociologist catch up to the actors. For this to happen, the sociologist must be capable of moving around in a world of "variable ontology" – time, space, size and existence are not absolutes, but matters of degree; variables that actors are constantly producing and re-shaping (ibid.: 78ff).

As with any good crime novel, the murder mystery is solved in the end. According to Latour, the tragic fate of Aramis should be blamed on the many engineers involved in constructing the transport system. If only they had been willing to open up their technological project to the necessary negotiations, discussions and uncertainties, Aramis would have stood a much better chance. If they had simply *loved* the technology a little more, they would have realized just how vulnerable it was, and how dependent it was on a broad range of external relations to the worlds of political and economic actors. To put this differently: In the end, the deadly blow was delivered to Aramis by the false beliefs of the engineers in the strict modernist divide between technology and society.

If we now consider the story of Aramis from the point of view of methodological and analytical strategy, then the main point is that Latour strives to produce a tailor-made and "disposable" explanation: "One single explanation to a singular, unique case; and then we throw it away" (Latour 1996a:

131). Sociological theory does not provide answers to any specific research question; such answers have to be discovered through the hard work of inquiry. This insistence on the "unique adequacy"[8] of explanations may well be considered an ideal of the sociology of associations; an ideal that calls for an empirical, contextual and problem-centered approach. As such, and as Latour states, "our sociology" prefers local histories to grand theoretical narratives. At the same time, however, we should note the implicit social ontology of such an openness and uncertainty regarding social explanations. The social universe of Latour is always marked by radical contingency and indeterminacy: Aramis *could* have been realized, and only retrospectively – after having done the appropriate sociological detective work – can we understand why, in fact, things played out the way they did.

Social order: From inter-subjectivity to inter-objectivity

Up to this point, we have seen how, with his sociology of associations, Latour attempts to radically distance himself from what he sees as a dominant sociological paradigm: the sociology of the social. Whereas this latter paradigm regards society, or the social domain, as the source of explanations for all kinds of social phenomena – from esoteric science to interactions in a classroom – the motto of the sociology of associations is (as noted) that "society explain nothing" but must itself be explained. This methodological approach points in the direction of an empirical and practice-oriented sociology, and thereby also in the direction of Latour's own historical and sociological studies, such as *Aramis* and *The Pasteurization of France* (see Chapter 2).

At the same time, we have also seen that Latour's break with the sociological tradition is not entirely definitive, since his sociology of associations is inspired by Garfinkel and his ethnomethodology. In particular, this inspiration manifests itself in the overall methodological injunction to analyze those practical activities, or ethno-methods, by which actors create, negotiate and maintain the connections that comprise actor-networks. In other words, despite the fact that Latour's rhetoric is often extremely critical of sociology, he does in fact adopt what may well be considered the most basic question of sociology: specifically, the question of what holds a social situation together – or, in Latourian language, what holds an actor-network together? In classic sociological terminology, this is known as the problem of social order: Why are there relatively durable and repeated patterns in social relations – rather than chaos, anarchy or the "war of all against all" that Thomas Hobbes wrote about in *Leviathan*? The sociology of associations is sociological to the extent that it (re)appropriates this question. As is often the case with Latour, however, the response is rather unconventional, especially since material objects are once again given a crucial – and sociologically unfamiliar – role.

We have already encountered the question of social order a number of times in this book: One basic question in the Latourian anthropology of science and technology has always been how certain socio-technical orders gain ground, stabilize and become distributed (see Chapter 2). In his early science studies, Latour develops such concepts as inscription devices, immutable mobiles and centers of calculation to explain these kinds of stabilizations, and thereby also the production of hierarchical power relations. Some socio-technical orders gain ground at the expense of others – and certain socio-technical innovations (such as Aramis) remain virtual and unrealized. As noted (in Chapter 2), the model of the actor in this early part of Latour's work is often appropriated from the world of politics or war: Techno-science is depicted as a matter of power, strategies, trials of strength and compromises. In parts of his anthropology of science, Latour thus has a tendency to "solve" the problem of social order by referencing asymmetrical power relations: Some socio-technical orders ("black boxes") gradually become sufficiently strong to ensure that no other actor can mobilize enough allies to challenge their supremacy.[9]

Indeed, this is a decidedly classic solution to the problem of order in the sociological tradition. However, if one seeks to explain why some orders are actually accepted by actors – that is, why they are considered legitimate – then the problems that arise from such assumptions are equally well-known in social-science history. Hobbes deals with the question of legitimacy via his famous *contract model* – but right from the beginning of his authorship, Latour explicitly rejects this theory and aims to replace it with notions of representation as translation (see Callon & Latour 1981). This also explains why the concept of representation plays such a crucial role in Latour's more political–theoretical thinking – and in his philosophy of modernity (see Chapters 3 and 4).

Despite such Latourian tendencies toward the emphasis on power and domination as solutions to the problem of order, which are manifested in certain parts of his work, it would be misleading to present this as an axiom of the sociology of associations. To the contrary, one characteristic of Latourian sociology – in contrast to so-called interactionist sociology – is that it includes very few ideas about the general and abstract features of social actors. Once again, inspiration from semiotics is evident here: The actors in the Latourian universe are, in fact, actants. That is, they are participants in a series of events – with their shapes, characteristics and roles entirely dependent on context. An actant is any entity that makes a difference in a series of events; and Latour states explicitly that "the competencies of the actor will be inferred *after* a process of attribution" (1996c: 237) – that is, *after* the series of events. Via semiotics, Latour is thus able to reject the choice among different actor models, including the deep dualisms of norms and values versus interests and strategies that run through all sociologies of action. The analyst should make no such choice once and for all – instead, he should follow the actors and *their* choices.[10] By adopting this position, Latour also commits himself to saying that there can be no general answer to the question of social order – that is, to the question of how actors construct actor-networks in practice. Or, more precisely: The answer cannot be located in any particular kind of inter-subjective relationship among people – whether based on shared norms and values, common symbols and language, or some contractual agreement.

This also helps to clarify why the sociology of associations is not some new version of the theoretical school in sociology known as symbolic interactionism – or, more broadly, "interpretative" sociology. Within this tradition – and based on philosophical hermeneutics – social order is ultimately explained with reference to shared constructions of meaning, shared symbols and a shared language.[11] Of course, Latour would not deny the importance of interaction, symbols or language – but he refuses to base his sociology on the notion of such phenomena enjoying ontological precedence. This refusal is expressed in a highly provocative – but also very entertaining – manner when Latour compares the problem of social order in human society to the same problem among chimpanzees and baboons. In this context, Latour argues that symbolic interactionism would be perfectly suited if one wanted to describe primate societies, but is very badly equipped for human society! (See Latour 1996c.) The reason for this somewhat surprising claim is that primates have only themselves, their bodies, their mutual favors, their trials of strength – in short, their complex social interactions – to keep the collective of "baboon" together. The situation is entirely different for the human collective, which includes a whole range of non-human actors – tools, walls, tables, money – that play decisive roles in framing interactions. Anyone who doubts the veracity of this observation should simply try to imagine how he would solve the problem of excluding someone from some local interaction if he was temporarily unable to mobilize the actant known as "a door" (see Johnson [Latour] 1988).

Against this backdrop, Latour argues that human interaction is basically not a matter of inter-subjectivity, but rather of "inter-objectivity" – another term added to his long list of neologisms, expressing the fundamental interweaving of humans and things (Latour 2005b: 193). Further, when Latour talks about the "framing" of social interaction – using a term borrowed from symbolic interactionist Erving Goffman – such framing should not be understood as purely symbolic, but rather as something material; as buildings, room divisions, fences, computer networks, etc. Social interaction among humans cannot take place without some such prior framing, a point that was already illustrated via the example of classroom interaction between teacher and students.

In relation to the problem of social order, moreover, it is worth noting that non-human actants tend to act in more long-lasting, durable and reliable ways than humans. To illustrate this claim, one need only to think of an everyday phenomenon like speed bumps on roads, called (for good reason) "sleeping policemen" due to their ability to affect the action of drivers (1999b: 186). Latour seeks to generalize this observation: "Any time an interaction has temporal and spatial extension, it is because one has shared it with non-humans" (1996c: 239). Once again, material objects thus come to play a

116 *Sociology of associations*

central role in Latour's thinking – this time, as the closest we get to solving the classic problem of social order, of keeping social relations together, in the sociology of associations. However, what is ordered or held together is obviously not a society in the traditional sense of the term; rather, we are held together in a collective that consists of humans as well as non-humans.

Latour has summarized this discussion of inter-objectivity in three rules of thumb for the practice of sociology (1996c: 240). The first rule of thumb is, as noted, to treat things as social facts. The second concerns the agency/structure debate, or the relationship between interaction and society; in this respect, the Latourian advice is to forget such dualisms altogether and instead focus on the exchange of characteristics among human and non-human actants. As pointed out, this amounts to a reformulation of the theoretical aims of sociology: The main problem will no longer be individual–society relations, but rather the whole dualism between society and nature (Schinkel 2007: 713). Third and finally, Latour suggests that sociology should end its eternal theoretical obsession with the so-called micro/macro issue, and instead empirically follow the processes by which "local interactions" as well as "global overviews", respectively, are created.

This third effect that stems from the sociology of associations (regarding the micro/macro issue) is discussed in more detail in an upcoming section. Before we get to that, we want to take a look at some empirical cases that demonstrate how Latour combines the concept of inter-objectivity with the necessity of specific ethnographic studies – this time, taken from outside the sphere of techno-science. This illustrates Latour's growing interest in different *types* of social relations; i.e., the "generalization" of his interest in knowledge regimes, which also marks the transition in "phase" (or face), from his anthropology of science to his sociology of associations.

Regimes enunciation: The objectivity of law and religious icons

In a great deal of the sociology of the social, modern societies are said to be "functionally differentiated"; that is, society is depicted as divided into relatively autonomous spheres, such as science, politics, economy, religion, law and mass media. This is, for example, a fundamental assumption in the neo-classical social theories of both Niklas Luhmann and Pierre Bourdieu. Latour, on the contrary, has always taken an ambiguous stand vis-à-vis this theory of differentiation, given that his anthropology of science has revealed the numerous gray zones and lines of connection between two major spheres of society: science and politics (see Chapter 2). However, Latour also emphasizes that his aim is *not* to abolish all boundaries between science and politics, but rather to re-describe and re-arrange our common world in such a way that the strengths of both practices will be respected (see Latour 1999b: 258ff). In general terms, Latour's sociology of associations seems to develop a certain similarity to differentiation theory: Law, science, religion, economy, morality, politics and organization are each depicted as having their own modes of existence, based on specific types of social circulation and chains of reference (Latour 2005b: 238f).

In this sense, to Latour, the non-modern world consists in a plurality of modes of existence or, as he also calls them, "regimes of enunciation" (Latour 2005d: 28).[12] Every regime of enunciation has its own specific mechanism for the production of truth, and in interviews from the early 2000s, Latour often says that his main intellectual project is to visit and document the various "truth-production sites" of our civilization (Crease *et al.* 2003: 16). Science still enjoys special status as a point of reference in Latour's thinking – precisely, he would likely claim, as is the case with science in Western society more generally. But given that science studies has radically transformed the image of science, it becomes necessary to also search for up-to-date re-descriptions of the remaining regimes of truth. And this is indeed a new project that Latour is already deeply immersed in.

In 2002, Latour first published his version of a full re-description of legal objectivity, grounded in the sociology of associations. *La fabrique du droit* ("the factory of law"), as the book is called in French (Latour 2002b; English translation Latour 2010b), is based on Latour's own long-term ethnographic studies into the *Conseil d'État* ("Council of State"), the supreme court of administrative law in France. True to his usual style, Latour follows state councilors through the striking architecture of the court corridors. He keeps a keen eye on the minute details of each of the procedures whereby legal reasoning, negotiation and decision-making is made possible. Latour analyzes everything from career and recruitment patterns to the iconic significance of the artwork decorating the walls. His main interest, however, focuses on the elaborate mechanisms of verification and objectification required for the production of justice. In this context, the overall point is that the production of law rests on particular forms of inter-objective ordering processes – in keeping with the "homeostatic" or conservative role of the court, and its emphasis on continuity, precedence and legal predictability (Latour 2010b: Chapter 6). This continuity is secured not least of all by a tight closure around a homogeneous textual and material universe, made up of endless numbers of files, notes, laws and declarations, the internal relations of which make up the core of law itself. As such, when numerous case files mount up on the desks of judges, this is only a surface sign of disorder: Each and every file is equipped with precise rules for how it should be handled, ordered and coded. As soon as a verdict is passed, the case may be closed and order reinstated – these cases, Latour notes, can be opened and closed at will, like any other record-keeping system (ibid.: chapter 2).

Latour undertakes an explicit comparison between the legal production of verdicts and the scientific production of facts. He does this in order to highlight the many contrasts that make up their entirely different chains of association. Whereas science employs endless chains of circulating references – the credibility of which is constantly being put to the test (see Chapter 2) – law, on the other hand, is a matter of producing "chains of obligation" that facilitate legal qualification, deliberation and decision-making. In the production of law, empirical facts never take center stage, Latour observes. Instead, the key issue concerns the solidity of those connections that can be forged to existing legal rules; that is, to existing obligations (Latour 2010b: Chapter 5). As such, the entire judicial process involves a gradual distancing from the particular aspects of some case. Indeed, the process of legal reasoning consists in myriad mechanisms for creating distance: from the disengaged language used by the judges to the sheer number of formal procedural rules. Paradoxically, then, objectivity is to be found in the courts of law and not in the laboratories of science – provided that we think of objectivity as disinterestedness (ibid.). But, as Latour remarks, what the law entails is an *object-less* objectivity: In the end, judges must produce a justice whose only anchor and point of reference is to be found in other parts of the edifice of law. Unlike the sciences, the law has no option of appeal to an indifferent and stubborn non-human world. Latour sums up his analysis of the (inter-)objectivity of law with a succinct aphorism: "Scientists speak inarticulately about precise objects, lawyers speak in precise terms about vague objects" (Latour 2010b: 237).

These rules of the game will once again be entirely different once we cast our gaze on a third regime of truth-enunciation, to which Latour has given increased attention since the late 1990s: the religious. Such a religious – or, more precisely, (Catholic) Christian – regime of enunciation has never been entirely absent in his thinking.[13] In autobiographical remarks and in texts on religious topics, Latour makes no attempt to conceal the fact that he considers himself a practicing Catholic – if perhaps not a very pious one, as he puts it (Latour 2005d: 27). Alongside his formal studies in theology, this Catholic faith has inspired Latour to deal with religious chains of association in a manner far more respectful and humble than the usual approach found in the sociology of religion.

Throughout the entire epoch of modernity, Latour argues, the critical impulse of sociology and society alike has attempted to marginalize religion, to unmask its fake fetishes, and to smash and destroy its icons. This very theme was the subject of the *Iconoclash* art exhibition in 2002, arranged and co-curated by Latour.[14] The Latourian post-critical and non-modern philosophy of religion, on the contrary, depicts religion as one of the most important ways in which we may be shaped as persons, and thus as a significant mode of existence. According to Latour, religion (or rather, Christianity) is a matter of producing a specific kind of personal *presence*; presence in a uniquely full and intense moment. Latour compares this to the "love speech" of everyday life: The statement "I love you" means nothing beyond the sheer conviction with which it is presented and (hopefully) received. Much like love-talk, religious statements deal in performative transformations – that is, literally, in "conversions": Before, you were absent; now, you are present (Latour 2005d: 30). There is nothing hidden, cryptic or esoteric about religious speech. Religious actants – from angels to gods – simply perform a kind of existential work that requires humans to apply subtlety and care if we are to practice and register the truth-effects of religion.[15]

As was the case with law, Latour also draws a direct comparison between religious regimes of enunciation and the scientific production of facts – and this time, the contrasts are even more striking. In fact, the thrust of Latour's argument in this context is that the entire modernist debate about some alleged conflict between religion and science is one big misunderstanding. There is simply no point of contact at all, Latour argues, between science and religion: Like the nightingale and the frog, they never meet in any ecological competition (Latour 2005d: 33). The modernist misconceptions on this point run deep: Science is imagined as dealing with the concrete and visible world; but in fact, scientists spend their time constructing technological mechanisms that bring them into contact with still more invisible and unknown worlds (see Chapter 2). By contrast, religion is generally said to deal with something distant, transcendent and invisible – but in fact, none of these adjectives captures the person-transforming presence that is precisely the hallmark of religion. If anything, Latour stresses, religion always remain local, mundane and visible.

Latour illustrates this by pointing to the famous depiction of an angel standing in front of the empty tomb of Jesus on Easter morning. The message here is: "Do not search among the dead, but among the living" – and it is precisely this message that turns the observer back toward a local and meaningful present. In this vein, Latour sums up his religious reflections, as based on his sociology of associations, by reformulating the Christian prohibition against images and idols: The problem never lies with idols as such; problems arise if one "freezes the frame" – that is, if one breaks the flow of religious connections and clings instead to one particular image (Latour 2002e: 37). Such a freeze-framing may lead to highly problematic forms of fanaticism or fundamentalism – much as may also happen, Latour stresses, with the tendencies of the modernists toward an iconoclastic critique of religion. The unbroken movement through chains of religious enunciation, on the other hand, remains one of the essential ways in which truth may be created in a pluralistic, non-modern collective.

In this section, we have made an acquaintance with the specific version of "differentiation theory" that is emerging from the Latourian sociology of associations: The non-modern world consists of a plurality of regimes of enunciation, as exemplified here by science, law and religion. In this respect, and perhaps paradoxically, Latour the monist seems more attuned to radical differences than most of his sociological colleagues. The Latourian regimes of enunciation are not just different from each other; in a certain sense, they never overlap ontologically – as we saw in the case of religion and science. As such, regimes of enunciation verge on the incommensurable. Exactly for this reason, one of the general points that emerges from the sociology of associations is that, in order to describe these various enunciation regimes, we need a sensitive vocabulary that will respect the unique aspects of the phenomenon under study – its unique methods of stabilization, its own mechanisms and style of objectivity. According to Latour, any attempt to describe the regimes using a general sociological meta-language – such as fields, systems, norms or power – is doomed to fail. Again, what exactly makes up the social world remains an open and metaphysical question – and one that can only be answered sociologically by studying its many irreducible modes of existence.

Localization and globalization: The different scales of social life

Our journey within (and around) the sociology of associations is nearing its end – but one crucial point, so far left untreated, still lies ahead of us. That point is: The social world is not simply differentiated "horizontally" into a plurality of regimes of enunciation and existence. It is also, and importantly, differentiated "vertically" into small and large actors, and into local and global actor-networks. Or rather: According to Latour, much of the dynamics of the social world turns around this exact issue of how differences in the levels and scales of social life may arise, and how such differences become durable or get transformed. This, then, is yet another case of Latour adopting a classic problem from the sociology of the social – this time, the so-called micro/macro issue. The sociology of the social generally brims with large and dominant macro-phenomena: capitalism, bureaucracy, nation states, the military–industrial complex, world systems, etc. Needless to say, Latour approaches these rather intangible and invisible social phenomena with a certain degree of skepticism – this already follows from the contextual approach of his sociology of associations. Yet Latour still wants to acknowledge that large and dominant actants *exist*; actants that work to macro-structure social life. His point in this respect is simply that differences between micro and macro – that is, between small and large actants – are not in any way natural or permanent, but are rather created, negotiated and transformed through ongoing social processes. Or, as Latour pointedly puts it: "Scale is the actor's own achievement" (2005b: 185). The empirical task of sociology, then, is to study those processes – of localization and globalization – by which both local micro-interactions and global macro-effects, respectively, are created in social life.

The importance of the micro/macro issue is nothing new to Latour: In fact, the arguments that we just highlighted belong to the earliest products of his anthropology of science and technology, as summarized in a 1981 article (co-authored with Michel Callon) titled "Unscrewing the Big Leviathan." This article was published in an anthology on the very topic of integrating micro- and macro-sociologies. As such, this article illustrates an early commitment on Latour's part to take up an explicit debate about sociological theory, and it underlines the specific importance that ANT accords to the problem of micro/macro thinking.[16]

As so often before, Latour is here inspired by the famous theory of Thomas Hobbes about the constitution of the social body: Hobbes' sovereign, the Leviathan, is a macro-actor who solves the social paradox of part and whole. The sovereign does not stand *above* his people; he embodies and expresses the will *of* the people – he *is* the people, simply in a different state of being.

Latour (and Callon) wants to draw far-reaching sociological implications from this peculiar arrangement envisaged by Hobbes: Social differences in level, size and scale are not inherent to actors, it seems, but are instead the result of battles or negotiations (Callon & Latour 1981: 278 ff). The basic sociological issue, then, is how a micro-actor becomes a macro-actor – or how actors grow, so to speak. To Hobbes, an agreement on some social contract is key to explaining the construction of a macro-actor, but Latour and Callon replace this notion of a contract with the much broader concept of translation. Put briefly, translation concerns the construction of authoritative spokespersons who speak on behalf of a long chain of other actors (as described in Chapter 2). Differences of scale in social life – between the micro and the macro – are thus closely intertwined with power and authority given that, by definition, spokespersons of actor-networks occupy powerful positions. This is exactly the point that is embedded in the concept of "black boxes." Within such boxes, long chains of science and technology become packaged in such compact ways that they make the small handful of spokespersons, who occupy central and strategic positions in the network, extremely powerful. On this note, Callon and Latour sum up their text by defining macro-actors as "micro-actors seated on top of many (leaky) black boxes" (1981: 286). Here, the fact that such black boxes are "leaky" suggests that the process of scale-construction should never be regarded as complete – even the most powerful macro-actor is no stronger than its weakest link.

Oligopticon

As Latour has pointed out elsewhere (1996c: 242, note 25), his anthropology of science primarily depicts all macro-structural effects as the performative results of elaborate and distributed practices of inscription and instrumentation. These are the effects that are summed up in the concept of "centers of calculation" (see Chapter 2). The center of calculation is a macro-actor that – by virtue of its many connecting lines to other data-producing sites – is capable of collecting and disseminating global overviews in the form of simple inscriptions, such as graphs and tables. By doing so, the center of calculation coordinates a wide range of scientific practices, spread out in time and space.

With the inherent "generalization" of such an interest in knowledge regimes implied by the sociology of associations, Latour now needs to explain similar mechanisms of coordination in social regimes other than science. To this end, he introduces the concept of "oligopticon." This notion is, of course, modeled on the somewhat more familiar "panopticon," but Latour arrives at it by substituting the Greek word for "a few" (*oligo*; known, for instance, from the economics of "oligopoly," referring to a state of limited market competition). Unlike the panopticon – Jeremy Bentham's 18th-century vision of an ideal prison involving the complete surveillance of inmates – the Latourian oligoptica are in no position to produce such "total overviews."[17] Via this neologism, Latour wants to signal an ontology that is already implied in his early text on the micro/macro issue: namely, that there simply *is* no such thing as a single, overarching macro-actor (or Leviathan) in social life. Instead, what we have are plural and competing macro-actors; or in other words, rival oligoptica.

An oligopticon, then, is any kind of network configuration that creates a limited, but solid, representation of the social: military command centers, newspaper editorial rooms, corporate boardrooms, offices of statistics, courtrooms, United Nations agencies, etc. Such places indeed all macro-structure parts of the social world. But they do so in concrete and localized ways, where any social effect to be produced will depend on the ongoing circulations of information between the oligopticon and its many points of connection. Oligoptica are star-like shapes – they manifest an extensive actor-network. Hence, the production of macro-structural effects is always localized concretely in the social landscape. For this reason, Latour argues, there is no need to invoke those intangible social structures – from the invisible hands of capital to those of patriarchy or empire – that critical sociology always finds lurking in the background of social life.

Panorama

Oligoptica, however, are not the only mechanisms for macro-globalizing social life – if for no other reason than simply because, as noted, they fail to satisfy our fantasies of global and total overviews. With those social devices that Latour now dubs "panoramas," the opposite is the case: here (as any film enthusiast knows), a viewer finds himself completely absorbed by a 360-degree exhibition and projection room. This panorama enacts a frame, a totality, around its audience. Every time some newspaper editorial, research report or expert opinion addresses "the world economic condition," "the history of democracy," "the effects of globalization" and such similar topics, we find ourselves confronted with a Latourian panorama: literally, an *image* of some imagined whole, in which local interactions may be interpreted and classified. Unlike oligoptica, panoramas see the whole – only with the small addition that, because the image production of the panorama is sealed off from the outside world, any possible relation of the image to other localities and actants will be inescapably uncertain. Panoramas see everything – and nothing – at the same time (Latour 2005b: 183ff). This does not necessarily make them useless. Quite the contrary: As social maps used by actors to navigate the world, panoramas help them coordinate their actions and imagine alternative futures.

According to Latour, it is only when viewed this way that some sociological macro-narrative – such as Ulrich Beck's theory of the "risk society" – may be valuable: Beck's panorama is socially performative and politically relevant, to the extent that it serves to prepare its audience (the social actors) for the future political task of composing a new collective. Interestingly, this may well work quite independently from the fact that it remains fundamentally uncertain and unclear whether such a thing as "risk society" or "reflexive modernization" has even happened at all (see Latour 2003b). Here, it is worth noting that Latour himself is also a producer of panoramas: The stories of non-modernity (see Chapter 3) and parliaments of nature (see Chapter 4) are socially performative in the sense that, ideally, they pave the way for their own realizations. According to Latour, the only thing that one should *not* do with a panorama, then, is to confuse it with the social territory as such. For such tasks, it will be more appropriate to deploy oligoptica, exactly because their macro-structuring lines of connection remain visible and detectable.

With oligoptica and panoramas, Latour suggests, we have now acquired the tools needed when, as sociologists of associations, we want to follow the production of macro-phenomena in the social world – including, of course, the very notions of "globalization" and "world society." Still, it is important to note that the Latourian dictum – "scale is the actor's own achievement" – remains symmetrical in its effects: Although macro-structuring is indeed socially produced, what does *not* follow is the idea that local interaction, everyday life and subjectivity should then provide a more concrete or basic starting point for sociological analysis (Latour 2005b: 193ff). Rather, the whole point that Latour strives to make is that localization – to exactly the same extent as globalization – is a socially produced end-product of a long and prior framing process.

To again use the example of the classroom: Here, a wide range of elements – walls, schedules, tables, language structures, authority relations, etc. – must already be in place for any interaction between teacher and pupils to ever occur. Moreover, Latour argues, the same point applies to all the qualities that we would normally think of as integral parts of individual subjects, such as identity, rationality and morality.

In short, Latour's somewhat polemical and anti-individualistic point in this respect is that subjectivity is something we gain; something we partake in through social relations, not something with which we are naturally equipped (Latour 2005b: 213ff). In this context, he speaks of "plug-ins" as some kind of propositions for subjectivity that circulate within the social. One straightforward example of this is the notion of an individual calculative rationality that underlies the workings of markets, according to economic theory. Such calculative rationality, Latour maintains, is not something one simply possesses or not, but rather something one may or may not achieve by gaining access to a range of extra-subjective resources, such as prices, product standards, spreadsheets and accounting norms. These resources, and their proper combination, are what enable the framing (and localization) of action within a market.[18] However, it would make little sense to say that such calculative actions *are* either local or global, micro or macro. Relations of scale and size – from micro to macro – should be seen as the emerging and transformable *results* of social life, not the given and fixed points of reference for sociological analysis.

In sum, Latour argues that social life may be empirically analyzed as the uninterrupted chains of practice that, as ongoing effects, produce both local interactions and global macro-phenomena. This observation corresponds to the kernel of accurate intuition that inspired the sociology of the social to articulate the micro/macro issue in the first place. What the sociologists did not realize, however, is that the ongoing enactment and re-construction of this very micro/macro issue is exactly what sociality is all about. On this note, what the sociology of associations contributes is to equip the actors *themselves* with the means to solve micro/macro questions – which will then no longer have to occupy the sociologists as a basic theoretical problem. Latour even goes so far as to argue that this micro/macro insight is in fact the most crucial contribution of ANT to social theory.

Apart from the analytical point, this is also a *normative* point for Latour. If relations of scale and size are what is constantly being negotiated in social life, then any sociological freezing of such relations – into predefined coordinates of large and small actors – would invariably operate to the benefit of strong macro-actors. They would be "immunized," so to speak, against the deconstruction of scales (see Callon & Latour 1981). One example of this might be the macro-determining roles that so-called critical sociology often grants to multinational corporations and imperialist nation states (notably the U.S.). According to Latour, such *a priori* distribution of roles and power is not especially critical – sociology only becomes critical if it makes visible those long chains of practical and material work that allow these actants to dominate others. Hence, one cannot be critical at a distance: The "critical distance" cultivated in critical sociology, Latour claims, is in fact an entirely safe and uncritical formula. To become critical, one must move *near* the object of interest – only in close proximity can one gain glimpses of the meticulous work, the contingencies and the fragility (Latour 2003a).

In this context, Latour once again draws his inspiration from sociologists Luc Boltanski and Laurent Thévenot, who managed to show that critique and justification are entirely practical activities that actors use to negotiate the relative "greatness" and "smallness" of themselves and others (Boltanski and Thévenot (2006 [1991]). As Latour writes, with reference to Boltanski and Thévenot: If there is one thing the sociologist cannot do in the actor's stead, it is to decide where they stand on a scale going from small to big – because at one turn an actor may mobilize all of mankind, France, capitalism or reason; while in the next moment, the scale may change abruptly by the actor entering into some local compromise (2005b: 186). Just think of the climate changes discussed in Chapter 4: How are we to prioritize our concerns about scientific uncertainty, planetary survival, future generations, coral reefs, French industrial growth, car-driving habits, identity constructions via the market, etc? How would we decide – on behalf of the actors – which of these entities and concerns are big or small; which ones have "global significance," and which are merely for "local debate"? If anything, micro and macro, small and large, are *moral* issues. And on this point in particular, the sociologist of associations needs to follow the actor's own sudden shifts in scale, if he wants to trace the gradual construction of the collective. Only then may the sociologist hope to gain political relevance, as one among other actors in the ongoing re-organization of the social.

Conclusion: Latour in the treadmills of sociology

In this chapter, we have become familiar with the peculiar ambivalence that characterizes Latour's approach to the science of sociology, from which he gains much inspiration – and which he even practices in some respects. On one hand, Latour argues that something has gone terribly wrong with sociology ever since the time of Durkheim, because the discipline has imagined its own mission as one of providing social explanations for the many phenomena, fields and structures of society. Society and the social, Latour claims, explains nothing in and of themselves – rather, they are in need of *being* explained. Sociologists who acknowledge this point will also discover that "society," understood as a purely human community, does not even exist – and hence, must be replaced by the notion of a heterogeneous collective consisting of both humans and non-humans. This transformation entails some fundamental changes to sociological activity, both in terms of basic theoretical questions and methodological rules of the game. Indeed, this is exactly Latour's intention.

With the sociology of associations, the relationship between individual and society – agency and structure – no longer constitutes the theoretical core of sociology. This core instead consists of relations between society and nature, or more correctly, between human and non-human actants. The social is no longer a specific domain of reality, but instead a movement; a particular way in which previously unconnected elements come to be associated – that is, *become* social. Likewise, sociology is no longer a meta-discourse about society, a provider of "strong" explanations – but rather a "weak" and abstract infra-language. Its foremost duty is to trace, and permit, the actors' own enactment of the changing geography, ontology and metaphysics of the social. Finally, the sociologist is no longer a passive and elevated observer of social life, but instead a performative participant, whose methods are not necessarily stronger, more significant nor more adequate than the "ethno-methods" of the actors themselves (Latour 1996a: 299). The Latourian sociology of associations, then, is nothing less than a manifesto for a radical transformation of sociology. As such, it ultimately represents Latour's respectful attempt – despite his skepticism toward the dominant self-understandings of the discipline – to remain faithful to the vocation of sociology.

126 Sociology of associations

In light of his philosophy of modernity and his political theory of representation (see Chapter 3), it should be obvious why Latour perceives the need to fully redefine sociology in these ways. Only in the form of the sociology of associations will sociology, as one among other disciplines, be equipped to provide useful and constructive contributions to that "due process" by which collectives must, from now on, constantly re-create themselves (see Chapter 4). In Latour's depiction, the political relevance of the sociology of associations is precisely its ability to renew the repertoire of the ingredients of the social; that is, to suggest new candidates for social existence (Latour 2005b: 258ff). Sociology, Latour tells us, is the science of living together – but prior to thorough study, we have no way of knowing exactly who is included, or *should* be included, in this collective "we."

On all accounts, then, Latourian sociology is far removed from any popular notion of critical deconstruction – by contrast, he adopts a post-critical attitude, whereby sociology becomes a matter of reconstructing the good life together. And this concludes the Latourian ring, so to speak. We are now back at the analytical starting point – back at the anthropology of science and technology, and back at the explosive increase of new hybrids that shape Latour's diagnosis of our times. Due to the dynamism of the techno-sciences, we presently live in a social world that constantly mixes "chemical reactions and political reactions" (see Chapter 3), and a world in which scientific questions about genetically modified organisms (GMOs) must be handled together with protests from non-governmental organizations (NGOs). In this context, the modernist depiction of Nature and Society is increasingly shaky – and this is why we need the heterogeneous conception of the social found in the sociology of associations. Ultimately, then, the question is whether one accepts the non-modern project. As Latour concludes: "If you really think that the future common world can be better composed by using nature and society as the ultimate meta-language, then ANT is useless" (2005b: 262). In the end, the sociology of associations makes sense only as an act of participation in the cosmopolitics of the non-modern world – and thus as a specific type of involvement in heterogeneous, collective and diplomatic processes (see Chapter 4).

So far, so good. Given the radicalism of this project, it should come as no surprise that the Latourian sociology of associations has already been met with – and *can* indeed be met with – a series of more or less basic sociological objections. Any thorough discussion here would take us off course, but let us briefly outline four of the weightiest objections that have arisen thus far.

First, one may argue that the very definition of sociality adopted by Latour leads him to over-emphasize the role of change, instability and "fluidity" in social life – to the detriment of a more thorough theorization of the durable, stable and structural aspects of social life (see Elder–Vass 2008). One classic domain for this type of discussion is the question of capitalism: One might ask whether the sociology of associations is capable of handling, within its own conceptual universe, such an abstract, structured, ubiquitous and historically far-reaching mechanism?

Second, one might ask (as a number of sociologists of science have actually done) whether Latour – given his abolition of the distinction between the social and the natural – perhaps puts himself in a situation where the very opportunity for sociology to *explain* social phenomena will have to be abandoned? (See Collins & Yearley 1992.) Whatever one thinks of the explanatory capacities of such "social" factors, one ought to recognize that Latour tells us surprisingly little about the impact of social class, profit maximization, norms, prestige, gender, ethnicity and other such similarly "traditional" explanatory variables of sociology.

Third, one might point out that Latourian social ontology seems strangely bifurcated, in that he seems to alternate between two "extremes" in social life: one metaphysical–ontological, the other empirical–contextual (see Guggenheim & Nowotny 2003). For instance, in his account of the Aramis project, Latour alternates between abstract considerations about the variable ontology of techno-social networks on the one hand, and very specific descriptions of technical details and the concrete individuals involved in the development of the transport system on the other. Such a depiction of sociality may appear somewhat fragmented and unmediated, in that it downplays relatively stable social institutions, discourses and roles – like organizations, families and public media – all of which may precisely function as "connecting links" between the (ontological/empirical) extremes.

Fourth and finally, many self-declared critical sociologists have undoubtedly already reached the conclusion that the Latourian sociology of associations lacks both normative clout and critical social potential (see Saldanha 2003). In any case, it seems fair to say that the possibilities for criticizing the various injustices of society, by way of being based in the science of sociology, look rather different for Latour than they do for the majority of his sociological colleagues.

As noted, any detailed examination of these matters here would take us too far astray. Hence, our listing should mainly be considered as a way of pointing to a number of the key debates and controversies that the Latourian sociology of associations will inevitably encounter on its voyage through the scientific and sociological public. Nobody can expect to be greeted with applause by the guardians of a discipline when they come marching in, claiming that most of that discipline has it completely wrong – indeed, Latour the anthropologist of science should be the first to realize this!

Given that this chapter has been an introduction to Latour's sociological thinking – and not an introduction to the criticism of this thinking – it seems reasonable to hand over the last word to the main character himself, at least in this context. Hence, let us briefly outline some of the counterpoints that Latour either *has* made, or *could have* made, in response to the objections raised. As is characteristic of Latour's intellectual temperament, such an exercise will have to rely on more of the latter and less of the former – that is, more on what he could say than what he has actually said. Other than some polemical attacks, Latour has simply not engaged in very elaborate or constructive dialogues with sociologists on the notion of the social. What follows, then, should be read with the important caveat in mind that, to a large extent, it represents our *interpretation* of the sociology of associations.

With regard to the first point of criticism – change versus stability – one might say that Latour has carefully kept a string of escape routes, or "lines of flight," open for his sociology of associations. Depending on the context, Latour might *either* answer that ubiquitous change is simply an essential characteristic of the world, particularly now that the epoch of modernity has come to an end; *or* he might adopt a more methodologically compromising position, by saying that the sociology of associations is not some universal sociology, and that it should only be used in those very situations in which the social is manifestly undergoing rapid transformation. Alternatively, he could of course question the entire assumption that his theory really *cannot* explain the relative stabilizations of social life – note, for instance, his discussions of inter-objectivity, framing and oligoptica.

This last reply will hardly convince the Marxists, however, for whom the solidity of capitalism is so overarching and (almost) trans-historical that it cannot be grasped as a Latourian material–semiotic stabilization process. To this counterargument, Latour would probably reply that Marxist notions of capitalism suffer from an over-emphasis of its continuities, and an under-appreciation of its variability, frailty and dependence on changing practices. As Latour notes, "Capitalism" as such has no credible enemies – but *every* concrete manifestation of capitalism *does*, whether we think of a global company like Microsoft, a specific property right or the World Bank. The term "Capitalism," in short, represents an unjustified objectification, which in fact contributes to a freezing of existing power relations. Confronted directly with the question, "What to do against capitalism?" Latour answers: First, one has to stop believing in it! (See Callon & Latour 1997) [19]

The other objections to Latourian sociology can be addressed more quickly, since we have, in a sense, already gone through Latour's responses. With regard to the second criticism – the abandonment of the possibilities of social explanations – the obvious answer must be: Yes, this is exactly the point of the sociology of associations. According to Latour, sociology will no longer be about social explanations, but about social descriptions that – if carried out in a sufficiently thorough way – may become a kind of "disposable" and uniquely adequate explanation, capable of verifying itself within the specific context from which it has emerged. Another way of saying this is that, by undergoing this transformation, sociology becomes much more akin to history and narrative semiotics.

With regard to the third point of criticism – the apparent bifurcation of social ontology between empirical and metaphysical matters – Latour might (we believe) accept the premises here, but he would nonetheless deny that we should be facing any problem. To the contrary, the sociology of associations deliberately calls for a new fusion of metaphysics and sociology, where questions about the ontology of the social world are treated as the result of the actors' own metaphysical efforts. The sole task of the sociologist, in this respect, is to be sufficiently abstract, so that none of the variable ontological possibilities will be excluded *a priori*. This is also the point when, as noted, Latour describes his own intellectual style as "empirical philosophy."

Finally, with regard to the objection on a lack of critical potential, Latour would probably accept the implication that the critical abilities of sociology will suffer some decimation by his theory – but he would most emphatically not accept that this should be problematic. Rather, the Latourian critique of critical sociology is precisely that it has become an all-too easy, automatic, opaque and unaccountable affair. Against this backdrop, Latour would not *ethically* defend the notion of critical sociological distance – only critical proximity makes sense as a sociological type of involvement in a legitimate political process. In this respect, Latour shares the approach of his French colleagues Boltanski and Thévenot: The most fruitful way of relating to critique is not as *critical* sociology, but rather as a sociology *of critique* – its practice, its justifications and, not least, its moral status.

We freely admit that our account here is kind to Latour: He gets the last word, exactly as in his own texts. One way of justifying this kindness is to argue that, presently, Latour is still somewhat of a marginal figure in the social sciences. Actor-network theory is only gradually finding its spot in the accepted firmament of sociological theories; and there are still considerable variations within different national sociologies in this respect.[20]

At the risk of some unwarranted generalizing, it seems reasonable to argue that, within extensive circles of sociology, Latour is still perceived either as mainly a philosopher (of science), or as being solely of relevance to rather narrow discussions within the sub-field of the sociology of science. As should be clear from this chapter, however, such a characterization is increasingly misleading. Against this backdrop, we may cautiously suggest that the sociology of associations provides a refreshing and potentially fruitful contribution to any sociological effort that wishes to reflect upon the social, as it moves beyond the narrow limits of "cultures," "nation states" and "social structures."

6 Conclusion
The enlightenment project of Bruno Latour

> For the last 20 years I have carefully hidden my big project under a screen of apparently disparate types of studies. . . . Even though I have always held positions in sociology, and have sometimes been accepted as an honorary anthropologist, and feel much loyalty to the little field of science and technology studies, and have also dabbled in social theory, I have never left the quest for philosophy.
>
> Latour, 2010a

Latour: Thinker of the contemporary world

At the beginning of this book, we first met Bruno Latour by a lakeside in Teresopolis, Brazil, engaged in conversation with a concerned American psychologist. Here, we related an anecdote about the wider intellectual confrontation between the natural and human sciences, now generally labeled the "science wars." In the eyes of the psychologist, this French theorist of science had unleashed a potentially dangerous "relativistic," "social constructivist" and "post-modern" attack on time-honored ideals as to how science grants us access to "true reality." Viewed through Latour's eyes, however, the source of amazement and concern is entirely different: How, he asks rhetorically, is it possible that an intellectual culture (modernity) has reached a point at which reasonable people (scientists) may ask each other – in all seriousness – whether they "believe in reality"? Do we now live in a time when reality has once again become a matter of religious belief? Which abyss of mutual epistemological confusion must we face in order to understand how such a question can even arise?

Having gone through the five preceding chapters of this book, we hope that our readers now have a clear sense of the overall shape of Latour's own answer: As always, our thinking is led astray by the many misleading dichotomies of the modern Constitution – dichotomies of society and nature, subject and object, language and reality. As such, we face no other realistic option than to develop an alternative to this modern Constitution. In this endeavor, Latour's thinking is clearly "beyond modernity," just as the American psychologist correctly perceives; however, his thinking is non-modern, not post-modern.

Likewise, Latour's alternative epistemology is resolutely constructivist, moving beyond the confines of scientific "realism" – but it is in no way *social* constructivist. Finally, his conceptual universe is thoroughly "relationalist," which, however, does not make him a relativist. Subtle differences like these are utterly crucial, and Latour's intellectual project revolves around attempts to articulate the differences clearly and distinctly. In his world, there *are* no science wars. However, the task of articulating a non-modern language, enabling us to see the *real* challenges of today's world in more adequate perspectives, constitutes an enormous intellectual and practical challenge. If we wish to follow Latour in his forays into the hybrid world of non-modernity, we are thus forced to re-think the basic constitution of the most essential ingredients of modernity – starting with science and technology, and moving on to eventually include everything from politics, society, law and religion to nature, the environment and ecological risks.

In such a portrayal, Latour seems in pursuit of an ideal of intellectual "holism," which in many respects was lost with modernity's specialization of knowledge into separate disciplines and problem horizons; a specialization that appears increasingly inadequate in today's "risk society" (see Latour 2008a; Bertilsson 2003). Latour's ideas develop within – and influence – a world of dynamic changes; a world in which the boundaries separating science from politics, society from nature, and people from technology appear still more indistinct, fluid or even erased. His characteristic intention to traverse all established analytical divisions resonates here with wider developments in which inter- and post-disciplinary cooperation has come to be perceived as a necessary step toward socially relevant science (see Nowotny *et al.* 2001). Latour's intellectual project can be seen as paradigmatic for such cross-disciplinary efforts. His thinking may be inspirational on many levels: descriptively as well as normatively; theoretically as well as empirically; methodologically as well as metaphysically. These levels are inter-connected and cannot be separated in any strict sense; to work with "Bruno Latour" the actor-network, then, is to actively contribute to the "non-modernization" of the world. As Latour would have it: Knowledge is performative, and it must be evaluated by its often unpredictable consequences.

Taken together, what this means is that the most relevant way for us to conclude this book is by asking: What critical–constructive resources does Latour offer to us, if we aim to restructure relations between science, society and nature at the beginning of the new millennium? In this respect, it seems particularly fruitful to consider whether, hidden behind the at times "deconstructive" façade, we may unearth the contours of Latour's "reconstructive" project for non-modernity – and to ponder the possibility that, deep down, this project really represents an (a-)critical project of enlightenment? In this concluding chapter, we let ourselves be guided by the same basic idea that also shines through in preceding chapters – namely, that Latour's thinking increasingly focuses on the affirmative assembling of a non-modern collective of humans and non-humans, beyond the "purified" Nature and Society of the modern Constitution.[1] Latour is now in the process of answering questions that inevitably turn up in the wake of his thinking: If we have never been modern – then what have we been? And what should we *strive* to become?

Such questions are accentuated in times when "globalization" generates new encounters – peaceful and violent – between the "modern" West and a range of other collectives around the globe. In this context, it is important to note the desire to diagnose our contemporary world that is inherent in all parts of Latour's thinking. The basic idea – as put forth in *We Have Never Been Modern* (1993) – is that, in a "Western" context at least, we are progressively ceasing to be what we have never really been anyway: that is, modern. Put more affirmatively, the many hybrids produced by science (albeit in unacknowledged ways) are gradually taking over the stage when it comes to the concerns, conflicts and aspirations of "the West." Latour's diagnosis has far-reaching implications: In a basic sense, contemporary life is depicted as going in the direction of increasing complexity and ever-more intense forms of hybridization.

Such interweaving occurs on many levels: as breakdowns in the social differentiations of modernity (between science, politics, etc.); as a crossing of boundaries between nature and culture (through biotechnology, environmental risks, etc.); and as a gradual loosening of "the nation state" as the defining border-limit of society, as social life moves in the direction of both localization and globalization.

Such arguments by Latour seem somehow familiar when it comes to diagnosing the present conditions of our life. They carry echoes of such well-known concepts as the risk- and knowledge society; and the entire idea of a "parliament of things" finds clear parallels in ecological politics, notably in the so-called principle of precaution (see Chapter 4). On closer inspection, however, Latour's thinking turns out to be considerably more radical than suggested by such resemblances. Compared to Ulrich Beck's notion of a world risk society, for instance, Latour's polemical point is that it remains an open and hotly disputed political question as to whether something like a common "cosmos" of nature and culture even exists (see Latour 2004b). In relation to popular notions of a present-day knowledge society (see e.g., Gibbons *et al.* 1994), one of Latour's central points is that the interweaving of science, state, market and nature is no historical novelty as such; it is simply that ongoing hybridizations have only become visible with the gradual collapse of the modern Constitution. Finally, in Latourian political ecology, it makes little sense to posit precaution as a "principle" that is to be formalized in political, economic and legal directives (see Latour 1998c; Dratwa 2002). Rather, precaution names one aspect of an ongoing moral challenge, which includes questions about the moral status of animals, rivers and the climate, and which leads into fundamental considerations as to how the non-human world may be "salvaged" from ecological apocalypse (Latour 2010a). Within all of these domains (and certainly many more), we may reasonably claim that Latour's theoretical universe offers us a set of inventive, provocative and wide-ranging resources for re-describing a world that (maybe) we thought we already knew.

However, Latour himself would entertain no illusions: His work is simply the beginning, if we aim to "non-modernize" our collective life (see Latour 2004d). For whereas Latour's work always takes place in close dialogue across intellectual fields, philosophical sources of inspiration and contemporary public concerns, his conceptual and pragmatic thinking often remains somewhat abstract and "speculative." In what follows, we aim to suggest how these ideas may nevertheless be assembled as critical–constructive resources that help us address the many challenges faced by today's globalized "knowledge and risk society." The guiding idea here is to try to pinpoint an (a-)critical enlightenment project that runs through all parts of Latour's thinking. At the same time, we seek to clarify the ways in which Latour's thinking has shifted subtly since the 1980s, often in dialogue with various critical voices. Finally, we provide a more personal assessment of how, as interpreters, we stand to gain the most from Latour's analytical efforts. In short, our recommended approach is to engage with his vision of a hybrid non-modernity, in an open-ended, empirically sensitive and experimental fashion. This, we hope, will prevent readers from being overwhelmed by Latour's "holistic" universe.

A post-social, globalized and contested world?

If we turn to Latour's overall understanding of the world as consisting of hybrid actor-networks, we seem to be confronted with something like a "post-social" vision (see also Knorr Cetina 1997). In contemporary "society" – according, at least, to one of Latour's central messages – our connections to other people are almost always technologically mediated. Furthermore, we entertain a number of meaningful and emotionally significant relations to diverse non-human actants. One needs only to think here of the close companionships that many people develop with pets, childhood landscapes, cars or favorite books (see also Haraway 2003). Latour clearly possesses an (almost) unrivaled eye for the constitutive importance of non-human actants in today's social world. For this same reason, he is at times associated with the concept of "post-humanism" (Hayles 1999: 291). Often, this term is meant to carry a certain normative charge, suggesting that, alongside other "post-humanists" such as Michel Foucault and Judith Butler, Latour has left behind, abandoned or somehow depleted humanism.

This interpretation, however, is misleading. Rather, Latour's main point is that we shall never know, once and for all, what constitutive significance the non-human world carries in shaping our very humanism. As such, the human remains open to negotiation. If we are to attach a general label to this style of reasoning, "non-humanism" seems more appropriate than "post-humanism." Thus, we emphasize that Latour has not abandoned humanism – on the contrary, he is deeply concerned with how, as a collective, we constitute and define ourselves. But he rejects the notion that there should be an underlying, original or essential humanism, unaffected by the events of the non-human world. In Latour's view, such a purified version of the human is yet another unsustainable product flowing from modern patterns of thought.

The Latourian actor-network – his non-human relations, so to speak – crisscrosses local and national boundaries. This unruly and shape-shifting geography is another key element in his thinking. To take a banal example: Any ordinary Nokia mobile phone (itself a symbol of our technologically mediated sociality) is officially deemed "Finnish," but it consists of components from a variety of countries: It is typically assembled in some industrial park in Beijing; and it potentially connects millions of users spread across the globe (see Hess & Coe 2006). In such a hybrid and post-social world, the Latourian concepts of actor-networks and "collectives" should be seen as posing an overall, radical challenge to re-think habitual understandings of exactly who and what we are connected to; where in time and space these connections are situated; and what social, moral and emotional qualities these different types of connections entail. In this context, it is important to note that Latour adopts a self-critical attitude vis-à-vis the term "network" – simply because this term has come to be used in so many different contexts that the meaning of the word is now potentially confusing. Latour's use of the term, for instance, overlaps only superficially with widespread perceptions that, in recent years, the Internet and globalization have together heralded a new epoch of the "global network society" (see Castells 1996). Similarly, a world of difference separates Latourian actor-networks from widespread sociological writings on the increasing significance of personal and social networks to anything from career options to the choice of spouse and political alliances. In the Latourian sense, "network" is first and foremost a heuristic tool; a methodological handle that continuously warns us against the self-assured fallacy that we already *know enough* about the multiple and varying boundaries, relations and influences of the social world.

Following from this, and keeping Latour in mind, we should maintain a skeptical attitude toward popular narratives of globalization as representing a new stage in the development of capitalism, accompanied by growing degrees of "global interdependence" and "cosmopolitan consciousness" (see Beck 2004). In this domain as well, the Latourian analytical starting point is that, since the 1600s, the sciences have been deeply implicated in what was often violent and imperialist forms of globalization through the spreading of "delegates" (technologies, laboratory equipment, knowledge, etc.) to the non-European world (see Chapter 2). Latour would even go so far as to argue that, historically, sciences such as cartography and geometry to a large extent *produced* our very notions of what "the global" – and hence, globalization – really is. This distinct approach to globalization and the role of technoscience also implies, however, that the production of a common, global reality is a never-ending process – and one that, at every moment, threatens to fail or collapse into conflict. This is precisely the point of the term "cosmopolitics," with which Latour wishes to emphasize that we cannot assume, prior to testing it, that we actually live in the same cosmos – the same common reality – as our scientific critics, political opponents or moral enemies. Whether or not this is the case needs to be resolved through gradual, careful and diplomatic experimentation; and in this respect, Latour's model of the parliament of things provides an outline for such "cosmopolitical" processes (see Chapter 4).

At the same time, Latour's notion of cosmopolitics contains a more wide-ranging historical and political–philosophical dimension when it comes to theories of modernity. In brief, this dimension concerns the collapse of Western "ethnocentrism" – an ethnocentrism closely implicated in the global effects of the modern Constitution. In different contexts, this history has been known as Westernization, progress, development, civilizing, imperialism or simply modernization. Common to these otherwise quite diverse expressions and practices is that they all presuppose what Latour – following the German philosopher Peter Sloterdijk – has termed "the metaphysical Globe" (see Sloterdijk 1999). The metaphysical Globe refers to a particular European tradition of thinking about the cosmos, cosmopolitanism and universalism that is traceable from the Greek Stoics to Galileo and Descartes, Kant and Hegel – and further on to contemporary thinkers such as Ulrich Beck, Jürgen Habermas and others. Despite their differences, these thinkers all imagine a cosmos that consists of one single, common, universal and transcendent reality, recognizable via the faculties of reason and science. However, with the collapse of the modern Constitution, Latour argues, even such basic coordinates can no longer be taken for granted. This is especially the case when, voluntarily or involuntarily, we are forced to sit at negotiating tables with non-Western collectives, for whom the illusory qualities of this Constitution have always seemed rather more obvious. In such a context, any attempts to invoke universal truths – whether scientific, political or religious in nature – risk bordering on ethnocentric fundamentalism (Latour 2004c).

This also helps in clarifying why Latour attaches such great significance to his "symmetrical anthropology" (see Chapter 3), and why he increasingly aims to *positively* articulate the non-modern regimes of existence and enunciation that the modern Constitution has previously kept from view (see Chapter 5). Symmetrical anthropology is Latour's term to describe the constructivist set of competences by which we learn to read, understand and identify radically different worlds – only to then pick up the work of comparison and juxtaposition in ways sufficiently abstract to actually encompass such multiplicity. In Latour's view, it is thus high time for Westerners to develop diplomatic skills that will enable us to deal with collectives whose basic assumptions about nature and culture are radically different from our own (see Latour 2002d). Only through symmetrical anthropology are "we," the so-called modern world, rendered comparable – and then hopefully, also politically and morally compatible – with so-called non-modern collectives. In the more-or-less diplomatic encounters that may result, it would evidently be helpful to possess a fairly accurate self-description to present to others.

This is the basic ambition embedded in Latour's idea of non-modern regimes of existence and enunciation. Indeed, on the whole, we may view his anthropology of science and technology, philosophy of modernity, political ecology and sociology of associations as so many suggestions on the competences that may assist us in the search for a more fruitful re-description of ourselves and the world. As Latour expresses this issue: It will make a crucial difference whether, in encountering other collectives, one seeks to defend Science (capital S); or whether, following Latour's suggestion, one wishes to defend an ideal of "circulating references" among well-articulated propositions (see Chapter 4; see Latour 2008a). Put briefly – and in all of its far-reaching simplicity – what is at stake is the examination of the conditions under which we may peacefully live together, beyond the now disassembled guarantees of the modern Constitution.

Displacements in Latour's intellectual project

As is evident from the chapters of this book, Latour's authorship is colorful, wild-growing and kaleidoscopic. It is characterized by a staggering range of sources of inspiration, analytical vocabularies and imagined communities of discussion. But despite such diversity, it still seems reasonable for Latour to sum up his project as one single, comprehensive empirical – philosophical effort to move beyond the modern Constitution (Latour 2008a). In other words, alongside diversity, his many books and articles simultaneously build up and maintain a clear sense of continuity. This is also the point when claiming, as we did in the opening chapter of this book, that Latour's intellectual project can be understood along two main axes: one thematic and one ontological–metaphysical. To summarize briefly: The thematic axis deals with consequences stemming from a basic observation in the anthropology of science that "facts are fabricated"; the ontological–metaphysical axis turns around a "monistic" thinking that emphasizes process, immanence and mediation as the fundamental components of the world. Likewise, continuities in Latour's thinking also explain why we have taken care to emphasize a range of connecting points between the four "phases" of his authorship: the anthropology of science and technology; the philosophy of modernity; the political ecology; and the sociology of associations. In fact, these four versions of his project should perhaps be seen less as "phases" and more as co-existing identities or intellectual personas, by which Latour continuously positions his thinking within the changing contexts of disciplinary concerns and real-world problems.

That being said, it still remains the case that a hypothetical reader, whose only encounter with Latour's work is based on *Laboratory Life* (1979), would most likely face considerable difficulties in recognizing the non-modern project and the far-reaching diagnosis of the contemporary world that we have just sketched. The Latourian intellectual project is obviously a dynamic entity undergoing constant change, with new elements forcing us to reconsider the significance of earlier formulations. For this reason, it seems expedient to take a summarizing look at three of the main aspects of Latour's writings, where one might reasonably talk about substantive displacements in focus, argumentation and sources of inspiration. These revolve around: the status of "the social" in Latour's version of constructivism; relations between descriptive and normative theories of science; and the political–philosophical significance of constructivist science studies. Displacements in focus and argumentation along these "problem axes" are best symbolized by a range of intellectual ancestors who Latour discovers and incorporates into his thinking over the years: namely, Gabriel Tarde (the social), Alfred N. Whitehead (normative theory of science) and John Dewey (political philosophy). The point of focusing on exactly these three axes of displacement is that they may be said to constitute Latour's implicit reply to criticisms frequently raised against his early anthropology of science and technology, or simply critiques of ANT. In many contexts, one still finds Latour's thinking, and ANT in particular, depicted as "social constructivist" (mostly in philosophy of science contexts; see Kukla 2000: 10); as "radically relativistic" (most vehemently during the science wars; see Sokal 1997); and as one-sidedly power-focused and "Machiavellian" (exemplified by the feminist critics; see Star 1991). These critiques are largely misleading, as we hope to have already shown. In the following, we briefly recapitulate why this is the case.

Latour and social constructivism

Social constructivism is a term that, like other "isms," may be interpreted in several, often contradictory ways (see Bertilsson & Järvinen 1998). Regardless of interpretation, however, it would be misleading to include Bruno Latour in this company. On the contrary, Latour's work – from the anthropology of science and technology and right up to the sociology of associations – has been a continuous and still more vocal questioning of the very conceptual category of the social, which social constructivists in various guises wish to apply for analytical, explanatory and critical purposes. In this respect, the displacement in Latour's thinking over the years is thus emphatically *not* a matter of him leaving a position (social constructivism) that he previously defended. Rather, the displacement entails an attempt on Latour's part to use still stronger rhetorical means and to make his constructivist alternative increasingly explicit, in order to avoid getting mixed up with the band of social constructivists.

This is also the context in which one may understand the prolonged (and still ongoing) theoretical controversies caused by ANT in more sociologically traditional areas of the science-studies (STS) field (see Collins & Yearley 1992; Bloor 1999). Ultimately, these controversies revolve around the relative weight assigned by different theories to social and natural factors, respectively, in the explanation of techno-scientific developments; and on this point, Latour remains consistently symmetrical, in that he refuses to assign any explanatory primacy to "the social" (see Chapter 2). Latour always portrays the social and the natural, Society and Nature, as elements that come into being – and become interwoven and stabilized – throughout one and the same hybrid process of weaving together human and non-human actants into actor-networks. In such processes, the social cannot be used to *explain* either Society or Nature; in fact, the social can only be *described* in its multiple and ever-changing associations (see Chapter 5).

Against this backdrop, it may seem surprising that the characterization of Latour as a "social constructivist" keeps popping up in the secondary literature. The main reason for this tendency, no doubt, is found in the fact that both the subtitle and the substance of Latour and Woolgar's *Laboratory Life* (1979) bear distinct imprints of a more "classic" social-constructivist sociology of science (see Collin 2011). In this respect, we have already mentioned how the word "social" disappeared from that book's subtitle in the second edition (1986). In our view, it is high time for Latourian interpreters to make a similar move: Latour is living proof that one may very well be a "hardcore" constructivist without enjoying the slightest connection to social constructivism![2]

Latour and relativism

The next displacement worth noticing in Latour's thinking is associated with discussions about "relativism," albeit in complex ways. As Latour is quick to point out, relativism functions in many contexts as an offensive term used against the more unconventional approaches to science studies, including his own anthropology of science, by various branches of so-called "realist" epistemology (see Bova & Latour 2006). In relation to some branches of idealist social constructivism, this accusation may perhaps carry some clout – and indeed, in certain new schools of thought within the sociology of science, the very concept of relativism is sometimes positively invoked and given a certain methodological significance.[3]

Once again, however, one needs to note that the term "relativism" seems entirely misplaced in relation to Latour's theory of science. In part, this has to do with Latour's understanding of "relativism," which has always carried stronger imprints from Einstein's theory of relativity than it has from the often quite unrealistic models of language–reality relations among philosophical epistemologists (see Latour 1988a). From his encounter with the theory of relativity, Latour draws a lesson that is most succinctly expressed by his French colleague and like-minded predecessor, Gilles Deleuze: Relativism is not "the relativity of truth," but "the truth of relations" (see Latour 2005b). The truth of relations is another way of describing the circulating references by which the sciences, in Latour's view, produce novel, challenging and robust chains of human and non-human actants. As such, Latour remains consistently "relationalist" in his thinking.

Within this consistently "relationalist" position, however, one may still point to a significant displacement over the years. In his work on political ecology in particular, Latour has come to preoccupy himself with questions of how to frame the circulating references of science in the language of an affirmative and normative theory of science, while also staying true to the insights of his earlier and more descriptive anthropology of science. As we saw in Chapter 4, Latour's solution to this problem primarily takes the shape of a dialogue with Alfred N. Whitehead and his criticism of the "bifurcation of nature" into primary and secondary qualities.[4] Inspired by Whitehead, Latour aims to establish some new criteria by which to distinguish well-articulated from poorly-articulated propositions – a distinction that brings him into (critical!) contact with a more classical philosophy of science (see Latour 2004a). Our point in this context is not so much to defend Latour's interest in Whitehead; in our view, the notion of well-articulated propositions contains strong theoretical potential, even as it should of course be subject to ongoing specifications of a critical–constructive kind (see Fraser 2006; Chapter 4). Rather, the more modest point here is that accusations of "relativism" entirely overlook and misinterpret Latour's basic faith in the ability of science to produce well-articulated circulating references, as well as his growing interest in affirmative and normative theories of science (see Latour 1999b).

Latour and political philosophy

This brings us to what is perhaps the most difficult and provocative part of Latour's intellectual project: his never-failing insistence on drawing out the consequences for political philosophy that might follow from his (and others') constructivist science studies (Latour 1991, 2004d). The point here is not simply the rather uncontroversial observation that the products of techno-science will usually have important social, cultural and political implications. Instead, Latour's more wide-ranging claim is that *any* solution to questions of social and political order will always be qualified by, and dependent upon, tandem solutions to questions of nature, science and epistemology. This is precisely the point when Latour refers to his political ecology as a "political epistemology" – with the further addition that *all* epistemology is "political" in this fundamental sense.

Against this backdrop, then, it is not hard to see why Latourian "anti-epistemological" thinking inevitably arouses concerns among more classical epistemologists, for whom questions of science (facts) and politics (values) *should* always be kept separate. Obviously, Latour's response to such concerns would be that the very distinction between facts and values is seriously misleading (see Chapter 4). Second – and more significant in this context – it is important to emphasize that, on this point exactly, Latour's thinking seems to have undergone a genuine transformation over the years, alongside a gradual displacement of his primary reference points in political philosophy. Throughout large parts of Latour's early anthropology of science and technology, Thomas Hobbes' notion of the sovereign (Leviathan) serves as the primary metaphor for political and scientific ordering. In terms of political philosophy, the implication seems to be that techno-science should be considered as one among several sources of power, dominance and stabilization, regardless of the degree of support and legitimacy vested in the resulting socio-technical order – hence, the accusations of power-focused "Machiavellism" (which, in the case of Latour, should then strictly speaking be called "Hobbesianism").

In his later political ecology, however, Latour is considerably more preoccupied with the question of how a "science-infused" social order might itself be made subject to more democratic forms of open, inclusive and diplomatic experimentation. As noted, the primary source of inspiration here is American pragmatist John Dewey and his (social–liberal) notions of democracy as a kind of "experimental collective intelligence" (see Bohmann 1999). This is what provides the impetus for Latour imagining the creation of parliaments of things, in which different forms of "social intelligence" – scientific, political, moral, economic – are to be applied simultaneously to the same matter of concern.

Again, our intention in this context is not to defend Latour taking inspiration from Dewey (see the discussion in Chapter 4); rather, the simple point is that allegations as to Latour's narrow focus on power and domination end up misrepresenting what is becoming a considerably more multifaceted and interesting political philosophy (see Brown 2009).

Does Latour have a critical enlightenment project?

Now that we have more clearly outlined Latour's intellectual project in general – and his far-reaching cosmopolitics in particular – readers might conceivably find themselves somewhat puzzled as to why Latour still refuses, with great vigor, to self-identify as a "critical" intellectual. In contrast to most of his (more or less) contemporary colleagues – from Pierre Bourdieu to Jürgen Habermas and Slavoj Žižek – we find in Latour's work only few explicit references to the glaring imbalances of power and forms of oppression characteristic of various globalized assemblages – from economic capitalism to political imperialism, military confrontations and techno-scientific projects. This unwillingness of Latour to clothe his thinking in the attire of some critical rhetoric has often given rise to the accusation that he simply lacks any "critical project" (see Saldanha 2003; Whittle & Spicer 2008). There is much to say on this subject (see Chapter 5); but in any case, it seems reasonable to assume that so-called "radical" social critics – in various shades of Marxist red – will continue to find themselves less than enthused by Latour's "a-critical" non-modernism.

However, before we accept this equation of Latour's a-critical attitude on the one hand, and some *uncritical* acceptance of all of the wrongdoings of the world on the other, we should ask ourselves whether – hidden somewhere in the Latourian universe – we might afterall uncover the outlines of some critical project of emancipation? Indeed, this is the hard question we pose in the following section, by attempting to narrow it down through the drawing of contrasts to alternative "paradigms," whose notions of critique differ in fundamental ways from those found in Latour's work.

Ever since Immanuel Kant wrote his notoriously famous essay in 1784 – "An answer to the question: What is enlightenment?" – the very idea of the "intellectual" as a social category has been carried by a certain humanist vocabulary, emphasizing the human capacity to exercise the transformative power of reason in independent, critical and public ways. Needless to say, Kant's own answer – that "enlightenment is man's emergence from his self-imposed immaturity" – has undergone a continuous stream of re-interpretation, updating and criticism throughout the successive centuries. The question of enlightenment has since been historicized ("the Age of Enlightenment"), geographically located (Scotland, The French Revolution), socialized (by way of inequalities in class, gender, ethnicity) and so on. With the emergence of post-modern and post-Enlightenment thinking since the 1960s, moreover, a string of novel, more relational, situated and dialogue-based models of intellectuality have gained ground (see Cummings, ed. 2005; Haraway 1991). If, during the days of Kant's thinking, intellectuals still held positions of cognitive authority as "legislators" in factual questions about the true nature of the world, it seems reasonable to assume that contemporary intellectuals are assigned a much more modest role as "interpreters" of the complex issues of our times (see Bauman 1989).

It almost goes without saying that Latour's non-modern empirical philosophy should be understood along these lines; that is, as an intellectual interpretation. His diagnosis of the age of hybrids is one among many others: It constitutes an interpretive offer among equal partners in a dialogue where no one can legitimately claim any *a priori* possession of absolute truths. In fact, it might be said that Latour's own theory of science offers a thorough depiction of the ideal figure of the modest, situated intellectual: Even the so-called "hard" sciences are no longer capable of providing an indisputable foundation for public discussion and conflict resolution. From now on, *all* of us must learn how to navigate in unsafe waters, where the best we can hope for is relative certainties (see Latour 1999b).

Such a pinpointing of Latour's self-reflexive role as an "interpretive" intellectual, then, is in itself a necessary maneuver, in order to capture the radicalism with which his non-modern thinking forces us to re-evaluate the very conditions of the Kantian problem of enlightenment. However, it is also insufficient. Here, in order to further narrow down the issues, we may point to three conceptual juxtapositions, already familiar in Latourian thinking.

142 Conclusion

Specifically, these are: a-humanism; the crisis of social critique; and the democratization of the sciences.

These issues have already been addressed in depth throughout the discussions in this book, and from different perspectives. But at this point, we find it fruitful to attempt to re-assemble the threads, by way of reflecting upon the possible meanings of "enlightenment" and "emancipation" in the context of Latour's intellectual project.

A-humanism

We have already highlighted how the theme of a-humanism shows up in Latour's work in a number of different ways: as an analytical movement in the direction of "generalized symmetry" across the nature–culture dichotomy (see Chapter 2); as a "post-social" diagnosis of the contemporary world; and as a question of the moral status of non-human ecological entities (see Chapter 4). Especially in this latter version of political ecology, it seems clear that Latourian a-humanism actually involves an element of enlightenment and emancipatory thinking – although more in relation to our ecological fellow-beings (animals, rivers, plants, climate) than to us as human beings (Latour 1998d). In this respect, it seems indicative of Latour's general a-humanist thinking that his only in-depth discussion of Kantian moral philosophy takes place in relation to questions of the moral status of non-human, rather than human, actors (see Latour 1998c).

However, and as already noted, it would be a grave misinterpretation to read a-humanism here as synonymous with "post-humanism" – not to mention "anti-humanism." Instead, the Latourian ecological enlightenment project revolves around the relationalist insight that the "common humanity" referenced by humanism depends, in a fundamental sense, on the multifarious connections of human beings to a shared, cosmic, non-human world. Or, as Latour himself expresses his relational–ecological ethics: A human being without elephants, rivers, ozone and plankton would be a human deprived of significant parts of his humanity (see Chapter 4). On closer inspection, Latourian a-humanism reveals itself as a kind of "extended" humanism.

Critical proximity

In the minds of most self-declared critical humanists and sociologists, no doubt, this Latourian a-humanism and his preoccupation with non-human actors nevertheless still seems an unfortunate distraction from the *truly* significant questions – by which they usually mean questions of power, inequality, critique and emancipation in the human, social world (see Vandenberghe 2002). Seen in isolation, this criticism appears to be misleading because it precisely implies the same *opposition* between humans and non-humans that Latourian a-humanism rejects. Needless to say, one may well discuss just how interesting, enlightening and potentially critical Latour's own analyses of primarily human phenomena – such as religion, law and politics – really are (see Chapter 5). However, disagreements on this level hardly justify the outright rejection of his intellectual project, as has been advocated by certain so-called critical social theorists (see for example, Fuller 2000).

As noted, it is Pierre Bourdieu, the acclaimed French sociologist, who represents the prime example of a theoretical opponent – and one to whom the Latourian intellectual project seems *fundamentally* erroneous. In his book on the sociology of knowledge, *Science of Science and Reflexivity* (Bourdieu 2004: 52ff), Bourdieu spends 10 pages accusing his younger fellow countryman of "using scientifically dishonest strategies," engaging in "a simple literary game of words" and, on the whole, of having created "a sociological work with absolutely no merit whatsoever." In order to understand this unusually harsh and uncompromising tone, it is most likely insufficient to consider only Latour's manifest observations on science and society – or, for that matter, Bourdieu's interpretation of these observations.[5] Instead, we need to understand the constitutive role played by social categories and criticism in Bourdieu's sociological paradigm – and, paralleling this, we need to re-evaluate the implications of the crisis which, according to Latour, is currently befalling this very same social criticism (see Latour 2004c).

The confrontation between Latour and Bourdieu may be depicted as a historical repetition, 100 years later, of the controversy between Tarde and Durkheim – a controversy that Latour deploys self-consciously in the presentation of his sociology of associations (see Chapter 5; see also Schinkel 2007). To Bourdieu, sociology is a science that aims to break with the self-understandings of social actors by way of theoretically re-constructing a social space (field), structured around inequalities in economic and cultural capacities (capital). Only in this way does sociology attain a *critical potential* via the objectification (Latour would say "revelation") of the unacknowledged inequalities of power that shape all domains of society, including science (see Bourdieu 2005). To Latour, on the contrary, the sociology of associations is a method that allows the researcher to follow how actors gradually build human and non-human networks, the precise contours of which remain a never-ending empirical challenge; only by tracing these networks does sociology achieve a *constructive* political and scientific relevance as a contributor to negotiations within the hybrid collective. In Bourdieu's view, the social can be used to explain and criticize. To Latour, however, the social explains nothing; instead, it should *itself* be explained through detailed empirical and historical studies. In Latour's view, then, the critical–humanist sociologist (read: Bourdieu) enjoys no privileged access to the realm of criticism; rather, as demonstrated by Boltanski and Thévenot (2006 [1991]), critique is an all-pervasive and quite mundane activity.

In Latour's appraisal, the sociologists of the social – from Durkheim through to Bourdieu – have all traded their ability to criticize for an implicit acceptance of how the modern Constitution divides the world ontologically into social and natural domains. Latour argues that, by doing so, the sociologists of the social are forced to ceaselessly oscillate between two equally unattractive positions: that of sociological self-aggrandizement (achieved via the explaining away of phenomena such as religion); and that of a misplaced reverence toward the "hard" facts of natural science (by accepting the modern purification of hybrids) (see Latour 2009a). Seen from the Latourian standpoint, this sociological bootstrapping is both scientifically untenable and arrogant (see Latour 2000b). Besides, it is not especially critical, given that sociological self-aggrandizement tends to stagnate in a few standard formulas on oppressive structures, which may be rather uncritically applied across the board (Latour would place Bourdieu's entire "neo-liberal capitalism" into this category; see Chapter 5).

On the whole, Latour adopts the non-modern view that it is high time to break with all of our deeply rooted traditions for critical iconoclasm – shaped by the vocabularies of revelation, sociologizing, unmasking and deconstruction – that have characterized the intellectual life of the West throughout the entire epoch of so-called modernity (see Latour 2002e). Instead, we ought to begin considering what it might mean to be a *constructive*, or *diplomatic*, intellectual (see Latour 2004d). Put differently: The Latourian project of enlightenment implies other sources of "light" and is populated by a different kind of intellectual figure than was the case under modern conditions. Ultimately, Latour adopts an "a-critical" stance: "Critical" is what a state of affairs or a situation might become if, as a researcher, one engages closely and deeply enough in its uncertain future. "Critical" is not a natural badge of honor designed for select intellectuals.

Democratization of the sciences

As a final element in this outline of Latour's a-critical project of enlightenment, we need to mention the democratization of the sciences, something that Latour explicitly declares as an ambition of his work. Ultimately, as we have emphasized, the Latourian vision consists of a pluralistic non-modern world, built up from regimes of existence and enunciation that enjoy equal ontological and epistemological standing. The specific truth conditions of these regimes all need to be understood, analyzed and respected. The crucial point to note about this non-modern world, then, is that it exists beyond the transcendental dominance of Science, Truth and Nature – a dominance that, according to Latour, was wielded by science over all facets of collective life, from religion to politics, throughout the epoch of modernity. This is the backdrop against which to understand the Latourian political epistemology: In a fundamental sense, what is at stake is a democratization of critical reasoning, by way of democratizing the current dominance of the sciences. In this sense, Latour basically advocates a kind of secularization of the sciences, which denies scientific explanations their unquestioned pre-eminence over other ways of recognizing, experiencing and acting in the world (see Latour 1999b). Such secularization, however, is supposed to simultaneously maintain our respect for the complex and intricate contributions that the sciences provide to the collective.

It is important to emphasize that Latour is far from being the only social theorist who currently raises questions about a possible democratization of the sciences – seen as a potentially progressive suggestion for how to extend, and fundamentally re-think, enlightenment issues of autonomy and liberation. Related discussions thrive among several of Latour's colleagues in the domain of science and technology studies (STS), as well as more generally among sociologists and political philosophers (see Stengers 2000; Maasen & Weingart, eds. 2005; Beck 1992; Turner 2003; Stehr 2005; Thorlindsson & Vilhjalmsson 2003). Across analytical divides, widespread agreement exists on the point that techno-scientific knowledge (in the fields of bio-medicine and nanotechnology, for instance) represents one of the most significant sources of political, economic and cultural power in the contemporary world. As such, this "sub-political" exercise of power ought to be brought under legitimate and democratic forms of control and debate.[6] In this context, practical experiences and experiments with such democratizations of expertise also play important roles. So-called consensus conferences, familiar primarily in the Danish context (see Bruun Jensen 2005; Blok 2007b) as well as much more unruly public clashes between researchers and activists (see Epstein 1995; Elam & Bertilsson 2003), are all part of these debates on the possible democratization of scientific knowledge.

At the same time, however, it seems reasonable to claim that Latourian ideas of how to reorganize relations between science, society and nature constitute the most far-reaching, radical and philosophically developed proposal of its kind, when seen in the context of our contemporary scene of social theory and political philosophy (see Lash 1999).[7] In this respect, Latour's sketch of the "parliament of things" is symptomatic of his desire and ability to fully deconstruct the usual intellectual habits of modernity – from epistemology to sociology, theology, political theory and moral philosophy – only to proceed by generating new models and imaginations of the collective life of non-modernity. As is characteristic of Latour's intellectual style, his work never stops with *de*construction; rather, the most significant moment lies in the *re*construction, understood as an affirmative articulation of the world, using new non-modern conceptual formulations. When seen through Latourian lenses, well-known phenomena change shape entirely: Scientific facts become circulating references; technological objects become stubborn actors; nature becomes the ground for political negotiations; and society is transformed into ever-changing associations of humans and non-humans. Wherever Latour casts his gaze of symmetrical anthropology, he extrapolates a world of practices and actions that is miles apart from the "official" versions of modernity, (social) science and philosophy.

It is precisely this unfaltering will to describe the world in deliberately "alienating" non-modern terms – of translations, actor-networks, hybrids, parliaments of things, propositions, regimes of existence and enunciation, and much more – that constitutes the true Latourian contribution to a critical project of enlightenment. His intellectual work offers an anthropology of the modern existence, the very gaze of which remains "imminently critical" in the sense that it forces us to constantly re-think apparently familiar problems, mental habits and institutional certainties. We should view Latour less as a thinker who wishes to criticize, and more as someone who radically re-describes, re-interprets – and thereby "re-enchants" – our so-called modern world. A re-interpretive "re-enchantment" of this type cannot be conjured by a distanced, deconstructive gaze. In Latour's work, then, it is instigated through an imminent critical proximity that strives to textually register the minute details of how the world is being built and re-built, in a variety of ways and in a plurality of locations, actor-networks and regimes of enunciation.[8] In this engaged, situated and constructive sense, Latour is definitely a critical intellectual (see Latour 2003a); perhaps even the first in a string of non-modern critics of modernity.[9]

Summing up, we may then answer the core question of this concluding chapter in the affirmative: Latour *does* in fact have an a-critical project of enlightenment. This project is best described in terms of a radically expanded humanism; an intellectual style that strives for critical proximity rather than critical distance; and a democratization of the roles played by the sciences in collective life. Although Latourian analyses are obviously relevant to our understanding of the contemporary global risk- and knowledge society, we should also recognize that part of his intellectual project is situated on a basic philosophical plane. His thinking calls for a willingness to problematize deeply held ontological assumptions – assumptions, in particular, about the orders of science, truth and nature. It is no coincidence, then, that the name of Latour is sometimes associated with the most radically critical thinkers of modernity, from Nietzsche to Heidegger (see Bruun Jensen & Selinger 2003; Riis 2008). But we should note that Latour himself prefers the company of Whitehead, Tarde and Dewey: Ultimately, his thinking is more "cosmological" and experimental than "post-structuralist" and uncompromising (see Keller 2002). This intellectual style also finds stylistic expression: Inspired by his mentor Michel Serres, Latour's ideal remains that of engaging different genres – from sociology to literature, and from science to mythology – which are then allowed to comment on each other, without being reduced to one dominant perspective (see Bowker & Latour 1987; Latour 2006b; Freed 2003). We wish to end this book with the suggestion that a similar basic "irreductionism" should be used in relation to Latour's own intellectual project.

Interpretive strategies: "Do you believe in non-modernity?"

Toward the end of our introductory chapter, we met a young Ph.D. student whose encounter with Latourian ANT turns out to be a disappointment: The theory seems poorly equipped to deliver those "explanatory frameworks" that, in the eyes of this student, are necessary to infuse the empirical observations of the social sciences with a sense of generalization and critical edge.

As readers, we are now in a better position to understand how this anecdote serves to cast the Latourian intellectual project in clear opposition to a kind of social-scientific "common sense." Unlike mainstream social science, Latour's primary focus is not on human actors, but rather on hybrid actants; and his networks are relational and processual chains of translation, rather than general social or technological forms. In addition to this, neither generalizations nor critical edge – in the usual sense of these terms – is on Latour's list of the intellectual virtues of non-modernity. Instead, he aims for an a-critical empirical philosophy that does justice to the unique qualities of its shifting analytical subjects. Finally, Latour emphasizes again and again that his thinking comprises a method, *not* a theory. His intellectual project assumes the shape of a set of tools for empirical and philosophical (re-) descriptions, rather than a catalogue of theoretical explanations for developments in the social world. If one attempts to read Latour as a "social theorist" – without first redefining the meanings of "social" and "theory" – this will invariably turn out to be a disappointing experience, just as it was for our anecdotal Ph.D. student (see Latour 2000b).

These precautionary remarks on the reception of Latour may seem relatively obvious, but it is nonetheless understandable if readers, at this stage, experience a certain feeling of exhaustion, perhaps even resignation, with regard to the Latourian project. Not simply because this project – as presented here – is multifaceted, complex and philosophically demanding. Latour's thinking *is* difficult to access. On the other hand, it is hardly more difficult than other contemporary projects on the firmament of the humanities and social sciences – and compared to these, Latour enjoys the distinct advantage of writing captivating, engaging and often humorous texts (see Harman 2009). As such, any experience of exhaustion might instead be attributable to precisely those characteristics that we have highlighted as the *strengths* of Latourian thinking: namely, the fairly high degrees of consistency and radicalism with which he conjures a non-modern alternative to our (apparently) familiar modern world.

This may at times leave readers feeling that we are dealing with a complete package here, in which the various elements – such as anthropology of science, philosophy of modernity, political ecology and sociology of associations – to a great extent presuppose, determine and mutually shed light on each other. If we accept this reading, however, we seem forced to acknowledge that Latour's intellectual project puts us face-to-face with a new "great theory" or "grand narrative"; that is, a theory and narrative of non-modernity. In an age marked by post-modern skepticism toward *other* such grand narratives – like those of progress, globalization, end of history and so on (see Lyotard 1979) – this may be somewhat disturbing to us. The question, it seems, is whether *too much* is at stake in the Latourian project?

Another way to approach a similar question – from a slightly different perspective – is to take Latour at face value when he proclaims that deep down, and behind the façade of his social-science engagements, he is ultimately interested in metaphysics (see the introduction to this book). In one sense, this is undoubtedly a provocation: Latour's interest in the "metaphysical" undergirds his desire to break away from the modern monopoly of the sciences when it comes to *the* one, true, empirical world (see Latour 2005c). At the same time, one may note that an interest in metaphysics often merges with an interest in cosmology in general and religion in particular; here, it is worth remembering that, after all, Latour was shaped as a scholar by traditions of Biblical exegesis (see Latour 2009a; 2008a). Perhaps we can think of good reasons as to why certain commentators read a kind of God-like presence in the Latourian relational ontology of mediation (see Holbraad 2004).[10] Regardless of the reasonableness of such an interpretation, however, one may be left with the impression that the hybrid world of Bruno Latour presents us with a kind of metaphysical cosmology – and that this cosmology precludes any freedom of analytical movement, calling instead for either complete acceptance or total rejection.

We want to emphasize, however, that this is not really the case – and there are several reasons why. Some of these reasons are evident in light of the preceding chapters; for instance, from the fact that we have consistently given priority to the sociological and anthropological readings of Latour. Against this backdrop, the statements just made appear to us as an unhelpful metaphysical reductionism. By writing this concluding chapter, moreover, we hope to leave readers with more solidly founded arguments to counter any kind of "ultimate" reading – that is to say, the kinds of readings that basically criticize Latour's project as a new "grand narrative" or a "metaphysical cosmology." This point can be stated simply, but it carries many implications: If we hope to learn anything from Latour's theory of science, it makes no sense to attempt to read *his own* intellectual project as one all-encompassing, essentialist, static and monolithic system of ideas – as a grand narrative or a deep metaphysical position. On the contrary, we should continue to insist that Latour's project is in *itself* an incomplete, dynamic, relational and only partially cohesive network. Although we have emphasized the fairly high levels of consistency and mutual connectedness among the individual components displayed in the Latourian intellectual universe, this does not imply that, as interpreters, we should necessarily feel trapped inside an immense and airtight system without cracks. Just as Latour demonstrates a high level of intellectual mobility, then we as interpreters need to similarly insist on our freedom of movement as we navigate through the different thematic compartments, disciplinary visions and empirical–philosophical knowledge interests manifested in Latour's extensive and hybrid universe. Indeed, as noted, one of the few things one should *not* expect to find in Latour's work is a novel, grand, positive theory about the definite characteristics of the social world.

What we find instead is a metaphysical thinking based on processes, immanence and mediation, making it possible to cultivate a strong analytical sensibility to the many hybridizations of this world, crisscrossing modernist boundaries between nature and culture. More than anything, Latourian metaphysics carry a negative lesson: it ought to vaccinate us against blithely assuming that – already, and once and for all – we *know* which significant elements make up the world, and how they are assembled. This is precisely the context in which Latour's self-description as an *empirical* philosopher needs to be taken seriously.

Indeed, in the Latourian universe, ontological–metaphysical questions never enjoy any privilege relative to the empirical analysis of human and non-human networks; on the contrary, such questions form central elements of any empirical inquiry. When describing Latour's project in terms of a democratization of the sciences, we should stress that this also implies a democratization of philosophical capacities: On Latourian premises, it is social actors themselves who raise and solve ontological–metaphysical questions. The primary task of the analyst is to follow the actors themselves – whether they are scientists, engineers, lawyers or social workers (see Elgaard Jensen 2001). How do hybridizations play out in such diverse temporal, spatial, social and technological contexts? This is an empirical question, and Latour's own case studies have merely scratched the surface when it comes to the diversity of the non-modern world.

As a counterpoint to the metaphor of a deep metaphysical system, it might then prove more appropriate to visualize Latour's empirical studies as a kind of non-modern cabinet of curiosities. Like a cabinet of curiosities, his studies exhibit a collection of strange and diverse elements – from failed technologies to religious icons – all of which obey stringent principles of ordering that are not immediately evident. Furthermore, there will always be room for new additions (new case studies) in the cabinet, whereby our experience of the whole (Latour's authorship) will need to be reorganized. This metaphor of the cabinet of curiosities has the advantage of allowing the non-modern world to emerge as a dynamic, never-ending project – not simply in the straightforward sense that Latour continues to reorganize his "cabinet," but more fundamentally, in the sense that any notion of final delimitation or closure would collide against the innate tendencies of the project. Latour himself prefers to borrow a term from American pragmatist William James to express this endless pluralism in action and experience: The non-modern world is not a "universe," but a "pluriverse" (see Latour 2004b).[11]

If the world is indeed a pluriverse – in the sense of being an endless and largely unknown space of possibilities – then this also amounts to claiming that our exploration of non-modernity has only just begun. In short, it is only by adopting an open-ended, investigative and experimental attitude in relation to his own intellectual project that we may remain in line with Latour's experimental spirit, as inspired by American pragmatists such as James and Dewey. As readers, interpreters and critics, we may inquire into the hybrid world of Bruno Latour on many different levels, coming from many different trajectories, and carrying many different aims in mind. We may orient ourselves toward different themes and disciplines; we may pursue empirical, metaphysical or political end-points; and we may attempt to follow Latour's own example of searching for new principles by which to divide and re-unite intellectual practices.

There is clearly no shortage of challenges; and by adopting Latour as our tour-guide through the non-modern landscape, we leave behind all *a priori* guarantees and certainties. What we gain instead is an offer of relative certainties, which may help us shed light on the profound transformations of our contemporary world: transformations in the relationship between nature and culture, between science and politics, between technology and society. As authors of this book, we hope to have made a small contribution to the inspiring process of following Latourian thoughts in and around our hybrid world. We hereby pass on to our readers the thread of the "Bruno Latour" actor-network. The result, as always, is in the hands of future users.

7 "We would like to do a bit of science studies on you..."
An interview with Bruno Latour

Introduction

Bruno Latour has published more than a dozen books and a huge amount of articles. The vast majority of these – including all of the central works mentioned throughout this book – have been translated into English. Therefore, in a certain sense, Latour is fully accessible to an English-speaking public. And yet, Latour is also unmistakably French. Although he has numerous international contacts, has held academic positions in the United States and England, and spent several years at the beginning of his career in California, he never hides the fact that he draws on a number of important French collaborators and gains inspiration from current French debates. Therefore, the majority of Latour's audience who reads English but *not* French (the authors of this book included) is left with a blind spot. We can see his "products," but there is something about his "circumstances of production" that remains obscure.

This situation is strangely reminiscent of the initial starting point for the anthropological studies of science with which Latour's career began. Latour and his contemporary colleagues noted that science was typically characterized by its final products (i.e., thoroughly established scientific facts), whereas only few descriptions existed on the "core" of science; that is, the scientific work practices themselves.

Therefore, as the authors of this book about Latour's "products," it struck us that it would be interesting to interview Latour on his circumstances of production, his practical engagements with the French intellectual scene, and to talk about the kinds of projects that his various books may be woven into. On this note, we contacted Latour and expressed our desire to make him the subject of a very modest form of science studies; not an anthropological field study of his scientific practice, but a list of curious questions – with the purpose of articulating his account of the resources, contexts and backgrounds of his finished works. Although Latour was officially on vacation, he kindly invited us to his private home in the countryside south of Paris. The following interview took place in August 2008.[1]

Mapping controversies

TORBEN ELGAARD JENSEN: You have been a professor at École des Mines for almost 25 years[2] and obviously engineers and technology play an absolutely crucial role in your work. We know that you teach a course called "Mapping Controversies,"[3] so we would like to know why you think that mapping controversies is important for engineers – now and in the future?

BRUNO LATOUR: First, you have to realize that French engineering schools are rather specific, especially École des Mines, which is largely an elite forming school based on the very Malthusian principle of the French elite. So we actually don't do much engineering; we do a lot of preparation, from mathematics and physics to administrative and directorial jobs, so it is a particularity of the French system.

There's a tradition in the École des Mines of having economics, management, history, law and sociology for now 45 years, I think. My own twist was that I changed a class – which was a compulsory class for first-year students, to form a presentation of social theory which did not really interest me and about which I actually know very little – to a more empirically-based STS practice, without teaching STS directly, but by making the students do things. So I thought the best way to do that was, OK, let's take an engineering project or science project, developed around a controversy, which is an old notion in history and sociology of science. It is a very powerful way of teaching STS to engineering students without telling them anything, which would scare them away, like sociology of technology or such. I mean, we don't say a word, you just make them do a controversy, which has to be alive, which has to be technical, of course; technical being taken in a very general sense – it can be esoteric, specialized knowledge – it doesn't have to be hardware, but it has to be alive, so no one has the answer. It is the principle of science studies, really.

And it has to be a web site. We found that asking students to create a web site was a powerful way to test many new techniques of presentation; the new quantitative tools that are now available to many . . . So we try to find ways of representing through the web – I mean, through "webby" techniques – what I now call "matters of concern," and not the technical art of it. So what started out as a small course is now part of a bigger consortium, together with MIT, Sciences Po, École des Mines and various places in Europe.

TEJ: I'm wondering how radical your intentions with this project really are. Because you could read that as sort of a pedagogical way to make engineering students understand some STS lessons, but you could also read this as a vision for the kind of role that engineers should play in the future of society . . .

BL: It is difficult to know. You can take it either as sort of a clever pedagogical way of teaching STS without telling anybody, or as an exploration of the basics of what will be education in technology in this century. My point – more in terms of design theory – is actually quite radical. I mean, it took about a century to produce – a century and a half, really – to produce the visualization of technology; the first piece from perspective drawing to geometry and so on, which is typically CAD design these days. You now have all this fancy technology, and you are still unable to represent any controversy about projects, about windmills and so on, which is now the normal state of affairs for technology. So, the magnitude of invention can be likened to perspective drawing.

This is to tell you that the cursor can go through a very simple idea about teaching, which is doing STS instead of teaching it. All the way to something that would be a very interesting project, which is to provide the tools for representing matters of concern, knowing that we will be engaged in those debates for the rest of our lives, so to speak. And as long as you have no way to represent matters of concern – except in the critical legion, which is the one from critical theory – you will never get anywhere because the engineers will not recognize their projects, and neither will the politicians nor the citizens.

ANDERS BLOK: I was curious about what you said about teaching social theory to engineers in a way that wouldn't scare them away, because, of course, when you read *Aramis* (Latour, 1996a), the whole genre, and the whole sort of setup of the story, is one of the coming together of an engineer and a sociologist. And at some point in the story, the engineer sort of revolts against this very strange sociologist who doesn't want to use social context to, let's say, explain or contextualize the technology. So there is a sort of joke, I suppose, on social theory and teaching social theory to engineers built into the whole story of *Aramis*. I was just wondering, is this based on your experiences in teaching engineers and how they actually react to actor-network theory, or is it something you invented?

BL: No, actually the whole discussion in *Aramis* is very biographical. It is based on work I did with a friend who is now a journalist with *Le Monde*. He was actually a young engineer from Telecom in Paris, so it is very . . . I mean, of course, it is fictionalized, but it is very much biographical. At the time, we questioned a classical way to describe technology: the social construction of technology . . . I think now it has changed, because of the ecological crisis, so what was still a sort of funny, ironic way of approaching the question in – what, that must be 1991 – 17 years ago, so a generation ago. I think now you can enter into discussion in a much more straightforward way, in which everybody is concerned with technology for ecological reasons, none of them is controversy-free; you are going to do that your whole life, you will be embroiled in tribunal suits, controversy where counter-effects will come at you. And this is common sense.

So, what I had to do in *Aramis* was to provide the theory of what it is to follow an object that is a technological project. Now I wouldn't even need a minute to do this – I mean, I would just say, "OK, this is the case. Now how do we represent it?" So, the whole impetus would be the next step, which is how, in practical terms, do you represent a project as a contested territory?

Cosmopolitics and ecology

AB: Let us continue to a different contested territory then. You wrote a book called *Politics of Nature* (Latour, 2004d), so of course the question of nature is implied in that very title – at least the title it got in the Anglo-Saxon world. Also you dedicate the book to, among others, David Western and his work with elephants in Kenya. Could you say a little about the role of these – in a more traditional sense – natural actants, to the way you approach the issue of cosmopolitics?

BL: It is precisely this book that allowed me to move to the argument of cosmopolitics, so to speak. With Nature, there is no way you can do anything. This was just before Philippe Descola's work appeared; now with Descola's (2005) work, which is a great help because I can now delegate to him the whole groundwork of comparative anthropology, I don't need to do it myself. But at the time, I had to do it by my own means in *Politics of Nature*.

And things move, because I still thought in *Politics of Nature* that you had to do a lot of work to show that ecology was not about nature, but was about the way we live – what [Peter] Sloterdijk would call breathable, livable atmospheres.[4] But I didn't know Sloterdijk at the time, and Descola was just beginning to publish his book. So what I did in *Politics of Nature* was a classical science-studies balancing act between nature and society, showing that it was not the two ... that there was another solution to the fact/value question, which is the heart of the book, and still, I think, useful – but still, in the old idiom of philosophy, I was detaching myself from. So now I wouldn't spare one minute to fight the fact/value distinction – it is now moot – but at the time, it was useful to do the work, because of all of the questions about realism and universality of science, and non-humans having no voice.

Now the question has again become: How do we represent – what are the practical tools to represent non-humans that are involved in contested sites? The question is the very, very practical question of equipping the citizens of a parliament ... with tools, very practical tools that allow them to visualize the dispute in which we are now embroiled; embroidered in a way which will not disappear anytime soon. There is no way – I mean, there are still people who think we are modernizing. The Chinese probably are still modernizing in great big ways, but everything is sort of ... there is something very outdated in the way the Chinese are modernizing themselves, so to speak. So we are trying to look at the modernism that is out of phase, even with the very powerful.

AB: Sure. I mean, that is all perfectly clear, but what does this mean in relation to a very pressing issue, such as climate change? In *Politics of Nature*, you suggest that we should "ecologize" our collective life. What would it mean to "ecologize" our way of going about thinking and acting and preventing climate change?

BL: I have no idea. Or, I mean, I have *some* ideas, but I would need to do the work. First, it will not be to economize it. Once we have done the work on ecology, you have to restart entirely again for the economy, and we're stuck with that because ecology is piece of cake, so to speak, compared to economics, which has not moved one inch from being the universalistic, taken-for-granted background of everything. So, what would non-economizing climate change mean? It will mean paying great attention to the representational instruments and finding a way of assembling the relevant parliament, which is – what is the shape of a parliament of climate . . .

Given the size of the problem, this is not an easy task; I would be greatly interested in participating in that. I have no . . . well, I can't tell just what it is, but it would have to be ad hoc; it would have to be at least specific for climate and, of course, lots of people do that. But this question is so big; it is difficult to get a hold on. Take for instance Petter Holm's analyses of fisheries in Norway.[5] On fish, you begin to see what sort of work can be done; what it means to de- or to dis-economize fish, by surrounding the economics into an ecology or cosmopolitics, although this is not the word he would use. This is a huge work of embedding, so to speak, the economics into the ecology, and the fact that you can do that on fish doesn't mean that you can do it on rivers or on the climate. On these tasks, we have reached the base camp, as they say in climbing. We are at the base camp. The rest of the work is there ahead of us.

AB: Maybe that was an unfair question . . .

BL: No, no – I mean, it is simply a difficult thing to answer without doing the work first.

AB: Can I ask one more question about the ecologists? Because one thing that strikes me when I read your work on – and I keep calling it "political ecology," and that's the point – I mean, you do claim that what you're arguing in terms of cosmopolitics has practical relevance for people who align themselves with political ecology, in the sense that if they would only know better, if you like, to what their practices of resistance against modernization were really about, it would give them a stronger political voice in the future. I mean, what is the basis of this claim – do you uphold this claim, and are there any signs of hope?

BL: That's the style in which the book is written; it is always books, and for me, books are very important. So, the book is written in this style – sort of old-fashioned style, and sort of Rousseauian style – saying that if people only were thinking differently, they would have a different life. Now, if you push on me, push this on me, I would say, of course, it is absurd; it is the role of the intellectual which we'll never manage to do. That is the style. It is the same thing with the word "constitution," "senate" and so on. So, that vaguely resembles the question which we raised before, for the representation of humans; and this stylistic question is very important – we are going to talk about it because it engages a set of metaphors. People say, "Ah, there is this guy who has worked out a political philosophy for non-humans, in a style that is vaguely recognizable." Now, it is also true – and here, probably I'm completely biased by my profession as a philosopher – that some problems actually, in some ways very cautiously, are caused or at least slowed down by the difficulty of having the right mind-set, so to speak. And that is where we can act. And in this case, I really think that nature is the blocking point of much ecological concern. So of course, it is a completely abstract and terribly difficult book, but it had to be done.

For readers, books are sort of at the same plane, but when you have written books for 25 years, 30 years or more, it becomes a form of movement. So I would say that *Politics of Nature* is – well, it did the job, which is now allowing me to do the next one, but it is slightly in the past, I'd say. The book will not change ecological partisans and yet, if any ecologists read the book, they would realize that this nature that they try to push on the rest of the world is only one of the four versions that exist. So I wanted to be the Karl Marx of the green ecologists in France, and I can't because there is no green movement to be the thinker of, because the movement disappeared. So that was a complete failure.

Art exhibitions and publics

AB: Again, the next topic follows from the previous one. We would like to know more about your practical engagements in the making of representational tools. Specifically, we would like to know about the large-scale multi-media exhibitions, in which you have been involved in Karlsruhe, the latest one being *Making Things Public* (Latour & Weibel, 2005).

BL: Yes, I am very proud of that. After all, I invested four years of my working life in it . . .

AB: Maybe one could say that the exhibition and the catalogue, in a radical sense, expand the concepts of the public and of politics. It is about sparking publics into being, so one way to ask about this would be: Is this your way of speaking *about* politics, or is it rather your way of speaking *politically*? What is at stake in these exhibitions, in your opinion?

BL: That is a complicated question. Several things – one of them is that I wanted to do field work on one mode of existence, which fictional art is a part of. I found that the only good way to do this was to do what has become an important feature now in art, contemporary art, which is curating. So I had the opportunity – the fabulous opportunity – to practice the exhibition as a medium. The second thing is, of course, connected with the question we raised before, which is to have a scale model of questions that are too big – too big if you get at them too fast. So, the climate change issue I couldn't answer because it is too big, so my reaction would be, OK, what would be the scale model of a question like that, either by doing science studies of many sorts, of course, or by a microtesting of assemblies? So the exhibition allowed me to change medium, from books to installations. But also to test hypotheses about what it is to treat these questions of representation in a very literal, lively, expansive, embodied way.

Now, the third element that is true for *Making Things Public* is also to explore what is very close on; namely, what publics are in the age of ecological crises. So, it's always back to this obsession with the representational tools. Your question about the adverbial form is, of course: is it politically correct – I mean, cosmopolitically correct? Yes, I guess the phantom – everything that makes the phantom public visible – is cosmopolitically correct, except, of course, the phantom did not really work in the show. I'm actually translating, and publishing next week, the French translation of the Lippmann book, *The Phantom Public* (1993 [1925]), "Le Public Fantôme," which will be quite a shock to the French, I hope.[6]

TEJ: I don't know if you will agree with this characterization, but at least my impression of *Making Things Public* is that it is not so much about a large violent conflict around an imagined center. Instead, there seems to be a form of friendliness amongst the participants. It seems like a foam, as Sloterdijk might perhaps say. I don't know if you'll agree with that . . .

BL: You're right; it is a foam, including in the way we had chosen the architecture. But it was also my goal to avoid the traditional antagonistic politics, which is the sort of common sense. The idea is, if I'm right in saying that we are moving from the "time of time" to the "time of space," we will have to co-inhabit, so all of the questions about antagonism are extremely important. What will this co-inhabitable, breathable space look like? The whole show was to try and find another set of passions for doing politics – not necessarily less violent, but not with the same coded definition of violence. In France, violence and the whole of politics is related to images of barricades with beautiful young girls, usually on the shoulders of guys that look tired. It seems to me that politics is difficult to practice in a politically interesting way. I'm very interested in the disappearance of politics, and the way of speaking about it. But it is a subject that I have trouble discussing with political scientists, even though I'm at Sciences Po now.

So the exhibition is also a kind of test of the inability of intellectuals to represent again what we are doing to another and different audience. It is a thought experiment – so yes, it didn't look political to the politically-minded people who came, but that was the goal. It should not be recognized as directly political, especially not political art, which is a very coded sub-set of art. For me, *Making Things Public* really is the beginning of a lot of work to be done and institutions to be created, because you need the institutions to do that collectively. I mean, there are already masses of people – about 300 people – involved, but that was just the people I knew; it is just my own connections. The set of passions that we have to cultivate for the next step, after modernism, will be very different from what we know now anyway, so we had better start at some point.

AB: That makes me think of an artist who seems to be compatible with your ideas about cultivating passions – Olafur Eliasson, the Danish–Icelandic artist. You met with him at Tate Modern in London, and his work also seems to escape a traditional definition of political art?

BL: Yes, we met in Venice and later at Tate, as you say. I immediately recognized dimensions of his work which move in the same direction as my project. All of us, I would say – what I call "the compositionists" – we are all sort of trying to see what will happen next, if we have never been modern, to use my terms. The compositionists all converge, I think – not converge, diverge, but explore, fanning out, so to speak – on this question of what we are, where we are, if we are not in Nature anymore. Olafur is one very interesting, very innovative explorer of this question. Perhaps I'm seeing too much congeniality in people, but when we talk, we immediately resonate.

Religion

TEJ: We would like to move on to a topic that we find exceedingly difficult – perhaps because we come from a rather secularized background. So it is about religion, obviously. On some occasions, when entering the science and religion debate, you have said that you would speak religiously rather than speak about religion. For instance, this was the case at the Sociality/Materiality conference at Brunel University back in 1999, where I was present. I recall that I was sitting in the middle of the lecture hall with a clean sheet of paper in front of me, ready to take notes. When I looked around, I could see a crowd of other conference participants with their clean sheets. At the end of your talk, my paper was still clean, and so were all the others' . . .

BL: Yes, it was very good. It was a pure provocation on my part. It was a very good sermon. It was a very scientific sermon, because I reproduced the phenomenon I was talking about, and that's why we're studying religion. The phenomenon itself has almost disappeared, so you have to reproduce it – if not, there's no way to study it, so there's a lot of reasons. One of them is that I'm Catholic. The second one is that I learned enormously from Biblical exegesis. I've just written my intellectual biography, and I realized from writing this that the study of exegesis in my Ph.D. was the first time I ever studied a series of mediations. In the case of theology, these mediations are indefinitely long, and yet they produce a truth condition. But only under very specific conditions, which are that we must produce the phenomenon we are transmitting, so to speak. So, my idea that mediation could be a sturdy way to produce reality and truth came actually from Biblical exegesis, through a very odd reading of [Rudolf] Bultmann.[7] Bultmann was doing a marvelous job of deconstructing the whole Gospel to extract about four sentences at the end, which would have possibly been pronounced – that, we don't even know – by someone who might have been called Jesus, Joshua. On the contrary, I took it positively. I said, "Look, through another mediation, they are still able to produce a phenomenon, a religious phenomenon, which is salvation; the difference between life and death." After all, this is a quite important difference. All of this is just stunning.

So, when I use that repertoire on science – for me, it was exactly the same, science is another series of mediations; not the same, of course, but a long, long series of mediations which were perfectly able, because they were long, to produce objectivity. So for me, the religious element is absolutely essential to the argument. I mean, not only because religion – contrary to what sociologists think – has not disappeared. On the contrary, it is taking on more and more importance. It is not only because, as a Catholic, I'm interested in retrieving some of these things. Religion also seems very important for ecology, as an alternative to the administrative and sort of hygienic repertoire of passions which have been developed around ecology. This alternative has to be found, and I don't think it is that very far-fetched. There is still a lot of the right energy in the idea that the Earth should be saved; and of course, it is not as religious as we imagine it. As an anthropologist of the moderns, I don't see how you could do this without religion, because, I mean, religion is such an important element of our life. So even though it has been secularized – and I don't believe at all in the secularization story, but . . .

AB: Neither do sociologists nowadays.

BL: Ah, good. It is always the same problem with secularization in the anthropology of the moderns. Religious value has been extracted in the history of the moderns, which is so important that it has effects on all of the other values. I mean, this has to be highlighted. Now, my provocative way of doing it is to say, "OK, religious studies. Those who are studying about religion are studying completely different things, such as how does a Muslim compare to a Christian." But that completely loses the phenomenon. It is a bit like trying to study science without doing STS, so to speak. It is a characteristic of religion that it is produced in the way it is spoken, because it doesn't deal with entities far away. It is about speaking in the right key. It is an extraordinarily interesting regime.

Sociological controversies

AB: Let us stay with the issue of sociologists and their misunderstandings a bit. When I read *Reassembling the Social* (Latour, 2005b), I got the feeling that you're engaging in a full-scale war against all of the sociologists of the social, many of whom happen to be French. How would you describe your own, sort of, terms of engagement with the discipline and history, of course, of sociology?

BL: Ignorance. First of all, ignorance. I'm too ignorant in sociology. It is not a fight, it is . . . I'm sneaking in at a party where there are already masses of people who are much more involved and interested. I'm just sneaking in and being mean because I want to develop one argument, which is completely orthogonal to sociology; which is connected to this obsession with non-humans and controversy. So, the reason I did this argument against sociology was to make the thing clearer, and one way of being clear is to be mean. But I'm not too proud of that, I have to say, because first, it is very unfair to the many sociologists who are doing something entirely different. So, it is a bit like a DNA specialist making fun of a specialist of guts or stomach. It is very unfair, because when you do have colon cancer, you need the guy who is a specialist in colon cancer – the one who studies DNA is actually useless. I mean, it is just a metaphor, but it is very unfair for DNA biologists to criticize organ people; and sociologists are organ people. They deal with family, with poverty, cities – and it is extremely useful, and they do an excellent job, but in order to make the central argument . . .

Again, it is a book; every book has its own strategy of writing. "What is to say what is to play" – it's a very French expression of saying, "You are wrong from beginning to the end, and I'm going to show you, and I never lie." That is the style effect – I mean, I wouldn't believe in it too much because the question is: Can the social be reassembled? And here, I think it is a perfectly fair critique that, even if the sociologists are right, they have not examined what they mean by "social" for a long time. So that is inspected, and I look at what is inside. And so even the rhetoric of this book is wrong – I mean, it is not wrong; it is a cliché, and I like clichés as a way of writing. I mean, *Politics of Nature* is a clichéd way of talking about constitutions and rights; I'm quite sure *Laboratory Life* (Latour & Woolgar, 1979) is a clichéd way of looking at anthropology in a way, if you want. That's the writing strategy for every argument – what counts is the argument. I don't think the argument in *Reassembling the Social* is of any interest for sociologists, for organ people. I think it is really orthogonal, and the only – I mean, my position is so bizarre and so completely a minority that I could be unfair. Maybe I'm justifying myself a bit too much here . . .

AB: No, it is really interesting, not the least with my own sort of disciplinary background [in sociology]. I mean, you do refer to Gabriel Tarde, and in this way, you articulate the history of sociology in a way that would imply that something did go wrong from the very beginning of the institutionalization of this discipline. Could you say a little bit more about your relationship to Tarde in that respect?

BL: Tarde is a useful way to re-open – I mean again, to stage a discussion that would have been impossible, if you had been a serious historian of sociology. See, there are lots of topics that, if you come to be too seriously scholarly about it, they just disappear. It is a defect of my own training as a philosopher, as a French style, but I sometimes think – I mean, I'm always respectful in my scholarly work, but sometimes it just hides the thing. So this is a very French way; we were trained to say, like Rousseau: "Laissons de côté tous les faits!" – let's leave aside all the facts for a while. It is not the way you are trained, if you are trained in Cambridge [England] or in Cambridge, Massachusetts, or whatever. I have a sort of weakness for this procedure, but you need specific conditions; you need to be not in a position of power, but a position of weakness – which we are in science studies – and you need to know that it is just a writing device.

Apart from that, we seem to be OK, so I just did that – not to dismiss, but also to elicit something, which has happened, I think. And that, I think, I could defend even on historical grounds, which is the fact that sociology, at least in France, has a much too close – too much of a role in the institutional work of the Republic. That's clear with Durkheim, but it is true all the way to Bourdieu anyway. And that this modernizing role, which they took for granted – this idea that they themselves, and we, need to clean up the number of entities we have to take into account, blind them to a lot of the things which I'm interested in. *Religion*, certainly, I mean the whole . . . you have no idea of the entire anti-religious attitude of the whole French social-science scene. It is really un-optimal to speak positively about religion there. *Science*, I mean not the science that the ideologists imagine, but scientific practice. *Folklore*, I mean the whole thing about underdogs, which the sociologists, on the other hand, are very proud of defending. And so on and so forth. So, even though my writing device for this book is a ploy, there is some truth in it, which is: Let's wait before modernizing, before sociology as a modernizing discipline – what else could we have done? And here, it is not only Tarde; it is also [Harold] Garfinkel. So these are the two pillars of my very limited sociological education – it is a big Garfinkel and a small Tarde, because I learned about Tarde much later. But I think all of this is still news for the sociologists . . .

AB: I can confirm that . . .

BL: They are too comfortable in their discipline, which is social, for the very simple reason that there is no physical sociology. If they had something like geography, it would be entirely different; if it were social geography, then sociologists would have a much more interesting life. So yes, in the end, I contradict what I said in the beginning. I still think that it was this infringement – that Tarde was an alternative, but he had absolutely no idea of what it was to create a discipline, just at the time when the whole intellectual establishment was done with discipline building. In addition – and here I'm seriously committed – the type of data point that Tarde envisaged is now available to us through the new digital technologies. So, even though my Tarde-mania – as someone, a French guy, said – has no historical ground, I think I will maintain it. Tarde now becomes again a resource because of the tools, which are now available. But I did not learn as much from Tarde as I did from Garfinkel. Garfinkel is completely unreadable in many ways, but the radicalness of Garfinkel is still unmatched. He is so mean to social theorists – he is really eating them! But, I must say that sociology is not a very happy topic. Sometimes, it is so pathetic – on French television every day, there is a sociologist speaking about every issue. I find it terribly, terribly sad. Sorry . . .

Writing

TEJ: Let us move on to a more positive topic then. We would like to know something about your views on writing as a social science practice: the craft of writing. For instance, in an interview for the *Chasing Techno-Science* anthology (Ihde & Selinger, 2003), you declare that you're not in the business of making a philosophy; you produce books. And further, in the last chapter of *Reassembling the Social*, you describe texts as the laboratories of social science. We have also heard that writing is a crucial part of what you teach PhD. students. So could you explain to us: What are your engagements and concerns with the craft of writing? Why is this so crucial?

BL: Yes, this is much easier than sociology, and I'm very committed to writing. There are four points here. It is a semiotic, plus an actor-network, plus an ethical, plus a sociology of science point. So, it is a semiotic point that we're writing texts – it is slightly obvious. But in the social sciences and in the natural sciences, it is completely obfuscated. In social sciences, we have what we call methodology. So you could have a whole course in the methods of the social sciences without ever having anything about the writing of texts – which is what you will be doing for the rest of your life, if you stay in academia. So the text is completely invisible – only method. It is the same to a natural scientist, although here it is forgivable. But it is unforgivable if you are a social scientist, because one of the questions that you are going to try to solve is to find a uniquely adequate writing strategy for the thing you study.

Second point is actor-network theory, which is this very complicated question of having mediators in the text, or making mediators *do* something instead of just being – so it is the whole argument about context. And here, if you make that actor-network point as a *theoretical* point, it takes only five minutes: "no context," et cetera. Now if you have to *write* it, it is a nightmare because, I mean – how do you do [that] without context? Immediately things come out, so to think that you have mastered actor-network theory just because there will be actants, non-humans, no context and so on – this is a very simplified version. I mean, you really need to be able to write it.

The third reason is ethical. The people you study deserve the respect that you have not borrowed your interpretation from somewhere else, so to speak. So I always try to restate the demand for unique adequacy, which Garfinkel (2002) had introduced, rightly, in the social sciences – I mean, the uniquely adequate text. If an argument is transported from one site to the next, it is probably a context or a meta-language that can be carried everywhere, a frame – "give me a framework." But if people have spent so much time supporting you, or being with you, they need to be able to be uniquely described, so to speak, and it is extraordinarily difficult to describe in that way. It is very easy to generalize, but it is very difficult to be uniquely adequate to the matters at hand. That is my experience in writing. Normally, to be scientific means to use as many general terms as possible – which is what my students mean by writing "scientifically." It is writing generally, in general terms. Now, writing in concrete terms is extremely difficult, and it requires more theory. So the paradox is always to avoid the general by being much more theoretical – we are never theoretical enough when we write.

TEJ: How exactly do you teach this? As you mentioned, this is not a standard part of courses on method.

BL: No, and I have never seen anyone else teach it. I teach a workshop on dissertation writing. It is fabulous for the students; it is a completely new experience. I have taught it now for 20 years or so – it is a most interesting thing to teach, absolutely fascinating. I've done that in Gothenburg [Sweden]; I've done that in Cambridge, Massachusetts; I've done that in many places. I learned that actually from my wife, who is a teacher in singing and sings herself. She was always complaining about the singing teachers – they're saying, "Well, just do this," but if they don't tell you *how* you do it, it is really useless. The good teacher is the one who says, "Put your feet here, and then the sound will come out like this." For me, it is the same with writing; it is a completely practical tool. It is not something to be said – it is something to be done. It is an entirely practical – ah yes, that was the fourth point I wanted to say – it is a science-studies point. It is, if science is a practice, and social science is a practice, then we need to know what sort of practice is writing. And it is very odd that, even in science studies, writing is supposed to be only by chance and feel. You will never collectively work on a chapter, on an article for three hours modifying the text, seeing what it does, seeing why people never write what they want – but something else, which is very far away, and why they are never faithful to the original idea of the people whose life they are documenting. It is very difficult to be faithful to the data.

In the natural sciences, it suffices – I mean, their writing style is terribly bad, but they have all of the inner resistance, so to speak, of the things they study. But not so in the social sciences. So, if you say, "The general context of the 17th century allowed for the emergence of the West and of the modern state" – I mean, who is going to contest this? And the more you do it, the more scientific it looks. So, it is a catastrophe, and it explains why the social sciences have lost completely . . . It is so surprising when, suddenly in a social-science article, you read something interesting in the middle of general comments. And sometimes, you have a quote and a commentary, and you say, "Wow, that's an original idea – much closer to what natural science used to mean." How do we in the social sciences manage to lose the most interesting aspects, just by . . . because we want to imitate the scientistic version of what natural science has never done in practice? It took me a long time to find the right way to write the book on law, *La fabrique du droit* (Latour, 2002b [2010]), because that is so obscure and complicated. It takes much time, finding the writing strategy. There is a literary element, of course, in it for me, but I always stop the exercise at writing well – it is not about writing beautifully. It is very amusing, because it seems to be so obvious, but my Anglo-Saxon colleagues in science studies miss the semiotic point. To them, the fact that writing is a medium is absolutely invisible – that's also why I was so interested in doing the art exhibition. I think this feel for the materiality of writing is a completely Continental thing. For others, ideas are floating around, and the fact that they are in this book and that book doesn't mean anything. It is ridiculous – I mean, everything in a book is an embodied intervention on a specific topic; it is a completely precise question. I feel responsible for what I have written if it is taken as writing. But as disembodied ideas? No!

Modes of existence

TEJ: We really should let you off the hook soon, but just to finish up, we want to ask you about your current work on regimes of enunciation and modes of existence. Could you tell us something about this project, its main ambitions – perhaps its status in your intellectual oeuvre, or perhaps its current status?

BL: Well, in fact, it is the real project of which the others are extracted. So as Graham Harman says, I'm the only philosopher who has worked simultaneously on "the first Latour" and "the second Latour."[8] Because, in fact, in parallel for now 20 years, I have actually done the enunciation regime or regimes in a hidden way, but I've done it systematically. So it is actually the real project, of which these different works on law and religion and politics are only instantiations or experiments, so to speak.

So it will not be easy to summarize, but the original point is simply to say: If we have not been modern, what have we been?

Most of the work I have done so far was actually about clearing the way, so that the anthropology of the moderns could be made positively and not critically. Of course, it is not a critical version; it is a completely positive version of the modern – almost too positive – saying, "OK, you presented yourself wrongly, so to speak, by saying that we are the ones who modernize the planet. This is now finished. You don't modernize, and in fact, the Chinese and Indians, Brazilians are doing it for you. So forget that – you are now in a position of post-domination or post-dominion, so things become interesting."

It is based on something I learned from studying science, where you defend science as a value in a way that is completely incommensurable with its own practice. So what are you selling: science or the practice of science? It is a completely different negotiation. This goes for law, technology, economy, et cetera. So, the project of the modes of existence is to say, "Let's compare the official version of each of these sets of values, so to speak, with each other and with their practice. Let us compare them two by two." Take religion and science, as an example. If you compare the two together at the ideological level, you get into the science and religion debate, which is completely hopeless. But when you compare at the level of practice, it becomes fascinating. Because you realize that it is science, which is about the far away; and religion, which is about the close up. And the two are equally different from common sense – science is breaking from common sense, and religion is breaking from common sense. One, because it provides access to the far away; the other, by getting you to the close up. So if you now imagine that there are 14 of these regimes, each of them has to be compared with the other 13, and they have to be compared at the real level – that is, both as the official version and as the practice. I think it is possible that you then get a positive and systematic description of the moderns – of what they are after. So, my project is a successor to the modernizing force, so to speak, which no one exactly knows what will look like. We have to end being modern because of the ecological crisis, but we have no idea how, and there is an out-of-sync process because the rest of the world is still modernizing in the old traditional way . . .

AB: Well, it sounds incredibly interesting. I'm sure we're both looking forward to reading it . . .

BL: It will be 1,000 pages in French, so . . .

AB: We'll look for the translation then. I'm very intrigued by the fact that – as far as I can tell – you are articulating a sort of European collective to use the terms of *Politics of Nature*, which, of course, then would lead me to ask the same question you ask in that book: How many collectives are we, and on what terms are we going to negotiate the common cosmos that we live in? Could you try to perhaps be a little more specific about the European collective – is your project a kind of elegy for the European civilization?

BL: That's a well-taken question. This project, it seems, does have a very European dimension. When I say "European," it is not the European Commission. It is just a question of being in that interesting part of the world – which used to be the strongest, but is now in a pluralist position – where you worry about being globalized by the Others, when before we were globalizing them. I mean, right now it is the case for Europe, not the United States so much. For Europe, it has a sort of practical value, this version of my project, I think. But as I said, it is not about creating a successor to Beethoven's "Ode to Joy," which is played at the beginning of all these European football matches. It is more like a slightly provocative post-colonial question, which suggests that all of those who are interested in colonial questions actually don't really give a damn about the others. The others are very strong – they get by, by themselves. Now let's take care of us a little bit. So it is a slightly touchy topic.

Let's say it is an argument like [Isabel] Stengers termed it: If you want to do diplomacy – and we are all engaged in this global diplomacy – you have to mandate the diplomats on what you really hold true.[9] If you do not, there is no margin of negotiation. If you send the diplomats out to say that science is universal laws, and there is no way we will accept any compromise, then the negotiation will stop, because what does "universal laws" mean? But if you send them out saying, "OK, forget about the laws of nature. But what you have to defend is circulating references" – this is what we really care about; the ways to nudge a production of scientific objectivity. Then negotiations speed up. And if you do that for all the sets of values – I know "values" is not a very good term – for those who think of themselves as European, then . . . But if you mandate the diplomat with an argument on all of his values, where there is a clear separation between the ideology of it and its practice, then there will be a margin of negotiation, which is opened up for the formerly strong, but now weak, Europeans. It becomes more interesting. I mean, there is a margin open – we don't know what will happen; maybe we will be globalized by China. But I think it is worth trying because we cannot count on the whole world now sharing our modernizing urge – it is not true in politics; clearly, it is not true even in economics, and our earlier form of Nature is now gone. So what would the repertoire look like, in which civilization will hold? That's the question.

Glossary of key terms

Actor-network theory (ANT) A particular approach to socio-technical analysis originally formulated by Bruno Latour, Michel Callon and John Law in the 1980s. ANT draws inspiration from Algirdas Greimas' work in semiotics, which posits that every word is defined entirely by its relations to other linguistic terms. ANT extends and applies this relational semiotics to all kinds of materials, actors and events. Therefore, ANT is also known as a "material semiotics." The analytical project of ANT is to investigate how certain entities (called "actants") become related to other actants, and how in certain cases, this process leads to the establishment of relatively durable and extended actor-networks. Such processes of network building are often described as *translation*, which is why ANT is also known as the "sociology of translation." Our book argues that ANT may furthermore be seen as a kind of codification of the anti-epistemological genre that Latour develops through his work in the anthropology of science.

Articulation A key concept in Latour's normative theory of science, especially in the later part of his authorship. The concept aims to clarify the difference between more and less successful claims to understanding, called "propositions" (from Whitehead). Articulation refers to a process whereby still more significant differences, finer nuances and active connections are acknowledged and recognized in the objects that make up the shared world of *the collective*. Rather than talking about scientific knowledge as true or false (absolutes), Latour suggests talking about knowledge – scientific as well as non-scientific – as being more or less well-articulated (degrees). The articulation of controversial *hybrids*, or matters of concern, is one of the central tasks to be handled by participants in the *parliament of things*.

Association A main Latourian concept of social relations, and a basic element in the type of sociology – called "sociology of associations" – to which *actor-network theory* gives rise. The term "association" refers to any connection established between human and non-human actors in a social sequence of events, and Latour uses the concept to highlight the dynamic process whereby new connections are created and changed.

Latour thus criticizes mainstream sociology for its understanding of the social as an already stabilized field, domain or structure. At the same time, he insists on understanding the social as a process that connects heterogeneous elements – people, technologies, institutions, tools and animals may all be associated. Association is largely equivalent to other Latourian concepts regarding the creation of actor-networks (such as *translation*, *mediation* and *hybridization*), but compared to these, association is more closely connected to a discussion on what holds a social *collective* together.

Center of calculation Latour's general term for scientific, economic, commercial or military organizations that routinely collect and combine streams of data or *inscriptions*. Over time, centers of calculation often accumulate significant strength, due to the fact that they summarize, speak on behalf of, and react to a wide range of other actants in a network.

Circulating references See *Scientific facts/circulating references*.

Collective, the A comprehensive and relatively enduring *association* of human and non-human entities that loosely corresponds to that which, in other contexts, is called "society" or "culture." Latour prefers the term "collective" because this term is not based on the premises of *the modern Constitution*, in terms of separating out society/culture as an ontological domain independent from non-human "nature." By way of the concept of "collective," Latour also avoids equating "society" with the nation state, as has historically been the case in much of sociology. In Latour's view, just how many collectives the world consists of, and how *local* or *global* they are relative to each other, remains an altogether open question.

Constructivism The philosophy of science position with which Latour aligns himself, and which is a driving force in his laboratory studies. Constructivism implies that *scientific facts* have a specific, material and social history of production, and that this process should be seen as constitutive for the validity of scientific statements. Unlike philosophical realism, constructivism does not perceive reality as existing independently of the technical and symbolic activities of humans, but instead as constituted through such practices. Latour's version of constructivism is distinct in that – unlike social-constructivist and deconstructive positions – he emphasizes the dynamic interplay between material and human factors in the creation of knowledge and the world, particularly within the framework of the technical–artificial reality of laboratories.

Critique/criticism May generally be seen as a practice whereby an actor defines a normative reference point to which a counterpart – the one criticized – does not live up. According to Latour, *the modern Constitution* is characterized by a wide range of opportunities for the exercise of specific forms of critique, based on the *purification* of nature and society. One version of this is known as critical sociology, a branch of sociology of which Latour is highly skeptical. Instead, inspired by Boltanski and Thévenot, he suggests that we should practice a sociology of critique; that is, to empirically analyze the critical competences mobilized by actors in specific contexts. In more normative respects, Latour's view is that critique may only be practiced responsibly through a sustained and profound analytic engagement in a particular subject matter. Latour calls this "critical proximity" to set it apart from the notion of a critically distanced intellectual.

Ecologization In Latour's terminology, "ecologization" is the positive counterpoint to *modernization*. Ecologization refers to an empirical and normative vision of extensive transformations in the collective life of humans and non-humans. By contrast to modernization, which divides *the collective* into nature and culture, ecologization is about recognizing the ever-more complex interweaving of humans, animals, ecosystems and technologies, which is made evident by our current ecological crises. In such contexts, uncertainty, precaution and collective ignorance are unavoidable conditions for political action. At the same time, ecologization points toward a relational ethics, in which the value of the non-human world is taken into explicit consideration; for example, in discussions about animal rights.

Empirical philosophy A term that describes Latour's intellectual style, characterized by the way he pursues philosophically charged questions by means of empirical methods, particularly those from anthropology. In relation to the philosophy of science, this approach suggests that epistemological questions about true knowledge should not be studied in a logically abstract way, but instead as empirically and historically situated. At the same time, it stresses that the social and cultural sciences ought to empirically study how actors themselves raise and solve philosophical questions about the characteristics of the world – in relation to, for instance, the constitution of time, space and the cosmos. Latour thus imagines a new division of labor between philosophy and empirical social research, whereby the two must remain in constant dialogue. This new division of labor is also referred to as *symmetrical anthropology*.

Globalization See *Localization/globalization*.

Hybrid/hybridization To Latour, the term "hybrid" generally designates a mixture of human and non-human elements, analogous to the common meaning of the word: a heterogeneous and compound phenomenon. Hybrids can be anything from Boyle's vacuum in the 1600s to the ecological issues of today, such as climate change and genetically modified foods. In Latour's philosophy of modernity, his key argument is that *the modern Constitution* has produced a distinction between nature and culture, which makes it difficult for the moderns to recognize hybrid phenomena. At the same time, the Constitution allows for an ever-expanding hybridization of the world, particularly through the establishment of scientific laboratories that repeatedly mix nature and culture in their daily practice – despite the modern Constitution's official imagery of a Nature separate from Society. Contemporary discussion on political ecology is now opening up a new recognition of the significance of hybrids, within the framework of a *parliament of things*.

Hybridization   See *Hybrid/hybridization*.

Immutable mobile   An object capable of being transported across distances without changing its shape. Immutable mobiles can be found in many forms: as *inscriptions*, machines, apparatuses or sometimes as people who have been trained to carry out a predictable sequence of actions. Immutable mobiles play a crucial role in the *global* distribution of techno-scientific networks – they may function as trustworthy delegates that can be sent out from *centers of calculation*, and that will eventually return to such centers.

Inscription   Refers to any process by which a material substance is transformed into a sign, a mark or a graph printed on a piece of paper. In his anthropology of science, Latour notes how inscription is obtained with the help of "inscription devices" (instruments, apparatuses), and he characterizes scientific laboratories as "factories of literary inscription." Inscriptions form one kind of *immutable mobile*; they may be transported without changing shape. Inscriptions may also be combined with each other in a variety of ways. Because of these properties, inscriptions play key roles, both within laboratories and in the construction and distribution of *global* techno-scientific networks. In this latter context, inscriptions are transported over long distances and assembled in *centers of calculation*, where they can be compared, summarized and in other ways assembled. Such processes may establish new higher-order inscriptions (like a gross national product or a geographical map). The inscription process may generally be described as an example of *translation*, since inscription connects two entities and allows one (the paper carrying the sign) to speak on behalf of the other (the "substance" or "phenomenon").

Localization/globalization   Two terms from Latour's sociology of *associations*, which together constitute an alternative to the standard sociological problem of micro and macro; that is, the question of differences in scale and level in social life. The main point to note is that differences between large and small social phenomena (groups, companies, states, etc.) should not be seen as essential and permanent, but instead as created and negotiated through continuous processes. "Localization" refers to any process by which chains of *actor-networks* become framed so that "local interactions" may emerge (such as in a classroom). "Globalization," by contrast, indicates any process by which phenomena spread across contexts and achieve an overarching status (in the form of, for instance, a scientific *center of calculation*).

Mediation   A term primarily used in the context of Latour's relational ontology, which describes the world as made up of changeable *actor-networks*, rather than categorical divisions and self-identical entities. Inspired by Michel Serres, the term "mediation" names a basic ontological–metaphysical process that transcends the boundaries normally drawn up between temporal epochs, spatial territories and analytical categories. In this sense, mediation is related to concepts such as *translation* and *hybridization*. Mediation, however, places more emphasis on the assumption that – in ontological terms – dynamic relations are primary, while static entities, such as "nature" and "society," are only temporary derivatives of such relations. The concept is also used in a narrower sense, in relation to chains of *associations*, in which links may be described as "mediators"; i.e., as potential sources of innovation and transformation.

Modern Constitution, the A thought construct that Latour uses in his philosophy of modernity. The modern Constitution is Latour's term for the most basic ontological rules that are assumed to constitute the so-called modern Western societies from the 1700s onward. The key assumption of the Constitution is that the world consists of two distinct domains: non-human nature versus human culture. This split, prescribed by the Constitution, manifests itself in how the moderns *critique* others; in their understanding of history; and in a range of practices that attempt to separate nature from culture (known as *purification*). However, modern society includes a range of practices that mix, combine and interweave nature and culture (known as *hybridization*). *Hybridization* results, for instance, from the *translations* produced in scientific laboratories. What the modern Constitution now prescribes is that the purified self-understandings of the moderns and their hybridized practices can never be explicitly related to each other. As such, the Constitution is based on a paradox. Latour argues that the modern Constitution has never been an accurate description of the world, and that it is becoming increasingly shaky. Therefore, he proposes an alternative *non-modern* constitution, also called the *parliament of things*.

Modernization Refers to the active ordering of the world according to the principles prescribed by *the modern Constitution*. This involves splitting *the collective* into "nature" and "culture," then to be represented by the natural sciences and the political system, respectively. This division also forms the basis for different types of modern *critique*. In this respect, Latour argues, modernization has been extremely productive. The official division between nature and culture has rendered all *hybrids* invisible; and in practice, this has allowed the moderns to create countless such hybrids without worrying about their consequences. According to Latour, however, the current ecological crises mean that such a carefree approach to *hybrids* is no longer possible. He presents *ecologization* as a positive alternative to modernization.

Non-modern/non-modernity A practice or a way of thinking that refrains from operating within the premises put in place by *the modern*

Constitution. Non-modernity typically involves transgressing the modernist nature–culture dichotomy, thereby making visible the role of *hybrids*. As examples of non-modern theories (or compatible analytical approaches), Latour includes Harold Garfinkel's ethnomethodology, Luc Boltanski and Laurent Thévenot's sociology of *critique*, and (of course) *actor-network theory*.

Parliament of things A thought construct used by Latour to explicate his ideas on political ecology. The concept of a parliament of things represents an alternative to *the modern Constitution*, in the sense of proposing an innovative way to order the *non-modern collective* of humans and non-humans. The parliament deals with *hybrid* phenomena in a way that considers both humans and things simultaneously, in a democratically legitimate process. As a replacement to the modern dichotomy between scientific and political representation – facts and values, nature and culture, objects and subjects – Latour imagines a new institution in which scientists, politicians, economists and moral authorities gather in the same *hybrid* forum. In the parliament of things, participants answer two fundamental questions in order to arrange a good common world beyond the division between nature and culture: "How many are we?" and "Can we live together?"

Purification The practical and discursive work of dividing nature and culture into two ontologically separate categories. Purification is, simultaneously, the process that makes *hybrids* invisible (see also *modernization* and *the modern Constitution*).

Regimes of enunciation See *Regimes of existence and enunciation*.

Regimes of existence and enunciation Common term for the kind of social grammar that makes up different forms of practice – like science, technology, religion, law, art and politics – which together constitute a pluralistic, *non-modern* world. Latour's sociology of *associations* gives rise to a careful in-depth exploration into the unique character of these different regimes, in terms of their specific chains of *mediation* and methods of stabilization. Hence, for instance, Latour shows how the practice of law deals mainly with chains of obligations, whereas religion concerns the production of a special kind of presence. The production of *circulating references* in science is thus depicted as just one regime among others for the recognition of, and action in, the world. Generally, regimes are seen to be ontologically equal and yet radically different – something that is particularly evident, Latour argues, in the case of science and religion.

Scientific facts/circulating references Epistemologists typically define "scientific facts" as statements that correspond to an externally given reality. In contrast to this notion, Latour depicts scientific facts as constructs; they result from an agonistic process that eventually – and only in particular cases – may lead to relatively stable chains of *translation*. Latour's *constructivist* description of scientific facts is based on his anthropology of science. Scientific laboratories transform material substances into *inscriptions*, which are then compared to other inscriptions, such as articles published by other laboratories. If all laboratories stop disputing a particular statement, and if the statement is widely distributed, then a scientific fact is established. It should be emphasized, however, that Latour does not see scientific facts as simply being the result of a socially negotiated consensus between social actors. Any statement that is no longer contested is the product of an extensive and heterogeneous network. The strength of the statement is based on a chain of stabilized *translations* between the statement, other statements, *inscriptions*, instruments, materials, laboratory animals and so on. Latour uses the term *circulating references* to describe such stable heterogeneous chains of *translation*. These chains are the actor-network on whose behalf a statement speaks. The concept of circulating references should be considered Latour's alternative to the so-called "correspondence theory" of the epistemologists – that is, the idea that scientific facts simply mirror reality. With circulating references, Latour points to the countless small and pragmatic *translations* that are established between things and words in scientific practice. This focus contrasts sharply to the epistemological notion of a wide gap between the world of things and the world of words.

Symmetrical anthropology   Latour's term for an anthropology that does not give precedence to the world-view of the moderns at the expense of the pre-moderns, and one that does not take as its point of departure the modernist dichotomy between "nature" and "culture." As its starting point, a symmetrical anthropological description of a *collective* adopts an analysis of the types – and extent – of *hybridization*. Distinctions at the level of types of hybrids create qualitative differences between collectives. Differences in the extent of hybridization allow some collectives to build more extensive actor-networks, to mobilize more entities, and thereby to attain a greater potential to dominate others. Latour's mapping of *regimes of existence and enunciation* represents a symmetrical anthropology of the Western world.

Translation   A concept derived from the work of Michel Serres, who uses it to describe a kind of *mediation* that simultaneously transfers and distorts a signal. In Latour's anthropology of science (and in *ANT*), translation denotes a process whereby two actors become related in such a way that one actor borrows some of the other's strength; in this way, the first actor ends up speaking or acting on behalf of the second. For instance, Latour maps a number of translation strategies by which advocates for a particular technological project may attempt to convince, mobilize and retain a range of necessary allies. Analyses of translation contrast strongly to theories of diffusion, which, according to Latour, provide an unrealistic account of the work and alliances needed to distribute innovations. Translation resembles Latour's other terms for the creation of actor-networks, such as *association, mediation* and *hybridization*. To a greater degree than these, however, translation connotes "Machiavellian" situations characterized by struggles, conflicts, shifting alliances and strategic attempts to mobilize allies.

Notes

Preface

1 In English: The Technical University of Denmark.
2 This latter approach, for instance, is the one pursued by Graham Harman in his excellent introduction to Latourian metaphysics, *Prince of Networks: Bruno Latour and Metaphysics* (2009). While Harman's book does a brilliant job of highlighting the philosophical importance of Latour's thinking, the reader will find only sporadic overlaps between his book and ours (although we certainly recommend reading both).

Chapter 1

1 The book *Higher Superstition: The Academic Left and Its Quarrels With Science* (1994) by biologist Paul R. Gross and mathematician Norman Levitt is a particularly prominent American example of the (misguided) criticism of Latour (and other "social constructivists") that emerges during these debates.
2 In this clearly provocative expression, Latour (2003c) plays on the common etymological roots of "fact" and "fabricated," with both stemming from the Latin "facere," meaning *to create* or *to do*.
3 For this section, we rely in part on the specific Wikipedia page dedicated to information about STS: http://stswiki.org
4 Readers interested in wine can learn more at the vineyard's web page: http://www.louislatour.com
5 See: http://www.bruno-latour.fr/index.html
6 In English: Center for Art and Media, Karlsruhe.
7 Paraphrased from a Latour quotation in Crawford (1993).
8 In English: "Exegesis and Ontology: An analysis of the texts of resurrection."
9 In English: The French Scientific Research Institute for Development and Cooperation.
10 In English: Center for the Sociology of Innovation.
11 For a description of this event, see http://tarde-durkheim.net
12 Latour is summarizing the laboratory studies by quoting his STS colleague, Karin Knorr Cetina (1981).
13 In his study of the dispute between Émile Durkheim and Gabriel Tarde in the early years of French sociology, Terry N. Clark (1973) uses the terms "cartesianism" and "spontaneity" (vitalism) to describe a similar difference in the configurations of historical ideas. Building on this, and with his inspiration from Tarde in mind, it would be possible to describe Latour's thinking in mainly vitalist terms. In this context, it should thus be emphasized that Latour draws inspiration from the three most important vitalist philosophers: Spinoza, Nietzsche and

176 Notes

Bergson (see Lash 2005; Bruun Jensen & Selinger 2003). On the subject of Nietzsche, Latour himself says that he was "my first philosopher" (interview, Crease *et al.* 2003: 21).

14 This line of inspiration, as well, should be considered in relation to Leibniz' monads and Whitehead's process philosophy – both make up components in Deleuze's self-conscious attempt to construct a tradition of philosophical monism, in contrast to prevailing forms of cartesianism (see Deleuze 1993).

15 "Actant" is yet another Latourian conceptual loan – this time, stemming from semiotician Algirdas J. Greimas. We provide more information on this later in this chapter and again in Chapter 2.

16 Part of the reason as to why Latour gains so much inspiration from Garfinkel, no doubt, is the fact that Steve Woolgar, co-author of *Laboratory Life* (1979), is a self-declared ethnomethodologist.

17 We should stress here that, while we latch on to Latour's own self-designations as a thinker, our way of talking about and partitioning his various disciplinary engagements (with anthropology, sociology and so on) does not necessarily, or in all respects, coincide with his own sense of positioning. This is where we take a bit of liberty as interpreters and translators.

18 It should be noted that our experiences as authors are rooted mainly in a Danish context. From our common participation in international STS environments, however, we have reason to believe that a division into two main ideal–typical reception groups will resonate in other contexts as well.

19 In the Danish context, we should mention the establishment, in 2006, of the first Danish association for STS studies, called DASTS. Interested readers should refer to the association's (English-language) web site: www.dasts.dk. One of the authors of this book, Torben Elgaard Jensen, is chairman of DASTS. We are neither dispassionate nor uninvolved observers of the Danish and international STS environments.

20 See, for instance, the critical and sophisticated – but otherwise quite different – discussions in Hacking (1999), Fuller (2006) and Collin (2011). This type of serious philosophical reception should be clearly distinguished from the kind of bland and lazy rejections with which Latour's work is sometimes met by various "science warriors" (see Weinberg 2001 for a good illustration).

Chapter 2

1 As mentioned in Chapter 1, Latour seldom maintains a consistent conceptual vocabulary throughout all of his writings. The term "inscription device" is used in Latour & Woolgar (1986), whereas the term "instrument" is preferred in Latour (1987).

2 Latour and Woolgar share their constructivism with colleagues in the field of laboratory studies (i.e., Lynch, KnorrCetina, Traweek). Later, Latour further develops constructivism into ANT. It is pivotal to distinguish this position from "social constructivism" – more on this later.

3 Latour's analyses of the relationship between techno-scientific discoveries and new social groups are, in many ways, similar to the so-called "social construction of technology" (SCOT) approaches, developed as a branch of the sociology of technology during the 1980s (e.g., Pinch & Bijker 1984). Once again, however, it is important to note that Latour's analyses are not "social constructivist" in character: For Latour, it is *fact-builders* who create new social groups, rather than the other way around (as is usually the case in SCOT).

4 The strategies that we do *not* mention here are ways in which fact-builders can: create completely new goals for some technology; conceal detours from partici-

pants; win the battle over the credit for the project; and finally, how fact-builders may make themselves indispensible (see Latour 1987: 115–21).

5 According to Latour, diffusion theory is particularly prevalent in the following academic disciplines: "The history of ideas, or the conceptual history of science, or epistemology" (Latour 1987: 134). To this list, one might well add, from a contemporary perspective, archeology, art history and neo-institutional organization theory. Several disciplines, such as anthropology, ethnology and cultural studies, have had strong diffusionist research programs in the past, but have now more or less abandoned this perspective.

6 We return to the principle of symmetry later, as this is a significant element in ANT. In this context, it is important to note that Latour was later to become entangled in a heated dispute with David Bloor over the correct interpretation of the principle of symmetry. Bloor is one of the main founders of the so-called "strong program" in the sociology of science of the 1970s and onward. Over the years, this program has expressed a great deal of criticism of Latour's ANT (see Bloor 1999).

7 The term "techno-science" was first suggested by Belgian philosopher Gilbert Hottois in the late 1970s.

8 Latour shares this interest with several colleagues, most notably British sociologist John Law, who at the time (early 1980s) was conducting a detailed analysis of how the Portuguese established trade routes to India in the 15th and 16th centuries (Law 1986). Law discusses how a particular type of ship (the carrack) acts as an efficient machine because it holds its parts (hull, sails, rigging, navigation instruments) together while keeping various allies and enemies in place (crew, wind, pirates).

9 Latour is fully aware that a number of other analysts have already described the importance of the printing press for the expansion of the West; in particular, he refers to Elizabeth Eisenstein. Latour's own original contribution, however, is a very focused (Machiavellian) analysis of the mobilizing effects of writing and imaging technologies whenever actors strive to gain persuasiveness.

10 For example, the meteorological institute might combine its data for temperature fluctuations over time with other data on greenhouse gas emissions – and thereby instantly become relevant to the most controversial "global weather phenomenon" of our times: anthropogenic climate change (see Chapter 4).

11 For a more systematic classification of Latour within the landscape of theories of knowledge, see Ward (1996). See also this book's concluding chapter.

12 For more detailed introductions, we refer in particular to the work of John Law (1992, 1997).

13 ANT has also been called *the sociology of translations*; see, for example, Callon (1986).

14 The *symmetry principle* was originally put forward in the 1970s by David Bloor, a social-constructivist theorist of science. Bloor criticized sociologist of science Robert K. Merton for playing on two registers in his explanations. When scientists are right, Merton argued, then Nature manifests itself in their articles. But when scientists are wrong, it is due to social factors – for example, fraud or incompetence. With his principle of symmetry, Bloor argued that the successes and failures of scientists must both be explained by the *same* types of factors. According to Bloor, both outcomes are social constructions. ANT agrees with Bloor in his criticism of Merton and inherits the ambition of sticking to one type of explanation. But as we have seen, the explanatory register of ANT includes actants of all kinds, human *and* non-human. Therefore, actor-network theorists talk about a *generalized* principle of symmetry while, at the same time, they criticize Bloor (and other social constructivists) for adhering to a kind of social determinism.

15 For John Law, this criticism inspired a further development of ANT that increasingly focused on the absent and the excluded (e.g., Law 2004). Michel Callon, on the other hand, does not seem affected by the criticism; one example is his work in the sociology of markets, which is largely formulated from the perspective of market builders (Callon 1998).
16 See Chapter 5, where we refer to Latour's analysis of various so-called "regimes of existence and enunciation." See also the concluding chapter and the interview with Latour.

Chapter 3

1 *We Have Never Been Modern* (*Nous n'avons jamais été modernes*) was first published in French in 1991 and appeared, in a slightly revised edition, in English translation in 1993.
2 This formulation is inspired by the pamphlet *War of the Worlds*, in which Latour provides a condensed version of his philosophy of modernity: "There are many ways to interpret modernism and its history, but I have become convinced that the best way is to treat 'modernism' as an anachronistic interpretation of the events in which the West participated" (Latour 2002d: 19).
3 The most famous visual depiction of this view is found on the front page of Thomas Hobbes' book *Leviathan*. It portrays a ruler whose gigantic body consists of a large number of small citizens. The sovereign is depicted as one "body politic," at once the sum of, and the ruler over, the will(s) of the people. For a discerning analysis of this and many other visual representations of the social whole, see Gamboni (2005).
4 According to Latour, Shapin and Schaffer engage in a *constructivist* analysis of how knowledge about Nature is established, while still subscribing to the *realist* assumption that Society simply exists out there. For this reason, Boyle is more closely scrutinized by the authors than Hobbes. Latour argues that both nature and society are the purified results of hybrid-translation processes, and by implication, that both forms of representation need to be studied in constructivist terms.
5 Note that this is a very specific interpretation of the dynamics of modernity. In Latour's work, for instance, modernity is not seen to derive its force from new Enlightenment ideals and a new mentality (Kant); the establishment of democracy and civil liberties (Tocqueville); a sudden change of productive forces (Marx); nor in exploitative relationships to the non-modern, non-Western world (Wallerstein).
6 Latour emphasizes that the work of translation is neither secret nor unacknowledged. The moderns are fully aware of what they do, and they face no problem in mobilizing their work of translation as a basis for criticism. Latour's point is simply that practices of translation are never explicitly juxtaposed with their paradoxical counterpart, the work of purification.
7 Boltanski and Thévenot identify six regimes of justification, known (in English) as the civic, market, inspirational, fame, industrial and domestic (Boltanski & Thévenot 2006 [1991]).
8 We adopt this example from Jagd (2007), who discusses it further.
9 This picture is particularly recognizable to anyone familiar with the way engineering researchers depict themselves in public contexts (such as one of the authors of this book). The stories that appear in the internal newspaper landing regularly on this author's desk seem to be written using the following formula: Researchers at our university have just created a new breakthrough that will change the world.
10 "Hvem er bange for Det Etiske Råd" by Robin Engelhardt, *Information*, February 15, 2008.

Chapter 4

1. In *Politics of Nature* (2004d: 252, note 4), Latour explicitly states that it will be advantageous to read these two books closely together.
2. This concept is named after Russian agronomist Trofim Lysenko, who was put in charge of Soviet biological science under the Stalin regime. Among other things, he is known for having rejected biologist Gregor Mendel's theory of genetic heredity, based on "historical materialist" grounds.
3. In the post-World War II era, this criticism is particularly paradigmatic in the early work of Jürgen Habermas (see Habermas 1970).
4. Serres' book *The Natural Contract* became the object of extensive debate in French intellectual circles of the 1990s, particularly when Luc Ferry attacked it for being "anti-humanist" and "undemocratic." See Whiteside (2002: chapter 4) for further details.
5. Perhaps under the influence of some still more "catastrophic" prospects of global climate change, the underlying tone of Latour's political ecology has recently taken a somewhat new turn: Under the rubric of "eco-theology," he now explicitly asks, "Will non-humans be saved?" (Latour 2009a).
6. According to Latour, this double respect is a "scarce resource" in our contemporary society, where no sphere is "more inviting for irony, satire, debunking, derision" than the political (Latour 2005a: 29).
7. The expression "anything goes" – and the philosophy of science ideas that gave rise to this expression – is presented by Feyerabend in his book *Against Method* (Feyerabend 1993 [1975]).
8. The analytical dimensions mentioned here stem from a new model of "science's blood flow" that Latour develops in *Pandora's Hope* (1999b: chapter 3). Due to space constraints, we do not delve into further details about this model, which in many ways represents a standardized version of the Latourian anthropology of science.
9. As already suggested in the introductory chapter, Latour considers Stengers to be one of the most significant contemporary francophone philosophers of science (see Latour 1997).
10. The example of elephants is not chosen at random: Latour is familiar with, and deeply fascinated by, the work of Kenyan ecologist David Western, as it concerns the rights of the Masai people, the plight of elephants, conservation and safari tourism. Latour even dedicates *Politics of Nature* to David Western – alongside Isabelle Stengers and her colleague, Vinciane Despret.
11. In several places throughout his work, Latour sharply distances himself from Heidegger's philosophy, precisely because (in Latour's view, at least) Heidegger suffers from a lack of respect for the sciences (see Latour 1999b: 3). The relationship between these two intellectuals is, however, more complex than such explicit criticisms would suggest (see Riis 2008).
12. The concept of "hybrid forum" originates in the work of Latour's colleague Michel Callon (Callon & Rip 1992). However, Latour often borrows the expression and uses it as largely synonymous to his own "parliament of things." See, for instance, Kastrissianakis' interview with Latour (2003).
13. The official title of these forums is "Commissions locales de l'eau"; i.e. local water commissions.
14. Whether or not such bureaucratic tendencies in environmental politics represent more than a "Western" phenomenon is a long and difficult discussion (see Meyer et al. 1997). However, it is not a discussion that Latour takes up – his analysis is based on French (and, more generally, European) experiences.
15. As Latour points out (1998c), such a fading away of environmental movements would be analogous to the hygiene movement of the 1800s, which was gradually made redundant by general health politics.

180 Notes

16 Although Latour does not mention this explicitly, it is worth noting that one of the most influential social-science paradigms in the study of environmental policy is precisely called "ecological modernization" (see Mol & Spaargaren 1993). Latour's theoretical diagnosis thus finds resonance in the wider literature of environmental sociology.
17 Latour quotes Immanuel Kant's famous definition of morality from *Critique of Pure Reason* – according to which "only man [. . .] is an end in himself" (quoted in Latour 1998c: 231).
18 As far as we know, Latour has never explicitly reflected on the question of *human* rights. Critics typically portray Latour – for related, but slightly different reasons – as an "anti-humanist" (see, for instance, Vandenberghe 2002; Fuller 2000). However, it seems more reasonable to assume that Latour simply views human rights as one historical "experiment" that is over and done with (in theory, at least), whereas questions about the rights of animals and other non-humans are still very much open and uncertain.
19 "Finality" is the term used by Latour himself (1998c: 233). The concept is reminiscent of Aristotle's notion of final cause (*causa finalis*), but should be understood here in a less restrictive sense. For an Aristotelian reading of Latourian political ecology, see de Vries (2007).
20 "Deliberative democracy" refers to a branch of democratic theory that sees the public discussion among free and equal citizens as essential to the legitimacy of political decisions. In contemporary democratic theory, this view is mainly represented by Jürgen Habermas (see Habermas 1992). In this context, the specific contribution of Latour's political philosophy clearly concerns the role of things.
21 Latour's argument in *Politics of Nature* is quite detailed on this point (2004d: chapter 3), but due to space constraints, we have to move quickly. We recommend that interested readers take a look at Latour's own exposition, which is not too difficult to follow through this passage.
22 In addition to these four considerations, Latour imagines the existence of three further functions in the parliament of things: a sharing of power between the first and second chambers; a "staging" of the totality of the collective; and a diplomatic negotiation with other collectives (Latour 2004d: chapter 5). We do not comment here on the sharing of power or the "staging" function, but we briefly come back to the role of diplomacy toward the end of this chapter.
23 Latour (2004d: 162f) provides a full and comprehensive overview of the respective contributions of each of the other professions, which makes for interesting reading, particularly if one is looking for a glimpse of what Latour (the person) might think of, say, politicians and economists.

Chapter 5

1 To take one example, Latour criticizes Bourdieu's tendency to exaggerate the "socialization" of scientific work in the following way: "When the second [Bourdieu] speaks of fields of power, then science, technology, texts, and the contents of activities disappear" (1993: 6). It should be noted that Bourdieu actually responds to Latour's criticism in *Science of Science and Reflexivity* (2004). We return to a Bourdieu-inspired criticism of Latour's thinking – and why it is less than satisfying – in the concluding chapter of this book.
2 Latour has spent his entire career re-describing what we understand by the concept of "science" – in particular as it applies to the natural sciences. Against this backdrop, it comes as no surprise that Latour is similarly skeptical of the term "social science." In this chapter, however, we focus on Latour's re-definition of the "social," given that we have already taken an in-depth look at his re-definition of "science" in the preceding chapters.

3 It is important to note that, in this context, Latour uses the term "relativist" in line with his interpretation of Albert Einstein's theory of relativity from theoretical physics – something Latour has written about elsewhere (Latour 1988a). As such, the meaning of "relativism" here has nothing to do with the normative epistemological position that "all knowledge is equally valid." In this respect, Latour fully agrees with Deleuze, when Deleuze writes that "relativism is not the relativity of truth, but the truth of relations" (Latour 2005b: 95, note 119). Latour thus uses the term "relativism" synonymously with the word "relationalism."
4 In light of Latour's later controversies with Bourdieu, it is somewhat ironic to note that Latour and Woolgar actually borrow the concept of the cycles of credit from Bourdieu.
5 The best example of this development in Latour's thinking is the fact that the word "social" disappeared from the subtitle of *Laboratory Life* in the second edition: In 1979, it was called "The Social Construction of Scientific Facts," and in 1986, it had become simply "The Construction of Scientific Facts." See Chapter 2 for more details on Latour's position vis-à-vis social constructivism.
6 Latour's argument against social explanations here comes close to Karl Popper's normative epistemological critique of non-falsifiable theories. However, unlike Popper, Latour has no intention of turning epistemology into a "super-science" with which we may pass final judgments on the validity of other theories. Latour is well aware that there really are no fully decisive experiments, in either sociology or physics, capable of settling theoretical questions once and for all. For this reason, he cannot claim absolute truth in his rejection of the sociology of the social – all he can do is indicate an alternative and more fruitful road ahead (Latour 2005b: 109f).
7 Latour states that "it would be rather precise to describe ANT as half Garfinkel and half Greimas," given that Greimas – as noted – remains Latour's primary source of inspiration with regard to semiotics.
8 Latour borrows this formulation and its underlying ideal from Garfinkel (2000b: 112).
9 This forms the basis of a whole range of critical discussions on ANT, which on the whole is accused of a kind of "managerial Machiavellism" – that is, the idolization of struggle, dominance and the strong winner. See our discussion in Chapter 2, as well as Latour (1999a) for one response.
10 Actor models based on rationality and norms, respectively, have to a great extent dominated the theoretical traditions of sociology ever since Weber and Durkheim (see Joas 1993). Rather than developing an alternative to such models, Latour mainly seeks to avoid the debates altogether – something that contributes to the impression that he has developed a quite unorthodox reading of sociology.
11 Symbolic interactionism has been very significant to the field of science studies, where Latour finds his most important discussion partners. See Clarke & Leigh Star (2008) for an introduction.
12 Latour adopts the notion of "modes of existence" from the French philosopher Etienne Souriau, whom he reads also in the context of both Whitehead and the American pragmatist William James (see Latour 2006b).
13 Latour has yet to put together his thoughts on religion into a book on the topic (in English); but he has written a number of articles, both in French and English, that form the basis of our discussion here.
14 The exhibition took place at ZKM in Karlsruhe, Germany; the same location as Latour's other major art exhibition, *Making Things Public*, in 2005 (Latour & Weibel 2005).
15 Latour clearly inherits his interest in angels as mediators (messengers) from his mentor, Michel Serres, who wrote an entire book on the subject (Serres 1995a). Another source of inspiration is most likely William James, who famously wrote

182 Notes

about varieties of religious experience (1902 [2007]), and who Latour refers to in some of his more recent writings on knowledge as a mode of existence (e.g. Latour 2008a).
16 Well-known sociologists, such as Anthony Giddens, Niklas Luhmann and Jürgen Habermas, likewise contributed to this anthology on micro- and macro-sociologies (Knorr Cetina & Cicourel, eds. 1981).
17 Bentham's panopticon was immortalized within social theory by Michel Foucault and his studies into the rise of the modern penal system in *Surveiller et Punir: Naissance de la Prison* (*Discipline and Punish: The Birth of the Prison*) from 1975. As such, when Latour discusses his notion of oligoptica by drawing contrasts to the panopticon, this likewise represents a somewhat implicit critique of Foucault.
18 In recent years, Michel Callon (Latour's close colleague) has been a leading figure in the creation of a new type of economic sociology that precisely focuses on the concrete, practical and material production of economic markets. See Callon (1998) for an introduction, and Latour & Lépinay (2009) for a comparable effort.
19 This is our own translation from the original French.
20 For instance, in the Danish context with which we are most familiar, it would be reasonable to say that the sociological reception of Latour is virtually non-existent – in part because this reception takes place in a range of interdisciplinary research environments inspired more by STS (Science and Technology Studies).

Chapter 6

1 In this context, we should note that, at the time of this writing (autumn 2010), Latour is allegedly putting the finishing touches on a giant work that aims to summarize his "affirmative" thinking about non-modern modes of existence, of which he seems to identify 14 in total. Although we are familiar with this work's (partial) existence, it is obviously not possible for us to anticipate its full significance for Latour's overall intellectual project. However, the interview with Latour that follows this concluding chapter gives the reader a small taste of what is to come.
2 It may be noted here that Gabriel Tarde has emerged as Latour's newfound sociological role model, precisely because his theories, in Latour's interpretation, embody a quite similar thinking about science and the social (see Latour 2009).
3 This applies in particular to the so-called "empirical program of relativism" (EPOR) of the Bath School, a theoretical program that grew in parallel with ANT in the 1970s and 1980s.
4 It should be noted that Latour's reading of Whitehead occurs in respectful dialogue with Isabelle Stengers, his favorite colleague in the contemporary philosophy of science (see Latour 1997).
5 However, it is worth noting that Bourdieu's criticism takes its point of departure in Latour's early anthropology of science and technology, as presented in *Laboratory Life* (1979). Many of Bourdieu's more specific points of critique may perhaps be defensible in the delimited context of this work, but they still emerge as misleading in light of later displacements in Latour's thinking.
6 The concept of "sub-politics" stems from Ulrich Beck's discussion of the risk society (1992), which we have previously mentioned.
7 One possible exception here would be Isabelle Stengers – with whom Latour maintains an ongoing dialogue (see Latour 1997).
8 To describe Latour's style as a "re-enchantment" of the world, as we just did, is obviously a play on Max Weber's famous notion of the modern, capitalist, rational world as fundamentally "disenchanted." Weber's diagnosis is open to various forms of questioning (see Bennett 1997); and, of course, Latour needs to raise critical questions as well: Since we have never been modern, we have also

never (really) been disenchanted. Still, the category of re-enchantment appears well-suited to describe some of the effects that Latour's thinking may have on the minds of more steadfast modernists than himself.
9 We say "perhaps" since, evidently, Latour has forerunners in this genre, especially in the form of his most significant mentor, Michel Serres (see Serres & Latour 1995). The pre-history of non-modernity, however, has yet to be written.
10 As interpreters, however, we personally lean toward the belief that such a suggestion is, in fact, misleading. This is by no means because we think that Latour's project should be exempt from religious interpretations, but simply because his ontology ultimately has more in common with a kind of sophisticated animism than it does with Catholicism (see Viveiros de Castro 2004; Bruun Jensen & Blok 2011).
11 On this point as well, Latour comes close to his French colleague Gilles Deleuze, who sums up his ontological position by way of the (only apparently) cryptic formula: "pluralism = monism" (Deleuze & Guattari 1987: 20).

Chapter 7

1 The interview itself lasted a little more than two hours and was conducted in English. The text published here has gone through rounds of processing and modification, but we have strived to reproduce the general "flow" and meaning of the interview.
2 Latour has since moved to a position as professor and Vice Dean of research at Sciences Po, also in Paris. This will emerge as a topic later in the interview.
3 The course, taught simultaneously at École des Mines, Sciences Po, MIT and three other universities in the spring of 2009, has the following web site: http://www.demoscience.org/ (accessed July 3, 2009).
4. The reference is to Sloterdijk's (2004) *Sphären* (Spheres) trilogy, released (in German) as *Blasen* (Bubbles), *Globen* (Globes) and *Schäume* (Foams). In his recent work, Latour makes much of his inspiration from Sloterdijk's work on spheres, to the point of stating that "I was born a Sloterdijkian" (Latour, 2009b).
5 See, e.g., Holm & Nielsen (2007). Also, Petter Holm has a Cyborg Fish research project web site: http://www.cyborg-fish.net/ (accessed July 3, 2009).
6 The book has since been released in French, in September 2008 (Paris: Demopolis), with a foreword by Latour (available at http://www.bruno-latour.fr/).
7 See Latour (2010a) for an elaboration of this point about Bultmann and constructivism in his intellectual autobiography.
8 Graham Harman is an American philosopher based in Cairo, Egypt, and author of an excellent book on Latour and metaphysics (2009). The exact source of Latour's quote is unknown to the authors of this interview, but presumably it stems from a private conversation with Harman.
9 Stengers develops her notion of diplomacy in a string of publications on the topic of "cosmopolitics," often in dialogue with Latour's work. For an introduction, see Stengers (2005).

Bibliography

Austrin, Terry and Farnsworth, John (2005): "Hybrid genres: fieldwork, detection and the method of Bruno Latour," *Qualitative Research*, 5(2): 147–65.
Bauman, Zygmunt (1989): *Legislators and Interpreters: On Modernity, Postmodernity and Intellectuals*. London: Polity Press.
Beck, Ulrich (1992): *Risk Society: Towards a New Modernity*. London: Sage Publications.
—— (2004): "The truth of others. A cosmopolitical approach," *Common Knowledge*, 10(3): 430–49.
Bennett, Jane (1997): "The enchanted world of modernity: Paracelsus, Kant, and Deleuze," *Cultural Values*, 1(1): 1–28.
Bertilsson, Margareta (2003): "The social as trans-genic: on bio-power and its implications for the social," *Acta Sociologica*, 46(2): 118–31.
Bertilsson, Margareta and Järvinen, Margaretha (eds.) (1998): *Socialkonstruktivisme. Bidrag til en kritisk diskussion*. Copenhagen: Hans Reitzels Forlag.
Betros, Gemma (1999): "François Furet: Finding 'Revolution' within the French Revolution," *Access: History*, 2(2): 53–64.
Bijker, Wiebe E. (1997): *Of Bicycles, Bakelites, and Bulbs. Towards a Theory of Socio-technical Change*. Cambridge, MA: The MIT Press.
Bingham, Nick and Thrift, Nigel (2000): "Some new instructions for travellers: the geography of Bruno Latour and Michel Serres," pp. 281–301 in M. Crang and N. Thrift (eds.): *Thinking Space*. London: Routledge.
Blok, Anders (2007a): "Actor-networking ceta-sociality, or, what is sociological about contemporary whales?," *Distinktion*, 15, no. 15: 65–89.
—— (2007b): "Experts on public trial: on democratizing expertise through a Danish consensus conference," *Public Understanding of Science*, 16(2): 163–82.
Bloor, David (1999): "Anti-Latour," *Studies in the History and Philosophy of Science*, 30(1): 81–112.
Bohman, James (1999): "Democracy as inquiry, inquiry as democratic: pragmatism, social science and the cognitive division of labour," *American Journal of Political Science*, 43(2): 590–607.
Boisvert, Raymond D. (1996): "Re-mapping the territory," *Man and World*, 29(1): 63–70.
Boltanski, Luc and Thévenot, Laurent (2006 [1991]): *On Justification: Economies of Worth*. Princeton: Princeton University Press.
Bourdieu, Pierre (2004): *Science of Science and Reflexivity*. Chicago: University of Chicago Press.

Bova, John and Latour, Bruno (2006): "John Bova in conversation with Bruno Latour: on relativism, pragmatism and critical theory," *Naked Punch*, 6 Issue 06 (Spring 2006): 107–121.

Bowker, Geof and Latour, Bruno (1987): "A booming discipline short of discipline: (social) studies of science in France," *Social Studies of Science*, 17(4): 715–48.

Brown, Steven D. (2002): "Michel Serres: science, translation and the logic of the parasite," *Theory, Culture and Society*, 19(3): 1–27.

Bruun Jensen, Casper (2005): "Citizen projects and consensus building at the Danish Board of Technology: on experiments in democracy," *Acta Sociologica*, 48(3): 221–35.

—— (2006): "Review essay: experimenting with political ecology," *Human Studies*, 29(1): 107–22.

Bruun Jensen, Casper and Blok, Anders (2011): "Techno-animism in Japan: Shinto cosmograms, actor-network theory, and the enabling powers of non-human agencies", under review in *Theory, Culture & Society*.

Bruun Jensen, Casper; Lauritsen, Peter and Olesen, Finn (ed.) (2007): *Introduktion til STS. Science, Technology, Society*. København: Hans Reitzels Forlag.

Bruun Jensen, Casper and Selinger, Evan (2003): "Distance and alignment: Haraway's and Latour's Nietzschean legacies," pp. 195–212 in D. Ihde and E. Selinger (eds.): *Chasing Technoscience. Matrix for Materiality*. Bloomington: Indiana University Press.

Burchell, Jon (2002): *The Evolution of Green Politics: Development & Change within European Green Parties*. London: Earthscan Publications Ltd.

Callon, Michel (1986): "Some elements of a sociology of translation: domestication of the scallops and the fishermen of St Brieuc Bay," pp. 196–233 in J. Law (ed.): *Power, action and belief: A new sociology of knowledge?* London: Routledge.

—— (1998): "An essay on framing and overflowing: economic externalities revisited by sociology," pp. 244–69 in M. Callon (ed.): *The Laws of the Markets*. Oxford and Keele: Blackwell and Sociological Review.

Callon, Michel and Latour, Bruno (1981): "Unscrewing the big Leviathan: how actors macrostructure reality and how sociologists help them to do so," pp. 277–303 in K. Knorr-Cetina and A.V. Cicourel (eds.): *Advances in social theory and methodology. Towards an Integration of Micro- and Macro-Mociologies*. Boston: Routledge and Kegan Paul Ltd.— (1997): "'Tu ne calculeras pas!' – ou comment symétriser le don et le capital", *MAUSS*, 9. Paris: La Découverte.

Callon, Michel; Law, John and Rip, Arie (eds.) (1986): *Mapping the dynamics of science and technology: sociology of science in the real world*. London: The Macmillan Press Ltd.

Callon, M. and Rip, A. (1992): "Humains, non-humains morale d'une coexistence," pp. 140–56 in J. Theys and B. Kalaora (eds.): *La Terre Outragée, Les experts sont formels!* Paris: Autrement.

Candea, Matei (2010): "Revisiting Tarde's house", pp. 1–24 in M. Candea (ed.) *The Social after Gabriel Tarde*. Milton Park: Routledge.

Castells, Manuel (1996): *The Rise of the Network Society*. Cambridge, MA: Blackwell.

Castree, Noel (2006): "Review: A Congress of the World," *Science as Culture*, 15(2): 159–70.

Cetina and A.V. Cicourel (eds.): *Advances in social theory and methodology. Towards an Integration of Micro- and Macro-Mociologies*. Boston: Routledge and Kegan Paul Ltd.

—— (1997): "'Tu ne calculeras pas!' – ou comment symétriser le don et le capital," *MAUSS*, 9. Paris: La Découverte.
Clark, Terry N. (1973): *Prophets and Patrons: The French University and the Emergence of the Social Sciences*. Cambridge, MA: Harvard University Press.
Clarke, Adele E. and Leigh Star, Susan (2008): "The Social Worlds Framework: A theory/methods package," pp. 113–38 in E. J. Hackett; O. Amsterdamska; M. Lynch and J. Wajcman (eds.): *The Handbook of Science and Technology Studies* [third edition]. Cambridge, MA: The MIT Press.
Collin, Finn (1996): "Bruno Latour og virkelighedskonstruktionens dimensioner", *Philosophia*, 25(3–4): 65–82.
—— (2011): *Science Studies as Naturalized Philosophy*. New York: Springer.
Collins, Harry M. and Evans, Robert J. (2002): "The third wave of science studies: studies of expertise and experience," *Social Studies of Science*, 32(2): 235–96.
Collins, Harry M. and Yearley, Steven (1992): "Epistemological chicken," in A. Pickering (ed.): *Science as Practice and Culture*. Chicago: The University of Chicago Press.
Crawford, T. Hugh (1993): "An interview with Bruno Latour," *Configurations*, 1(2): 247–68.
Crease, Robert; Ihde, Don; Bruun Jensen, Casper and Selinger, Evan (2003): "Interview with Bruno Latour," pp. 15–26 in D. Ihde and E. Selinger (eds.): *Chasing Technoscience. Matrix for Materiality*. Bloomington: Indiana University Press.
Cummings, Dolan (ed.) (2005): *The Changing Role of the Public Intellectual*. London: Routledge.
Deleuze, Gilles (1993): *The Fold: Leibniz and the Baroque*. London: Athlone.
Deleuze, Gilles and Guattari, Félix (1987): *A Thousand Plateaus: Capitalism and Schizophrenia*. Minneapolis: University of Minnesota Press.
Demeritt, David (2006): "Science studies, climate change, and the prospects for constructivist critique," *Economy and Society*, 35(3): 453–79.
Descola, Philippe (2005). *Par-delà nature et culture*. Paris: Éditions Gallimard.
Dewey, John (1927): *The Public and Its Problems*. New York: Holt.
Dratwa, Jim (2002): "Taking risks with the precautionary principle: food (and the environment) for thought at the European Commission," *Journal of Environmental Policy and Planning*, 4(3): 197–213.
Elam, Mark (1999): "Living dangerously with Bruno Latour in a hybrid world," *Theory, Culture & Society*, 16(4): 1–24.
Elam, Mark and Bertilsson, Margareta (2003): "Consuming, engaging, and confronting science: the emerging dimensions of scientific citizenship," *European Journal of Social Theory*, 6(2): 233–51.
Elder-Vass, Dave (2008): "Searching for realism, structure, and agency in Actor Network Theory," *British Journal of Sociology*, 59(3): 455–73.
Elgaard Jensen, Torben (2001): "Performing social work: competence, orderings, spaces, and objects," PhD Thesis. Copenhagen University: Institute of Psychology.
—— (2005): "Aktør-netværksteori – Latours, Callons og Laws materielle semiotic," pp. 185–210 in A. Esmark, C.B. Laustsen and N.Å. Andersen (eds.): *Socialkonstruktivistiske analysestrategier*. Frederiksberg: Roskilde Universitetsforlag.
—— (2008): "Future and Furniture: A study of a New Economy Firm's Powers of Persuasion," *Science, Technology & Human Values*, 33(1): 28–52.
Epstein, Steven (1995): "The construction of lay expertise: AIDS activism and the

forging of credibility in the reform of clinical trials," *Science, Technology & Human Values*, 20(4): 408–37.
Feyerabend, Paul (1993 [1975]): *Against Method*. London: Verso.
Finnemann, Niels Ole (1996): "Moderniteten – alt forladt eller blot fornyet? – Latour og det moderne", *Philosophia*, 25(3–4): 221–42.
Forman, Paul (1971): "Weimar culture, causality, and quantum theory, 1918–27: Adaptation by German physicists and mathematicians to a hostile intellectual environment", in R. Mccormmach (ed.): *Historical Studies in the Physical Sciences*. Philadelphia: University of Pennsylvania Press.
Foucault, Michel (1975): *Discipline and Punish: the Birth of the Prison*. New York: Random House.
Fraser, Mariam (2006): "The ethics of reality and virtual reality: Latour, facts and values," *History of the Human Sciences*, 19(2): 45–72.
Freed, Mark M. (2003): "Latour, Musil, and the discourse of non-modernity," *Symploke*, 11(1/2): 183–96.
Fuller, Steve (2000): "Why science studies has never been critical of science: some recent lessons on how to be a helpful nuisance and a harmless radical," *Philosophy of the Social Sciences*, 30(1): 5–32.
—— (2006): *The Philosophy of Science and Technology Studies*. New York: Routledge.
Furet, Francois (1981): *Interpreting the French Revolution*. Cambridge: Cambridge University Press.
Gad, Christopher and Bruun Jensen, Casper (2010): "On the Consequences of Post-ANT," *Science, Technology, & Human Values*, 35(1): 55–80.
Gamboni, Dario (2005): "Composing the body politic: composite images and political representation, 1651–2004," pp. 162–95 in B. Latour and P. Weibel (eds.): *Making Things Public: Atmospheres of Democracy*, Cambridge, MA: The MIT Press.
Garfinkel, Harold (2002). *Ethnomethodology's Program: Working Out Durkheim's Aphorism*. Lanham, MD: Rowman & Littlefield.
Gibbons, Michael; Nowotny, Helga; Limoges, Camille; Schwartzman, Simon; Scott, Peter and Trow, Martin (1994): *The New Production of Knowledge. The Dynamics of Science and Research in Contemporary Societies*. London: Sage Publications.
Gross, Paul R. and Levitt, Norman (1994): *Higher Superstition: The Academic Left and Its Quarrels With Science*. Baltimore: The John Hopkins University Press.
Guggenheim, Michael and Nowotny, Helga (2003): "Joy in repetition makes the future disappear. A critical assessment of the present state of STS," pp. 229–58 in B. Joerges and H. Nowotny (eds.): *Social Studies of Science and Technology: Looking Back, Ahead*. Dordrecht: Kluwer Academic Publishers.
Habermas, Jürgen (1992): *Between Facts and Norms: Contributions to a Discourse Theory of Law and Democracy*. Cambridge, MA: The MIT Press.
—— (1970): *Technology and Science as Ideology*. Boston: Beacon Press.
Hacking, Ian (1999): *The Social Construction of What?* Cambridge, MA: Harvard University Press.
Haraway, Donna (1980): "Review of B. Latour and S. Woolgar, Laboratory Life: The social construction of scientific facts," *Isis*, 71(3): 488–89.
—— (1991): *Simians, Cyborgs, and Women: The Reinvention of Nature*. London: Routledge.
—— (1994): "A game of cat's cradle: science studies, feminist theory, cultural studies," *Configurations*, 2(1): 59–71.

Bibliography

—— (2003): *The Companion Species Manifesto. Dogs, People, and Significant Otherness*. Chicago: Prickly Paradigm Press.
Harman, Graham (2009): *Prince of Networks: Bruno Latour and Metaphysics*. Melbourne: re.press.
Hayles, Katherine N. (1999): *How We Became Posthuman: Virtual Bodies in Cybernetics, Literature and Informatics*. Chicago: University of Chicago Press.
Hess, Martin and Coe, Neil M. (2006): "Making connections: global production networks, standards, and embeddedness in the mobile-telecommunications industry," *Environment and Planning* A, 38(7): 1205–27.
Holbraad, Martin (2004): "Response to Bruno Latour's 'Thou shall not freeze-frame'," available at http://nansi.abaetenet.net/abaetextos/response-to-bruno-latours-thou-shall-not-freeze-frame-martin-holbraad. (Last accessed January 7, 2011)
Holm, Petter (2007): "Which way is up on Callon?," pp. 225–43 in D. MacKenzie, F. Muniesa and L. Siu (eds.): *Do Economists Make Markets? On the Performativity of Economics*. Princeton: Princeton University Press.
Holm, Petter and Kåre Nolde Nielsen (2007). "Framing fish, making markets: the construction of individual transferable quotas (ITQs)," *The Sociological Review*, 55 (supplement 2): 173–95.
Ihde, Don (2003): "Introduction," pp. 1–7 in D. Ihde and E. Selinger (eds.): *Chasing Technoscience. Matrix for Materiality*. Bloomington: Indiana University Press.
Ihde, Don and Selinger, Evan (eds) (2003). *Chasing Technoscience: Matrix for Materiality*. Bloomington: Indiana University Press.
Jagd, Søren (2007): "Economics of convention and new economic sociology: mutual inspiration and dialogue," *Current Sociology*, 55(1): 75–91.
James, William (1902 [2007]): *The Varieties of Religious Experience*. New York: Cosimo Classics.
Jasanoff, Sheila (2003): "Technologies of humility: citizen participation in governing science," *Minerva*, 41(3): 223–44.
Joas, Hans (1993): *Pragmatism and Social Theory*. Chicago: University of Chicago Press.
Johnson, Jim [Latour, Bruno] (1988): "Mixing humans and nonhumans together: the sociology of a door-closer," *Social Problems*, 35(3): 298–310.
Kastrissianakis, Konstantin (2003): "Bruno Latour – We are all reactionaries today. An interview," *Re-public*, available at: http://www.republic.gr/en/?p = 129* (Last accessed January 7, 2011).
Keller, Catherine (2002): "Introduction: The process of difference, the difference of process," pp. 1–30 in C. Keller and A. Daniell (eds.): *Process and Difference: Between Cosmological and Poststructuralist Postmodernisms*. New York: State University of New York Press.
Knorr Cetina, Karin (1995): "Laboratory studies," pp. 140–66 in S. Jasanoff, G.E. Markle, J.C. Peterson and T. Pinch (eds.): *Handbook of Science and Technology Studies*. London: Sage Publications.
—— (1997): "Sociality with objects. Social relations in postsocial knowledge societies," *Theory, Culture & Society*, 14(4): 1–30.
Knorr Cetina, Karin and Cicourel, Aarob V. (eds.) (1981): *Advances in Social Theory and Methodology. Towards an Integration of Micro- and Macro-Sociologies*. Boston: Routledge and Kegan Paul.
Kuhn, Thomas S. (1962): *The Structure of Scientific Revolutions*. Chicago: University of Chicago Press.

Kukla, André (2000): *Social constructivism and the philosophy of science.* London: Routledge.
Lahsen, Myanna (2005): "Technocracy, democracy, and U.S. climate politics: the need for demarcations," *Science, Technology & Human Values*, 30(1): 137–69.
Lash, Scott (1999): "Objects that judge: Latour's Parliament of Things," pp. 312–38 in *Another Modernity, A Different Rationality.* Oxford: Blackwell Publishers Ltd.
—— (2005): "Lebenssoziologie: Georg Simmel in the Information Age," *Theory, Culture & Society*, 22(3): 1–23.
Latour, Bruno (1983): "Give me a laboratory and I will raise the world," pp. 141–70 in M. Mulkay and K. Knorr-Cetina (eds.): *Science Observed.* London: Sage Publications.
—— (1984): *Les microbes, guerre et paix.* Paris: Editions A. M. Métaillié.
—— (1987): *Science in Action.* Cambridge, Massachusetts: Harvard University Press.
—— (1988a): "A relativistic account of Einstein's relativity," *Social Studies of Science*, 18(1): 3–44.
—— (1988b): *The Pasteurization of France.* Cambridge, MA: Harvard University Press.
—— (1990): "Drawing things together," pp. 19–68 in M. Lynch and S. Woolgar (eds): *Representation in Scientific Practice.* Cambridge, Massachusetts: The MIT Press.
—— (1991): "The impact of science studies on political philosophy," *Science, Technology & Human Values*, 16(1): 3–19.
—— (1993): *We Have Never Been Modern.* New York: Harvester Wheatsheaf.
—— (1996a): *Aramis, or the Love of Technology.* Cambridge, Massachusetts: Harvard University Press.
—— (1996b): "On actor-network theory: a few clarifications," *Soziale Welt*, 47(4): 369–81.
—— (1996c): "On interobjectivity," *Mind, Culture, and Activity*, 3(4): 228–45.
—— (1997): "Stengers's Shibboleth," foreword, pp. vii–xix in I. Stengers, *Power and Invention: Situating Science.* Minneapolis: University of Minnesota Press.
—— (1998a): "Ein Ding ist ein Thing – a (Philosophical) platform for a Left (European) Party," paper presented at Cologne meeting "Innovation in Science, Technology and Politics". available at: http://www.bruno-latour.fr/poparticles/poparticle/p076.html (Last accessed January 7, 2011
—— (1998b): "From the world of science to the world of research?" *Science*, 280(5361): 208–9.
—— (1998c): "To modernise or to ecologise? That is the question," pp. 221–42 in B. Braun and N. Castree (eds.): *Remaking Reality – nature at the millennium.* London: Routledge.
—— (1998d): "'The man that freed the non-humans'. An interview with Bruno Latour,," *VEST*, 11(1): 61–66.
—— (1999a): "On recalling ANT,," pp. 15–25 in J. Law and J. Hassard (eds.): *Actor Network Theory and After.* Oxford: Blackwell Publishing.
—— (1999b): *Pandora's Hope. Essays on the Reality of Science Studies.* Cambridge, MA: Harvard University Press.
—— (2000a): "A well-articulated primatology – reflexions of a fellow traveller,," pp. 358–81 in S. Strum and L. Fedigan (eds.): *Primate Encounters.* Chicago: University of Chicago Press.
—— (2000b): "When things strike back: a possible contribution of 'science studies' to the social sciences,," *British Journal of Sociology*, 51(1): 107–23.

—— (2002a): "Gabriel Tarde and the end of the social," pp. 117–33 in Patrick Joyce (ed.): *The Social in Question: New Bearings in History and the Social Sciences*. London: Routledge.

—— (2002b): *La fabrique du droit. Une ethnographie du Conseil d'État*. Paris: La Découverte/Poche.

—— (2002c): "Morality and technology: the end of the means,," *Theory, Culture & Society*, 19(5/6): 247–60.

—— (2002d): *War of the Worlds: What about Peace?* Chicago: Prickly Paradigm Press.

—— (2002e): "What is iconoclash? Or is there a world beyond the image wars?," pp. 14–37 in B. Latour and P. Weibel (eds.): *Iconoclash*. Karlsruhe: Center for Art and Media/Cambridge, Massachusetts: The MIT Press.

—— (2003a): "Critical proximity or critical distance," unpublished (so-called) pop article, available at: http://www.bruno-latour.fr/poparticles/poparticle/P-113% 20HARAWAY.html (Last accessed January 7, 2011).

—— (2003b): "Is re-modernization occuring – and if so, how to prove it? A commentary on Ulrich Beck," *Theory, Culture & Society*, 20(2): 35–48.

—— (2003c): "The promises of constructivism," pp. 27–48 in D. Ihde and E. Selinger (eds.): *Chasing Technoscience. Matrix for Materiality*. Bloomington: Indiana University Press.

—— (2004a): "How to talk about the body? The normative dimension of science studies," *Body & Society*, 10(2–3): 205–29.

—— (2004b): "Whose cosmos, which cosmopolitics? Comments on the peace terms of Ulrich Beck," *Common Knowledge*, 10(3): 450–62.

—— (2004c): "Why has critique run out of steam? From matters of fact to matters of concern," *Critical Inquiry*, 30(2): 225–48.

—— (2004d): *Politics of Nature: How to Bring the Sciences into Democracy*. Cambridge, MA: Harvard University Press.

—— (2005a): "From Realpolitik to Dingpolitik, or how to make things public," pp. 14–43 in B. Latour and P. Weibel (eds.): *Making Things Public: Atmospheres of Democracy*. Karlsruhe: ZKM/Cambridge, MA: The MIT Press.

—— (2005b): *Reassembling the Social: An Introduction to Actor-Network-Theory*. Oxford: Oxford University Press.

—— (2005c): "What is the style of matters of concern? Two lectures in empirical philosophy," Amsterdam, April/May 2005. Available at: http://www.bruno-latour.fr/articles/article/97-STYLEMATTERS-CONCERN.pdf (Last accessed January 7, 2011).

—— (2005d): "'Thou shall not freeze-frame,' or, how not to misunderstand the science and religion debate," pp. 27–48 in J.D. Proctor (ed.): *Science, Religion, and the Human Experience*. Oxford: Oxford University Press.

—— (2006): "Powers of the fascimile: a turing test on science and literature," unpublished paper, available at: http://www.bruno-latour.fr/articles/article/ 94-POWERS-TURING.pdf (Last accessed January 7, 2011).

—— (2006b): "Sur un livre d'Etienne Souriau: *Les Différents modes d'existence*," unpublished paper, available at: http://www.bruno-latour.fr/articles/article/ 98-SOURIAU.pdf (Last accessed January 7, 2011).

—— (2007): "'It's the development, stupid!', or how can we modernize modernization?," in J. Proctor (ed.): *Postenvironmentalism*. Cambridge, MA: The MIT Press.

—— (2008a): "A Textbook Case Revisited – Knowledge as a Mode of Existence," pp. 83–112 in E. J. Hackett; O. Amsterdamska; M. Lynch and J. Wajcman (eds.): *The*

Handbook of Science and Technology Studies [third edition]. Cambridge, MA: The MIT Press.

—— (2009a): "Will non-humans be saved? An argument in ecotheology", *The Journal of the Royal Anthropological Institute*, 15(3): 459–75.

—— (2009b). "Spheres and Networks: Two Ways to Reinterpret Globalization," lecture at Harvard Graduate School of Design, Cambridge, MA; to be published in Harvard Design Magazine, 2009. Available at: http://www.bruno-latour.fr/articles/index.html (Last accessed July 3, 2009).

—— (2010a): "Coming out as a philosopher," *Social Studies of Science*, 40(4): 599–608.

—— (2010b): *The Making of Law: An ethnography of the Conseil d'État*. Cambridge: Polity Press.

Latour, Bruno and Woolgar, Steve (1979): *Laboratory Life: The social construction of scientific facts*. Beverly Hills and London: Sage Publications.

—— (1986): *Laboratory Life: The construction of scientific facts* [second edition]. Princeton: Princeton University Press.

Latour, Bruno and Weibel, Peter (eds.) (2005). *Making Things Public: Atmospheres of Democracy*. Cambridge, MA: The MIT Press.

Latour, Bruno and Lépinay, Vincent A. (2009): *The Science of Passionate Interests: An introduction to Gabriel Tarde's economic anthropology*. Chicago: Prickly Paradigm Press.

Law, John (1986): "On the methods of long distance control: vessels, navigation and the Portuguese route to India," pp. 234–63 in J. Law (ed.): *Power, Action and Belief: a new Sociology of Knowledge*. London: Routledge and Kegan Paul.

—— (1987): "Technology and heterogeneous engineering: the case of Portuguese expansion," pp. 111–34 in W.E. Bijker, T.P. Hughes and T. Pinch (eds.): *The Social Construction of Technological Systems*. Cambridge, MA: Massachusetts Institute of Technology.

—— (1992): "Notes on the theory of the Actor Network: ordering, strategy and heterogeneity". Centre for Science Studies, Lancaster University, http://www.lancs.ac.uk/fass/sociology/papers/law-notes-on-ant.pdf (Last accessed January 7, 2011).

—— (1994): *Organizing Modernity*. Oxford: Blackwell.

—— (1997): "Traduction/trahison: notes on ANT," Department of Sociology, Lancaster University, http://www.lancs.ac.uk/fass/sociology/papers/law-traduction-trahison.pdf (Last accessed January 7, 2011).

—— (2002): *Aircraft Stories: Decentering The Object In Technoscience*. Durham: Duke University Press.

—— (2004): *After Method: Mess in Social Science Research*. London: Routledge.

Lewowicz, Lucia (2003): "Materialism, symmetry and eliminativism in the latest Latour," *Social Epistemology*, 17(4): 381–400.

Lippmann, Walter (1993 [1925]). *The Phantom Public*. New Jersey: Transaction Publishers.

Lyotard, Jean-François (1979): *The Postmodern Condition*. Manchester: Manchester University Press.

Maasen, Sabine and Weingart, Peter (eds.) (2005): *Democratization of Expertise? Exploring Novel Forms of Scientific Advice in Political Decision-making*. New York: Springer.

McCright, Aaron M. and Dunlap, Riley E. (2003): "Defeating Kyoto: the conservative

movement's impact on U.S. climate change policy," *Social Problems*, 50(3): 348–73.
Meyer, John W, Frank, David J., Hironaka, Ann, Schofer, Evan and Tuma, Nancy B. (1997): "The structuring of a world environmental regime, 1870–1990," *International Organization*, 51(4): 623–51.
Miller, Clark (2001): "Hybrid management: boundary organizations, science policy, and environmental governance in the climate regime," *Science, Technology & Human Values*, 26(4): 478–500.
Mol, Arthur P.J. and Spaargaren, Gert (1993): "Environment, modernity and the risk society: the apocalyptic horizon of environmental reform," *International Sociology*, 8(4): 431–59.
Murdoch, Jonathan (2001): "Ecologizing sociology: actor-network theory, co-construction and the problem of human exceptionalism," *Sociology*, 35(1): 111–33.
Newton, Tim (2007): *Nature and Sociology*. London: Routledge.
Nowotny, Helga; Scott, Peter and Gibbons, Michael (2001): *Re-Thinking Science. Knowledge and the Public in an Age of Uncertainty*. Oxford: Polity Press.
Næss, Arne (1989): *Ecology, Community, and Lifestyle*. Cambridge: Cambridge University Press.
Pinch, Trevor J. and Bijker, Wiebe E. (1984): "The social construction of facts and artefacts: or how the sociology of science and the sociology of technology might benefit each other," *Social Studies of Science*, 14(3): 388–441.
Riis, Søren (2008): "The symmetry between Bruno Latour and Martin Heidegger," *Social Studies of Science*, 38(2): 285–301.
Saldanha, Arun (2003): "Actor-network theory and critical sociology," *Critical Sociology*, 29(3): 419–32.
Schinkel, Willem (2007): "Sociological discourse of the relational: the cases of Bourdieu & Latour," *The Sociological Review*, 55(4): 707–29.
Serres, Michel (1982): *The Parasite*. Baltimore: The John Hopkins University Press.
—— (1995a): *Angels: A Modern Myth*. Paris: Flammarion.
—— (1995b): *The Natural Contract*. Ann Arbor: University of Michigan Press.
Serres, Michel and Latour, Bruno (1995): *Conversations on Science, Culture, and Time: Michel Serres with Bruno Latour*. Ann Arbor: University of Michigan Press.
Shapin, Steven (1988): "Following scientists around," *Social Studies of Science*, 18(3): 533–50.
Shapin, Steven and Schaffer, Simon (1985): *Leviathan and the Airpump: Hobbes, Boyle, and the experimental life*. Princeton, NJ: Princeton University Press.
Sloterdijk, Peter (1999): *Sphären II: Globen*. Frankfurt am Main: Suhrkamp.
—— (2004). *Sphären I–III: Blasen, Globen, Schäume*. Frankfurt am Main: Suhrkamp Verlag.
Sokal, Alan (1997): "Professor Latour's philosophical mystifications," *Le Monde*, January 31 (in English translation).
Star, Susan Leigh (1991): "Power, technologies and the phenomenology of conventions: on being allergic to onions," pp. 26–56 in J. Law (ed.): *A Sociology of Monsters? Essays on Power, Technology and Domination*. London: Routledge.
Stehr, Nico (2005): *Knowledge Politics: Governing the Consequences of Science and Technology*. Boulder, CO: Paradigm Publishers.
Stengers, Isabelle (2000): *The Invention of Modern Science*. Minneapolis: University of Minnesota Press.

―― (2005). "Introductory notes on an ecology of practices," *Cultural Studies Review*, 11(1): 183–96.
Strum, Shirley and Latour, Bruno (1987): "The meanings of social: from baboons to humans," *Social Science Information*, 26(4): 783–802.
Teubner, Gunther (2006): "Rights of non-humans? Electronic agents and animals as new actors in politics and law," *Journal of Law and Society*, 33(4): 497–521.
Thompson, Charis (2002): "When elephants stand for competing models of nature," pp. 166–90 in J. Law and A. Mol (eds.): *Complexities. Social Studies of Knowledge Practices*. Durham and London: Duke University Press.
Thorlindsson, Thorolfur and Vilhjalmsson, Runar (2003): "Introduction to the special issue: science, knowledge and society," *Acta Sociologica*, 46(2): 99–105.
Tilley, Nicolas (1981): "The logic of laboratory life," *Sociology*, 15(1): 117–26.
Tucker, Aviezer (2007): "The political theory of French science studies in context," *Perspectives on Science*, 15(2): 202–21.
Turner, Stephen P. (2003): *Liberal Democracy 3.0: Civil Society in an Age of Experts*. London: Sage Publications.
Vandenberghe, Frèdèric (2002): "Reconstructing humans: a humanist critique of actant-network theory," *Theory, Culture & Society*, 19(5–6): 51–67.
Van Der Veken, Jan (2000): "Merleau-Ponty and Whitehead on the concept of nature," *Interchange*, 31(2–3): 319–34.
Viveiros de Castro, Eduardo (2004): "Exchanging perspectives. The transformation of objects into subjects in Amerindian ontologies," *Common Knowledge*, 10(3): 463–84.
de Vries, Gerard (2007): "What is political in sub-politics? How Aristotle might help STS," *Social Studies of Science*, 37(5): 781–809.
Ward, Steven C. (1996): *Reconfiguring Truth*. London: Rowman & Littlefield Publishers.
Weber, Max (1978): *Economy and Society: An Outline of Interpretive Sociology*. Edited by Guenther Roth and Claus Wittich. Berkeley: University of California Press.
Weinberg, Steven (2001): *Facing Up: Science and its Cultural Adversaries*. Cambridge, MA: Harvard University Press.
Whatmore, Sarah (1997) "Dissecting the autonomous self: hybrid cartographies for a relational ethics", *Environment and Planning D: Society and Space*, 15(1): 37–53.
Whiteside, Kerry H. (2002): *Divided Natures: French Contributions to Political Ecology*. Cambridge, MA: The MIT Press.
Whittle, Andrea and Spicer, André (2008): "Is actor network theory critique?," *Organization Studies*, 29(4): 611–29.

Index

Page numbers in **bold** refer to figures.

a-humanism 142
abstractions 45
actant 17
actor-network 3–5, 14, 105–6, 113, 120, 134
actor-network theory 3, 18, 47–50, 52, 162–3; defined 47
agency 48, 107
animal rights 90, 99–100
ANT *see* actor-network theory
anthropocentrism 90
anthropology: symmetrical 135, 145
anthropology of science 19–21, 26–51; actor-network theory 47–50; articles, types of statements and struggle between laboratories 33–5; background for the laboratory studies 28–9; breaking with diffusion theory 40–1; inscription devices 31–2; laboratory as a fact-producing factory 29–30; machines, alliances and "machinations" 35–41; translation 37–9; type 1 statements 34–5; type 2 statements 34; type 3 statements 33–4; type 4 statements 33; type 5 statements 33; worldwide techno-science 41–7
antidualism 12
Aristotle 180
articulation 83, 87
association 16, 18
Augé, Marc 7

Bauman, Zygmunt 105
Beck, Ulrich. 123
Bergson, Henri 176
bifurcation of nature 14
black box 35, 121
Bloor, David 41
Boltanski, Luc 62, 63
Bourdieu, Pierre 6
Boyle, Robert 56–9
Brahe, Tycho 45
Bultmann, Rudolf 159
bureaucracy 120
Butler, Judith 133

CAD (computer-aided design) 153
calculative rationality 123–4
Callon, Michel 8, 28, 47
capitalism 128
Carnot, Sadi: principles of thermodynamics 35–6, 40
cartography 105, 134
cascade 45
Castells, Manuel 185
center of calculation 27–8, 44, 45
Centre de Sociologie de l'Innovation (CSI) 7
Cetina, K. 28, 29
chains of obligation 117–18
chains of translation 76, 82, 147
circulating reference 81, 82
circulation 14, 15, 16, 18
climate change 73, 80, 89, 95, 100
collective 104–7, 165–6
Collin, Finn 186
Collins, Harry 186
common sense 96, 147
constitution *see* modern Constitution
constructivism 32
consultation 93
correspondence theory 26
cosmology 148
cosmopolitics 80, 84, 97, 135
critical proximity 142–4
critique 60–1

cultural relativism 67
culture vs. nature see nature vs. culture
cybernetics 35

de Spinoza, Baruch 176
de Tocqueville, Alexis 178
deconstruction 124, 126, 144
Deleuze, Gilles 14–15
deliberative democracy 92, 180
Derrida, Jacques 12
Descartes, René 12, 135
Descola, Philippe 53–4, 154
Despret, Vinciane 179
Dewey, John 92–3
Diesel, Rudolf 35–6, 38–9, 48
diesel machine 40
differentiation theory 116–17, 119
diffusion theory 40–1
Dingpolitik 81, 84–7, 87–8, 92, 97
double representation 77–81
Durkheim, Émile 9, 103, 175, 181

Eastman, George 38
ecocentrism 90
ecologization 81, 89, 90, 91, 92, 99
economy 108; knowledge 22; psychological 9
Einstein, Albert 138, 181
Elam, Mark 74
Eliasson, Olafur 158
engineers 11, 39, 152, 153
enlightenment 141; First 60; Second 60
enlightenment project 130–50; a-humanism 142; critical intellectual project 140–6; critical proximity 142–4; democratization of the sciences 144–6; displacements 136–40; interpretive strategies 146–50; Latour as thinker of the contemporary world 130–3; political philosophy 139–40; post-social, globalized and contested world 133–6; relativism 138–9; social constructivism 137–8
environmental movements 80, 87–8, 98
epistemology 81; political 76, 77–81, 84, 139
ethics 72–3, 90
ethnocentrism 135
ethnology 177
ethnomethodology 113
European Union 99

Ferry, Luc 179
Feyerabend, Paul 81, 179

field studies 26
finality 91, 180
formalisms 45
Foucault, Michel 6
framing 115, 119
French Revolution 61
fundamentalism 119, 135
Furet, François 61

Gaia 88
Galilei, Galileo 135
Garfinkel, Harold 17, 104, 110, 161–2
geometry 44, 48
Giddens, Anthony 182
globalization 105, 120–5, 134
GMO food 80
GMO (genetically modified organisms) 126
Goffman, Erving 115
Greimas, Algirdas J. 17
Gross, Paul R. 175
Guillemin, Roger 7, 28

Habermas, Jürgen 179
Haraway, Donna 187
Hegel, Georg Wilhelm Friedrich 12, 71, 135
Heidegger, Martin 85
hermeneutics 115
hierarchy 94
Hobbes, Thomas 56–9, 120–1, 140
Holm, Petter 155
human rights 180
hybridization 15, 18
hybrids 16, 70, 96, 179–80

iconoclash 6
Ihde, Don 21
immanence 10, 14–15
immutable mobiles 44, 45
individualization 109
industrialization 108
infra-language 111
inscription 121; devices 31–2; literary 31, 37
institution 94
intellectual 141; holism 131
Intergovernmental Panel on Climate Change (IPCC) 86, 96, 97
Internet 134
interobjectivity 113–16
intersubjectivity 113–16
irreductions 6, 52

James, William 149
juxtapositioning of documents 33

Kant, Immanuel 141, 178, 180
Kelvin, Lord 36
Knorr-Cetina, Karin 28, 182
knowledge production 57
knowledge society 1
Kuhn, Thomas S. 29

L' Ecole Nationale Superieure des Mines 7–8
La fabrique du droit 117, 164
laboratory: articles, types of statements and struggle between laboratories 33–5; background for the laboratory studies 28–9; as a fact-producing factory 29–30; machines, alliances and "machinations" 35–41
Laboratory Life 7, 26, 27, 46, 136–7, 138, 160
Lash, Scott 189
law 116–18, 166
Law, John 8, 28, 47
legal objectivity 116–20
Leibniz, Gottfried Wilhelm 12–13
Lévi-Strauss, Claude 67–8
Levitt, Norman 175
Lippmann, Walter 191
localization 120–5
Locke, John 14
Louis the 16th 45
Luhmann, Niklas 23, 116, 182
Lynch, Mike 29, 176
lysenkoism 77

Machiavelli, Niccolò 16
machiavellism 140
machination of forces 38, 39
machines 35–6
macro actor 121, 124
macro phenomena 120
mad cow disease 96
Maison Louis Latour 6
Making Things Public 6, 156–8
mapping controversies 152–4
Marx, Karl 178
marxism 6
matters of concern 86
matters of fact 57, 58
matters of opinion 57, 58
mediation 14, 18
Mendel, Gregor 179
Merton, Robert K. 177

meta language 16, 23, 109
metaphysical globe 135
metaphysics 14–15
method 53–4
metrology 43
micro actor 121
micro-macro-problem 102, 124
Microsoft 128
modalities 34
modern 54
modern Constitution 54–61; dynamism 59–60; Hobbes v. Boyle 56–9; and its practice **65**; purification and translation **56**; on the trail of 54–6
modernity *see* philosophy of modernity
modernization 123, 180
monism 12
morality 180

Næss, Arne 90
nation state 105, 129, 132
nature *vs.* culture 103–4, 132, 149
network 134 *see also* actor-network
Nietzsche, Friedrich 16, 146, 176
non-governmental organizations (NGOs) 126
non-human actors 8
non-modernize 133
Northwest Passage 15

object-oriented democracy 84–7
oligopticon 121–2
ontology 10, 15, 49, 112
ORSTROM 7

Pandora's Hope 2, 9, 77, 81–2, 109
panopticon 121–2, 182
panorama 122–5
paradigms 29
parliament of things 76, 78, 79, 80, 84, 86–7, 93–7, 101, 132, 140, 145
particular universalism 67
Pasteur, Louis 8, 42, 48
Pasteurization of France (1988) 26, 42–3
perplexity 93
perspective drawing 43, 153
philosophies of immanence 14–15
philosophy: empirical 22, 129, 141; political 75–6, 80, 97, 99–100, 139–40; process 10, 13, 176
philosophy of modernity 52–74, 77, 88, 115; anthropology, constitutional metaphor and thought experiment 53–4; modern Constitution and its

practice **65**; modern Constitution dynamism 59–60; modern critique exercise 60–1; origins of the modern Constitution 56–9; parliament of things 70–1; purification and translation **56**; radical consequences 64–70; on the trail of the modern Constitution 54–6
plane of immanence 14
plug-ins 123
pluriverse 149
political activism 89
political ecology 75–101, 155–6; between ecology, science and democracy 97–101; epistemology to articulation 81–4; four collective tasks in parliament of things **94**; to modernize or to ecologize 87–91; non-modern Constitution 92–3; object-oriented democracy 84–7; parliament of things 93–7; political epistemology and double representation 77–81; toward a new political ecology 75–7
Politics of Nature 9, 19, 75, 76, 79, 92, 154–6, 160, 165
Popper, Karl 11
postmodernism 46, 81
Powell, Colin 85
precautionary principle 98–9
primatology 82–3
principle of precaution 132
principle of symmetry: generalized 48
printing press 43, 177
productive paradox 55
proposition 13, 83
purification 55, 60

quasi-object 16

rationality 27
Realpolitik 84–7, 97
Reassembling the Social (2005) 9, 19, 103, 104, 160, 162
regimes: of existence and enunciation 27, 117–20, 136, 144, 178; of justification 62; market 88
relationalism 181
relativism 138–9, 181; absolute 67
relativity theory 107, 138, 181
religion 118–19, 158–9
representation 58, 78; political 58; scientific 58
rhizomes 14, 15

risk society 76, 123
Rousseau, Jean-Jacques 161

Saussure, Ferdinand 7
Schaffer, Simon 56
Schmitt, Carl 16, 80
Science in Action (1987) 26, 35, 43
Science of Science and Reflexivity 143
science studies *see* STS
science wars 77, 109, 130
scientific facts 26, 35
scientific realism 46
semiotics 48, 110
Serres, Michel 15–16, 37, 66, 79
Shapin, Steve 56
Sloterdijk, Peter 135, 183
social constructivism 46, 137–8
social engineering 105
social interaction 115
social order 64, 113–16
social science 181
society 40, 58, 104–7
socio-technical orders 113–14
sociological controversies 160–2
sociology 143; critical 102, 124; from inter-subjectivity to inter-objectivity 113–16; Latour in the treadmills of sociology 125–9; Latour-the-sociologist as techno-directive 111–13; Latour's sociological ambivalence 102–4; localization and globalization 120–5; objectivity of law and religious icons 116–20; oligopticon 121–2; panorama 122–5; social explanations 107–11; from society to collective 104–7
sociology of association 102–29
sociology of criticism 62
sociology of innovation 4, 102
sociology of translation 37
Stengers, Isabelle 83, 166
stoics 135
structuralism 6
Strum, Shirley 8, 82
STS 1, 39
subpolitics 145, 183
symbolic interactionism 115

Tarde, Gabriel 9, 12, 103, 160–2
technological innovation 8
technoscience 48, 105, 108, 114
Thatcher, Margaret 104
Thévenot, Laurent 62–3, 71
transcendence 14

translation 8, 14, 15, 16, 18, 37–9, 121
Traweek, Sharon 28, 29, 176

United Nations 122
Université de Bourgogne 6
Université de Tours 6
"Unscrewing the Big Leviathan" 120

Wallerstein, Immanuel 178
water parliaments 86

We Have Never Been Modern 9, 16, 18, 52, 53, 54, 61–2, 71, 73, 74, 76, 102, 132
Weber, Max 88
Western, David 154, 179
Whitehead, Alfred North 13–14
Woolgar, Steve 7
World bank 128
Writing 162–4

Žižek, Slavoj 140